Border Sanctuary

THE MEADOWS CENTER
FOR WATER AND THE ENVIRONMENT
TEXAS STATE UNIVERSITY

Kathie and Ed Cox Jr. Books on Conservation Leadership
Sponsored by The Meadows Center for Water and
the Environment, Texas State University

Andrew Sansom, General Editor

A list of other titles in this series may be found at the back of the book.

Border Sanctuary

The Conservation Legacy of the Santa Ana Land Grant

M. J. MORGAN

Texas A&M University Press • College Station

First edition

This paper meets the requirements of ANSI/NISO
Z39.48-1992 (Permanence of Paper).
Binding materials have been chosen for durability.
Manufactured in the United States of America

LIBRARY OF CONGRESS CATALOGING-IN-PUBLICATION DATA

Morgan, M. J., 1955– author.
Border sanctuary: the conservation legacy of the Santa Ana land grant / M. J. Morgan. — First edition.
pages cm
Includes bibliographical references and index.
ISBN 978-1-62349-320-2 (cloth: alk. paper) —
ISBN 978-1-62349-324-0 (ebook)
1. Santa Ana National Wildlife Refuge (Tex.)—History. 2. Wildlife refuges—Texas—Santa Ana National Wildlife Refuge—History.
3. Wildlife refuges—Texas—Lower Rio Grande Valley—History.
4. Wildlife management—Texas—Santa Ana National Wildlife Refuge—History.
5. Forest conservation—Texas—Santa Ana National Wildlife Refuge—History.
6. Forest conservation—Texas—Lower Rio Grande Valley—History. I. Title.
QL84.22.T4M67 2015
639.909764'4—dc23

2015002706

Border Sanctuary is dedicated to the one person who truly
gave it historical accuracy
and who truly gave me the will to persevere:
my husband, Thomas D. Morgan.

I also dedicate it to three people
belonging always to Santa Ana:
Benigno and Victoria Leal
L. Irby Davis

Contents

Foreword by Andrew Sansom ix
Acknowledgments xi

The Land of Santa Ana: Solving Mysteries 1

Chapter One. Saving the Santa Ana Forest 13
South Texas in the 1930s 15
The Symbolic Chachalaca 19
Perceptions of the Forest 24

Chapter Two. The Original Landscape of Santa Ana 30
Three Environments 34
Lessons of *Dicliptera* 36
Hunter of Flowing Habitats: The Jaguarundi 40

Chapter Three. First Changers: Hunters, Grazers, and Browsers 44
New Eco-Travelers: The Lure of Resilient Grasslands 47
Into the Forests 54

Chapter Four. The Early Leal Years: People of the River 59
The Leals and Their Neighbors: Families of the Mexican Grants 64
The Trees of Santa Ana 68
A House of Handmade Bricks 74
Mounted Raiders in South Texas 78

Chapter Five. The World Outside Comes to Santa Ana 83
Hard for People, Good for Trees 85
Horses on Santa Ana 88
Jaguars and Horses 90
Losing and Gaining Santa Ana 95
The Leal Fortunes 104

Chapter Six. Fire, Water, and Goats on Santa Ana: The Guzmán Dream 110
The Traveling Armadillo 110
The Way of Fire 112
The Eating of the Grass: Clues in the Twentieth Century 114
Santa Ana in 1880 119
The Dream of La Pechuga 125

Chapter Seven. Land Redefined 136
Surveys, Sales, and Rails 139
Santa Ana in the Great Depression Years 145
Epilogue: The Future of a River and Its Trees 150

Notes 159
Bibliography 187
Index 203

Color illustrations follow page **58**

Foreword

My first experience with the incredible biological diversity of the Lower Rio Grande Valley occurred when, as an employee of The Nature Conservancy, I had the privilege of adding part of the historic Tres Corrales Ranch to the Rio Grande Valley National Wildlife Refuge. The property was owned by a wonderful gentleman named Hale Schlaben and his family, and together, they had for many years preserved the rich natural brush that characterizes the habitat of the Valley and supports the cornucopia of birds, animals, and other living things that depend on it.

Mr. Schlaben understood the importance of protecting the brush country and had resisted the general practice throughout the Valley of scraping it to the ground in order to plant citrus, grain sorghum, and other agricultural products. For years, the US Fish and Wildlife Service had tried to buy his property, but he always refused, assuring them that he would protect it and that the government could spend its money on other, more threatened tracts. At some point, he got into debt and needed to sell, which is where I came in, because the Fish and Wildlife Service could not move fast enough to meet his financial needs. In order to fill the gap, The Nature Conservancy directed me to purchase the property and hold it until the government could get its act together and add the property to the refuge.

During this interim, I not only became extremely close to the Schlabens and their legacy of conservation, but I was also introduced to the remarkable natural and cultural diversity of this unique region, including the southern section of the original land grant awarded to Benigno Leal by Mexico in 1834, two years before the Texas Revolution. As M.J. Morgan so eloquently writes in this volume in the Kathie and Ed Cox Jr. Books on Conservation Leadership, this land became the second National Wildlife Refuge established in Texas in 1943, just over 100 years later.

From this beginning, the Santa Ana National Wildlife Refuge became the beachhead for conservation in the lower four counties of Texas, one of the most biologically diverse regions of the hemisphere, containing a documented 1,200 species of plants, 300 species of butterflies, and approximately 700 species of vertebrates, of which at least 520 are birds. The Valley is also one of the richest and most interesting cultural areas of the continent.

Today, the Lower Rio Grande Valley is the largest destination for birdwatchers in the world and home to the World Birding Center, not far from the refuge, which is all that remains to represent the original natural and cultural history of the old land grant that was once traded for a fiddle and a new suit of clothes.

All this and more awaits the reader here in Border Sanctuary, the third book from the pen and keyboard of M.J. Morgan, an accomplished researcher, teacher, and writer at Kansas State University. Publication here of her landmark study of one of America's true natural treasures would not have been possible without the generosity of Will and Pamela Harte, members of another great family of South Texas conservationists and ranchers. Now residing in the Davis Mountains, their legacy across the state of Texas becomes more significant each day.

As I prepared to close the transaction on my very first conservation land deal at the Tres Corrales all those years ago, Hale Schlaben had a massive heart attack and did not survive to see his dream come true and his financial issues put to rest. He would have loved this book and the rich heritage it recounts. I wish I could have introduced him to M.J. Morgan.

—Andrew Sansom
General Editor, Kathie and Ed Cox Jr. Books on Conservation Leadership

Acknowledgments

Because I live in another state, I have had to depend so often on the generosity and assistance of the people of South Texas. Nowhere could there possibly be a warmer and more enthusiastic group! I would like to thank most especially the managers and staff at Santa Ana National Wildlife Refuge who talked with me over a five-year period: acting manager Chris Hathcock, former refuge manager Jennifer Owen-White, staff member Laura de la Garza, and plant ecologist Kimberly Wahl. Kimberly read and edited a complex section of the manuscript, providing valuable insight into terminology. I also thank the following people in a variety of places across South Texas. First, I am grateful to Cecilia Venables at the Mary and Jeff Bell Library at Texas A&M University in Corpus Christi and to Beverly Pardue at the McAllen Public Library; they tracked down some obscure materials for me. Christina Mild, amazing botanist, provided much information and also generously donated personal photographs. To the archivists of Special Collections, University of Texas–Pan American, Edinburg, I owe a heartfelt thanks: George Gause and Janette Garcia answered every question and every e-mail, found sources I thought were lost (especially old maps), asked stimulating questions, and assisted in so many other ways. I also thank Sarah Williams, director of Frontera Audubon in Weslaco; Matthew Martin, Archivist and Curator of Old and Rare Books at Southwestern Oblate Historical Archives in San Antonio; Esteban Lomas and Barbara Stokes at the Museum of South Texas History, Edinburg; and Sonny Hinojosa, manager of Hidalgo County Water District #2 in Edinburg. All gave of their time to talk with me, and Sonny provided maps early on in my research that proved critically important.

Thank you to Shannon Davies, editor-in-chief at Texas A&M University Press. Through her patience and direction, this study found a new and better shape. I am *extremely* grateful to Dr. Beatriz de la Garza for her generous donation of personal time to help me with Spanish spellings, accents, and meanings. When I could not find a single professional translator willing to assist me, Dr. de la Garza's attention to the manuscript made all the difference in its accuracy and authenticity. Another person I sincerely thank is Coralyn Davis Lundell, daughter of Irby and Anna May Davis. She generously shared family photographs and information about her parents, important activists in the saving of Santa Ana. I also thank Amanda Dempster here in Kansas for her careful work in sizing and inserting historical images and for being cheerful throughout an often aggravating process. Last, thank you, Tom, my husband and *compadre,* for being with me every step of the way through the forest of Santa Ana and the telling of its story. Any inaccuracies are, of course, my own.

Border Sanctuary

The Land of Santa Ana

Solving Mysteries

In 1943, an old Mexican land grant gave its name to the third national wildlife refuge in Texas. Preceded only by the Muleshoe (1935) and Aransas (1937) refuges, Santa Ana National Wildlife Refuge included the southern portion of two leagues awarded to Benigno Leal over a century earlier. Santa Ana has been the name consistently associated with the tangled, gray-green sprawl of forest along the lower Rio Grande. The name persisted even as laborers cleared land around the woods for agriculture in the early twentieth century. Smoky air from burning mesquite seemed to obscure the edges of history and memory. Original Tejano landowners had passed on, those who once had ridden or walked every *vara* of their property and knew exactly where boundaries lay. By 1920, heavily planted furrows combed the black earth to the horizon, blurring the understanding of survey lines, of where edges of early grants met. The grants themselves had been subdivided, bought and sold, auctioned, reclaimed, inherited, and fought over in courts for over a hundred years. Even in 1909 a litigated court case arose, *Merriman v. Blalock*, contesting a piece of old Santa Ana.

The Mexican surveys of 1834, including those of Santa Ana, started at the Rio Grande using then-visible corner markers such as hackberry and mesquite trees, large boulders, and resacas. In a century's time, the only clear boundary lines were on maps. The old metes and bounds system of ownership had in many cases disappeared. This was also because of the changing channel of the Rio Grande and the eroding and building up of its banks. There were no constants along the river. By the time federal purchasers in 1940 "bought up" the old acreage of Mexican grants stretching north into the Texas plains, most South Texas people identified the wild, dense, surviving thorn forest as the "Santa Ana Tract" or "Santa Ana Groves." The towering trees along the Rio Grande had become permanently identified with Santa Ana. And yet, that tract was not clearly understood. It actually contained nearly two thousand acres of three grants: a slim edge of Agostadero del Gato (Pasture of the Cat); the portion of Santa Ana below the Military Road; and most of the acreage of Los Toritos below the road as well.

Los Toritos, or the Little Bulls, flanked the Santa Ana grant to the west. In the oral tradition of the area, Los Toritos is frequently shortened to El Toro, and on American documents and surveys, it is usually misspelled as Los Torritos. These three land grants shared an amazing riverine forest, but where their boundaries lay within the scope of the refuge as it opened to the public in 1943 remains somewhat obscure.

Discovering truths about the land named Santa Ana—its story, its shape, its people, even its basic legal parameters—has proven a challenging and mysterious venture. Where exactly were the boundaries of the original 1943 refuge? What was known and understood to be the Santa Ana forest? Where was the Santa Ana land grant within the refuge? Acquisition documents, including a survey, have not come to light. However, several maps can provide clues. The hand-drawn map below, sketched by naturalist Irby Davis working in the "Santa Ana Tract" in 1940, clearly shows the present-day outline of the wildlife refuge. Because Mr. Davis frequently led birding expeditions into riparian woods and was conducting a nesting census at the time, it is safe to say that this sketch also depicts the basic shape and size of the 1940 forest itself. Irby Davis used a dotted line to con-

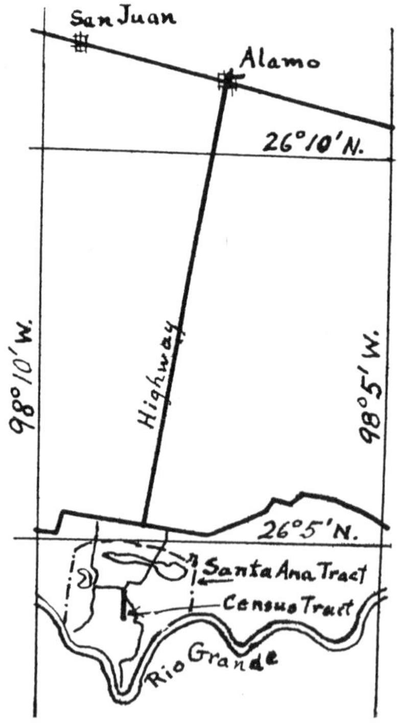

A hand-drawn map by Irby Davis, taking a nesting census in 1940 on what he called the Santa Ana Tract. As rough as this sketch is, the shape of the present-day Santa Ana National Wildlife Refuge is clear. From the National Archives.

vey the limits of the forest and also included two resacas. The enormous resaca near the northern boundary has had several names across the years. Today on the refuge it has divided itself into five smaller lakes known as the Pintail Lakes. The second, much smaller crescent lake to the west is today called Cattail Lake. It lies on the old Los Toritos land grant.

Like Santa Ana, the southern acreage of Los Toritos held a dense forest that provided continuity of habitat for birds and mammals. At the time of the original refuge creation, the forest on these two grants was a single, nearly impenetrable swath of trees and looping vines richly fed by the floodwaters of the Rio Grande. These woodlands were often described as "massive" or "jungle-like." The forest stood in a preserved, ecologically complex state: a tract of soaring, nest-filled woods measuring roughly two by two and a half miles. Nowhere else in Texas and nowhere else in the world was there such an extensive acreage of original subtropical thorn forest still thriving. A forest evolving near an ancient river is a startlingly virile living environment, filled with minihabitats and curious animal-plant relationships. On the land known as Santa Ana, differing water levels had created at least five different ecological terraces sloping up from the banks of the Rio Grande. Because of this biotic richness, as well as the enduring, brilliant green of the forest, Santa Ana has become known as the jewel of the National Wildlife Refuge System. It is certainly a jewel among the eighteen other established wildlife refuges in Texas, for on Santa Ana are found more endangered species than on any other refuge in the entire United States.[1]

In a way, we can view these woods as we might view the last members of a species—holding on in an environment that has become threatening to their survival. Yet unlike natural histories that detail the path to extinction, this history of the land of Santa Ana examines the path to survival. The chapters of this study, although they follow a chronological story, seek to answer these questions: How were these woodlands preserved? What natural and human history unfolded here that preserved these trees? A further goal is to understand the kind of environmental knowledge held by the Spanish, Mexican, and Tejano people who passed through and eventually lived on Santa Ana. For the preservation of the Santa Ana forest is tied to how the original occupiers understood their land.

If we do not know the history of the land itself, we cannot appreciate that the refuge exists today because of human choices and motivations. The actions of truly diverse populations across two hundred years of recorded history can reveal the connections people felt for a specific place along a historic river. Yet this history is an elusive, strangely patchwork one, with very little recorded information until after 1900, even though the story of change and adaptive survival along the Rio Grande unfolded well before that. It began in the late 1740s, when Spain decided to colonize the northern frontier of Nueva España (today, northern Tamaulipas, Mexico). The story ends almost exactly two hundred years later, in the 1940s, when the southern portion of the Santa Ana land grant became part of a national wildlife refuge. At that point, active and clearly identified policies began to protect the forest home of hundreds of species of resident and migratory birds. For the next seventy years, Santa Ana would continue to change, bird numbers would rise and fall, and species counts would indicate new distributions and habitat use. The people walking the trails there would be birders and visitors. The identity of Santa Ana as a wildlife refuge—a precious and preserved environment—remains its permanent face to the world.

This history of land perception, use, and preservation focuses on two "square leagues" of land, each 4,428 acres, the original Santa Ana grant. The refuge, lying below the Military Road, safeguards a remnant of thorn forest originally thriving on the Leal, Treviño, and Domínguez land grants. This study is not about the wildlife refuge in its entirety, nor is it about the refuge as it evolved and changed between 1943 and today. It is rather a history of a single 1834 grant, which today, if superimposed on a modern Hidalgo County map, would shoot north through the city of Alamo toward the once-vital South Texas Plains. A GIS map showing how this might look is provided on the next page. The green forest of Santa Ana National Wildlife Refuge sprawls and thrives across the floodplain of the Rio Grande on three Mexican land grants, lying also to the west in Los Toritos; but the Leal homestead site, the family cemetery, and the enormous, life-giving resaca on Santa Ana form the basis of this study.[2]

At the time of the original 1834 grant, three distinct environments were flourishing: the forest, the broken chaparral interspersed with woodlands, and the northern grasslands. This study examines what happened over time to those three environments: who held on to the land; who sold it and why; who bought it and with what dreams; what numbers of grazing animals thrived on its nutritious grasses; what happened to the land during an unprecedented agricultural boom in the early twentieth century—and finally, how the forest on the lower acreage survived through the 1920s and 1930s.

In telling this story, one obstacle was nearly insurmountable: there are almost no recorded human perceptions of the land until the first refuge managers arrived in 1940. As soon as these able and keenly perceptive men began to submit detailed reports of the refuge's earth and water, plants and animals, food sources and cover, the old land grant sprang to life in a way never seen before. To read the words of Earl Craven and Luther Gold-

A GIS map depicting how Santa Ana National Wildlife Refuge lies on the three 1834 grants of Agostadero del Gato, Santa Ana, and Los Toritos. The deed for the wildlife refuge on file at the Hidalgo County Courthouse confirms this distributioin. Map by Angela Schnee, 2013.

man, who sent quarterly reports to the National Wildlife Refuge System across an entire decade, is to suddenly have a window into the vast, unrecorded past, for these reports detail processes and relationships that had endured for millennia. The words of these men are truly the *only* existing record of how the forest, internal pastures, and grasslands of Santa Ana may have adapted and survived. Before the commonly accepted use of the word "ecology" in the 1960s, these managers understood it. Their descriptions of trees, thorny brush, grasses, and wildflowers also establish preferred habitat for these plants, where they probably grew over millennia on the old leagues. Manager observations about birds, mammals, reptiles, and insects also suggest ways those species thrived in a subtropical thorn forest and used the adjacent habitat of northward-stretching grassland. Thus, a single decade of rich biological data and perception holds the key to understanding the past on Santa Ana, because the observations of the managers occur at the point of transition in the 1940s; they provide a picture of the land just before work crews began to shape the acreage into a public-use refuge.

The irony is that two twentieth-century observers left more words in a single decade than any of the other human beings who lived on the leagues between 1749 and 1943. For the latter people—the members of the Leal and Guzmán families, the Mexican and then Tejano laborers, and also their relatives who moved on and off the ranches—we have no original words. (Victoria Leal may have dictated some of the phrases in her will of 1887.) What remains of the lives of Santa Ana people are entries in legal documents: deeds, wills, agricultural census data, and Hidalgo County tax rolls. And thanks to the efforts of passionate Mexican American genealogists, we have the reconstructed family trees and scanned church records from Old Spanish Nuevo Santander churches. But for most of this study of the Santa Ana land grant, the human beings who lived there can be glimpsed only through the environmental history of the land. Such a history must include people as part of the ecosystem; in this approach, the people and their relationships to the land they cared about are paramount.[3]

Today, the academic field known as Borderlands history is continuing to draw the efforts of skilled historians. This field has rapidly grown to include oral accounts, folklore and culture, music and literature, heritable land ownership, ethnic and labor relations, the history of women on both sides of the Rio Grande, the struggles for educational and political equality, and many other themes of identity and contested or shared experience. Yet Borderlands history has been strongly social history; until recently, it has not included much work in environmental or natural history, except for masterful studies of Hispanic and Tejano land tenure. The analysis of conservation practices has focused mainly on water management for agriculture. A leading historian of Hispanic farm and ranching experience in the Lower Rio Grande Valley, Armando Alonzo, has observed, "Very little is known about Hispanic and Anglo conservation practices prior to the twentieth century." Recent work on agriculture in the twentieth century has examined, for instance, the cotton industry in Texas during the New Deal or water management and water rights along the Rio Grande. In addition, Mexican soil and water specialists have produced important studies of land degradation south of the river. Yet there are almost no studies that address change on specific tracts of land over centuries of occupation and use, especially for the counties of South Texas. Almost all significant Borderlands environmental history derives from events in the twentieth century, and El Paso and New Mexico have yielded the most studies.[4]

The reason for this is lack of records in the eighteenth and nineteenth centuries, especially the kind of personal sources that might tell us about the people themselves: letters, diaries, photographs, handed-down stories, or preserved material culture. For the land grant of Santa Ana (and also for its flanking grants of El Gato and Los Toritos), we have none of the kinds of sources traditionally used to reconstruct the human role in environmental history. While we can reproduce the legal outlines of *porciones* and land grants and map the march of grants along the north bank of the river all the way to Laredo, we cannot easily know what kind of environmental knowledge the early settlers had, or how the Spanish, Mexican, and Tejano people of South Texas made decisions that impacted their land.

In a few memoirs of ranch life in Hidalgo County, we glimpse the pattern of drought and flood that stamped both agriculture and ranching efforts. For instance, from La Esperanza Ranch, operating by 1880 on the old El Gato grant, a descendant has written an account of how a farmer-rancher there carried a picture of San Isidro into his cornfields and marched it up and down the rows. He prayed aloud to San Isidro, the patron saint of farmers, when conditions became extreme: "San Isidro, farmer, take away the sun and bring the rain" or "San Isidro, farmer, take away the rain and bring back the sun." We have no surviving accounts like this for any of the people who may have lived on or passed through Santa Ana, whether Indian, Spanish, Mexican, Tejano, or Anglo-American. This study provides a way around that problem, an interpretive framework for understanding how dwellers on land including a vital thorn forest may have understood and preserved it, and why. Knowing why counters assumptions that the survival of the Santa Ana forest was a result of neglect, lack of interest, or happenstance.

Some histories of Mexican and Tejano ranch communities in South

Texas have been more successful with retrieving information. This is especially true for four important works: the history of the El Capote ranch community in the Pharr-Reynosa Bridge archaeological study of 1994; the award-winning history of the Santa Anita land grant, *I Would Rather Sleep in Texas* (primarily a study of the McAllen family, however); a study of the extensive Balli family, *The History of the Prestigious Balli Family: Story of the First Pioneer Settlers of the Rio Grande Valley*; and the history of the Vela land grant in the early chapters of *Petra's Legacy: The South Texas Ranching Empire of Petra Vela and Mifflin Kenedy*. These histories focus on people and their changing relationships. In addition, vital oral history projects being directed out of the University of Texas–Pan American are retrieving and preserving stories still available to us through interviews with descendants of land grant families. Sadly, to date it has not been possible to locate living descendants of the Leal or Guzmán families on Santa Ana who have memories and stories to share of their forebears; neither do we have much information about the early Domínguez family whose son, Máximo, acquired Los Toritos and then rapidly sold it. This study must therefore use different interpretive methodologies to literally find the people hiding among the trees of Santa Ana. We know that many human beings crossed the land of the refuge and rode horses north into the grasslands. We know their trails, home sites, and cemeteries. But beyond this evidence, we can also learn about them through studying the land they lived on.[5]

In researching the history of the Santa Ana land grant, an additional, important group of South Texas people has come to light: a small grassroots organization called the Rio Grande Valley Nature Club. This club was directly responsible for bringing the Santa Ana forest to the attention of the national wildlife refuge director. Club members were 1930s birders who met in each other's homes in the small communities of South Texas; yet, like the Leals and the Guzmáns, they left almost no discoverable records. Their president, Irby Davis, was a practicing lab chemist in Harlingen. He had such a passion for birds that he regularly sent in nesting census data to the precursor of *National Audubon* magazine, the journal called *Bird-Lore*. Members in the first Rio Grande Valley Nature Club of the late 1930s included men and women living in Alamo, San Benito, San Juan, Edinburg, and Harlingen. They identified their goals as "conservation and the advancement of knowledge of nature." As will be seen, through Irby Davis's persistent correspondence with the head of the US Biological Survey, this club saved the forest of the Santa Ana tract. Their efforts resulted in federal purchase of the woodlands for a wildlife refuge.

This study is therefore a thank-you to the Rio Grande Valley Nature

Club and an acknowledgment of the importance of the Leal family, especially Victoria Leal, the matriarch who alone held on to some of the original family land. It is also an acknowledgment of the Julio Guzmán family: Julio and his sons, Amado and Julio Jr., practiced mindful stock raising on the eastern league of Santa Ana. Their management did not result in overgrazing or forest clear-cutting. As Santa Ana celebrates seventy years as a wildlife refuge, we must honor the three groups of people whose actions and choices saved the Santa Ana forest for posterity. Yet since these people lived at widely different times, how the story is told must be carefully considered.

In two ways, this study departs from traditional histories. First, it opens with the moment in time when the Santa Ana forest was preserved: the creation of the wildlife refuge. The first chapter describes what was happening to South Texas counties during the Great Depression and explains how critically endangered the forest truly was. It also establishes the role of the Rio Grande Valley Nature Club through its correspondence with the head of the US Biological Survey. With this background, readers can understand the ecological rarity of Santa Ana and keep this in mind as they learn its life story. In the next chapters, the focus goes back—far back—to the time when the first Spanish settlers were arriving along the Rio Grande in the mid-eighteenth century. The description of their knowledge of the land and ways of using it, and of the impact of their livestock and hunting practices, sets in place the constant of environmental change. The story then moves steadily forward in time to trace the fortunes of Mexican grantees through two nineteenth-century wars, new citizenship in the United States, land loss and land reclamation in the 1850s, a cattle and ranching boom after the Civil War, a relentless drought and land sell-off in the 1890s, and finally, a dramatic agricultural explosion after 1900. By 1905, both original leagues of Santa Ana were in the hands of American land company agents. The last chapter explains what happened to the forest and northern grasslands of the old grant between the turn of the century and the creation of the refuge in 1943. The book thus comes full circle, arriving back at the moment Santa Ana became "an inviolate sanctuary."[6]

In addition, to understand how ecological processes operated on the Santa Ana grant across two centuries and to document changes in the land, a fresh methodology can be effective. The observations of the refuge managers in the 1940s are interwoven throughout the story. This means that the words of Luther Goldman, writing in 1944 about a searing drought affecting the refuge, can be used to understand what likely happened in other droughts that came in unceasing cycles to these lands. For

A 1944 photograph of the curving southern refuge boundary, the Rio Grande, carved out by the 1933 hurricane. This curve forms one of the twin "lobes" of Santa Ana today. Refuge managers worried about the steep erosion of the bank. From the National Archives.

instance, a September 1944 report noted: "Hardwood cover on the area was not so seriously affected as the herbaceous cover by the drouth. It seems possible that even a small percentage of the normal wood seed production occurred, but the birds had seed and fruits from the hardwoods that may have overcome this lack." The use of a twentieth-century assessment to suggest the ways trees and birds responded to drought in the eighteenth century *is* novel. Yet it is the only clear window we have into the ecological past on this land grant, aside from limited data gathered through archaeology and the few available travelers' logs. Using these manager reports, historical accounts, and modern biological studies in tandem teases out a story of constant change and adaptation, sometimes at an incremental level—a seed, a root—but often, vigorously visible.[7]

Most dramatically, when the Rio Grande changed, a domino effect occurred, rippling through the ecosystem. In 2008, the Farm Service Agency in Hidalgo County produced a poster showing two aerial photographs of the refuge. In the first image, from 1930, the river curves gently, dividing Texas and Mexico. Forested areas appear nearly black. By 2008, the same spot shows a profound, curving indentation where the Rio Grande leaped to a new channel during the Brownsville hurricane of 1933. The Rio Grande is now a meandering *W* shape, the twin lobes it created instantly noticeable on all subsequent maps. Photographs from the 1940s show the curvature.

The aerial images of 1930 and 2008 illustrate the dynamic character of this river, assaulted by incoming Gulf hurricane rains and high winds that scour, dredge, and redeposit bank soils. Shifts in the river are symbolic of the profound alterations in the valley itself. Altogether in the Lower Rio Grande Valley, perhaps 95 percent of the original habitat has been irrevocably altered. A study of vegetational change in Cameron County established that in this single South Texas county, native riparian woodland loss is 91 percent. Excoriating and permanent changes can be traced to the unprecedented agricultural expansion of the early 1900s; yet land greed did not destroy one dense, bird-filled forest stretching two miles north from the river. Thus, the story of Santa Ana must include explanations for the preservation of a habitat found nowhere else in the world. The extraordinary diversity of plants and animals in this protected forest includes threatened and endangered mammal species like the jaguarundi and ocelot. Over four hundred species of birds and half of all the butterfly species in the United States can be found here. And the forest, chaparral, and grasslands of the Santa Ana grant *will* speak if we look and listen closely enough.[8]

Although hiding or muffled in many places, a narrative exists of the Leals, their land, and their forest. Two of the three ranch locations on the Santa

Ana grant were inside or bordering the forest, as was an early ranch on the neighboring grant of Los Toritos. Documentary traces are slight, but knowing where those ranches lay allows us to sketch them in through an understanding of the environment. In this reconstructed story, readers can glimpse the people of South Texas who learned to know this land well, who were part of the Santa Ana ecosystem. In particular, we must credit the choices made by people of Hispanic descent—the Mexican and Tejano Leals, the Tejano Guzmáns—whose combined tenure on the grant was over seventy years of its nineteenth-century history. Their ways of responding to their land produced changes but also preserved Santa Ana. The settlers of the northern Spanish Empire who first arrived in the Rio Grande Valley in the 1750s and whose descendants were granted the Santa Ana leagues in 1834—here were actually the first conservers. They were not insignificant players. To tell their story, the narrative moves fluidly back and forth in time, connecting the land and people of long ago with the visible picture of the refuge acreage in the 1940s. The epilogue briefly examines Santa Ana National Wildlife Refuge as it is today. In this way, we can discern the ongoing vibrancy and responsiveness of the Rio Grande floodplain forests. This is a story of both human choice and miraculous survival.[9]

CHAPTER ONE

Saving the Santa Ana Forest

In the fall of 1943, the first manager of a new national wildlife refuge in South Texas ended his report on a note of satisfaction. "The Santa Ana Refuge has passed into Government hands . . . and a very fine little refuge was acquired," he wrote, typing carefully onto the provided legal form. These words are the last of his quarterly report, a document hidden away in boxes of such reports in the National Archives. Yet this single sentence marks a momentous legal safeguard for an endangered forest. Down in Harlingen, Texas, members of the Rio Grande Valley Nature Club could celebrate. After months of urgent correspondence with the head of the National Wildlife Refuge System, they had finally succeeded in saving a subtropical thorn forest poised on the edge of destruction. The Rio Grande Valley Nature Club was a modest organization that defined the civic lives of perhaps twenty men and women; it has now passed into obscurity, overshadowed by the much better known Texas Audubon chapters. Yet it was this club, these passionate birders and lifetime residents of the valley, who had perceived the treasure of Santa Ana Groves, as the forest was locally known.

During the bleak Great Depression years, members of this small organization had sponsored birding trips into the woods. When the fall and spring migrations changed the sky above the Rio Grande—tremulous miles of birds on the wing we can only wistfully marvel at today—men and women in sturdy walking shoes and canvas hats arrived by the Military Road. Through the 1920s and 1930s, they had seen the numbers of white-winged doves, for example, plummet from estimates of eight to twelve *million* a year in the lower Rio Grande to perhaps five hundred thousand by 1939. The arrival of these large blue-gray birds by the millions had become a phenomenon in the valley. Lured by those numbers, game hunters had also begun migrating to the area: annually, perhaps forty thousand hunters arrived to bolster the economy and spirits of a depressed region. Accounts by valley settlers in the 1930s mention community dove hunts as well. Farmers in the Alamo area had noticed that white-wings built nests on the first lift of the canal system but would fly to the second lift to feed. Doves had learned to use irrigation infrastructure that had been in place for only twenty years; one writer states that they were therefore "harvested with ease." In this atmosphere, where at times the borders of grain fields and scattered old-growth woodlands were literally packed with men, guns, and Model T autos, the Rio Grande Valley Nature Club members hiked quietly into the big trees of Santa Ana. They knew that in the end, the count that mattered was nests.[1]

The commitment of these birders to the trees and avian life of Santa Ana Groves represents a change in the mission of birding societies. In the late nineteenth century, formal ornithological clubs were composed of what one writer has called "bird-students"—young people, mostly men, fascinated by the scientific knowledge obtained through birding and the collection of nests, eggs, and bird carcasses. After World War I, these clubs began to shift toward a membership of bird lovers and observers; more middle-aged people joined, and more women. By the 1930s, hundreds of small birding clubs had formed all across the United States in communities and microregions like the Lower Rio Grande Valley. And in the late 1920s, a national movement was growing that confronted both market hunting and the collection of bird specimens and eggs. In 1929, a pamphlet appeared that Irby Davis and his membership may well have read: *A Crisis in Conservation: Serious Danger of Extinction of Many North American Birds*. This pamphlet insisted that policy makers consider the reality of species extinction; the authors warned about impending loss of species such as the whooping crane, trumpeter swan, ivory-billed woodpecker, flamingo, buff-breasted sandpiper, and upland plover. On the eve of the Great Depression, twenty-six other species were threatened.

The problem of collectors raiding unprotected natural areas was yet a concern in South Texas, although it is difficult to document the extraction of birds. In 1939, Irby Davis gave an informal address to a group of birders. He stated that a "greedy collector" had come down into the forests along the Rio Grande, seeking the rose-throated becard. This collector "took all that we had," Irby said. The haul included six birds and three nests. Irby concluded bitterly, "We have not seen a becard since." The rose-throated becard is described by ornithologist Timothy Brush as having always been rare or uncommon in the Lower Rio Grande Valley, so the extraction of becard nests was particularly distressing. Such personal stories underscored the message in *A Crisis in Conservation*. Issued as a wake-up call to the National Association of Audubon Societies, this pamphlet was also a critical publication for shaping grassroots activism. Yet the concerns of bird lovers in the Lower Rio Grande Valley were overshadowed—ominously—by the impact of the Great Depression and a decade of damaging droughts and hurricanes. The Rio Grande Valley Nature Club appears in the historical record in the late 1930s, founded in 1937 after a decade of privation and struggle.[2]

South Texas in the 1930s

Despite flourishing game bird hunting, in Hidalgo and Cameron Counties, as in most of America, the years 1929–33 were the bleakest of the Great Depression. Economists believe that income troughs, or all-time low levels, occurred for all social classes in 1933, including the wealthy agriculturists and cotton gin owners in South Texas. Cotton had gradually become the most important crop in Texas, luring many Mexican and Mexican American laborers northwest, even though the Matamoros-Reynosa area of Mexico had developed into a highly productive cotton farming region as well. Since as early as 1906, migrant tent communities had formed outside cotton-ginning centers; in the 1930s, these tent towns were proliferating in South Texas as well. The *Texas Almanac and State Industrial Guide* stated that in the early 1930s, 70 percent of the state population depended on cotton for livelihood—small cotton farmers, ginners, shippers, merchants, financers, and "employees." Of the 254 counties in Texas, 223 were growing cotton on what agricultural historian Keith Volanto has called "a tremendous increase in cotton acreage." The phrase "cotton employees" meant both resident and migrant workers in the fields, many of whom also labored in the citrus crop industry.[3]

In Hidalgo County, Mexican American and Mexican day laborers, both legal and illegal residents, often pieced together a living by raising a few chickens, cows, and especially goats; they ran these animals near the river, in the lower acreage of grants like Santa Ana where grazing leases were generally held by absentee owners. There, woodland and broken chaparral that could not be irrigated provided browse for domestic animals. The trees of the remaining forested areas furnished firewood. Poverty of an immediate, visible nature stamped the former ranching landscape, as migrant camps for displaced people arriving by rail sprang up outside towns and cities. One historian suggests that the communities of South Texas and the southwestern part of the state had "the most serious problem" with numbers of destitute migrants, possibly referring to the living conditions of poor Mexican farm workers. (However, the Great Depression had generally been a time of repatriation to Mexico of thousands of laborers. Waves of border crossings to the United States picked up again only in the 1940s.) Migrant camps outside Harlingen, Weslaco, Mercedes, Edinburg, and Alamo have been documented in photographs taken between 1935 and 1945 by workers from the Farm Security Administration–Office of War Information. These camps were occupied mainly by white migrants; one photograph is even captioned "White migrant workers in the mesquite." Not too far from the old Santa Ana grant, especially to the north of the Military Road, the landscape was defined by redundant cotton crops and displaced people.

In impoverished South Texas, economic recovery from the paralyzing Depression years was paramount. During the decade when the Rio Grande Valley Nature Club formed, two critical events overshadowed concerns about diminishing habitat for birds. The first was the federal government's intervention in cotton production, a dramatic statewide initiative now termed the "Great Cotton Plow-Up." Along with the cotton farms of central Texas, the broad, steamy, manure-laden fields on old porciones and land grants were yielding a glut of cotton in the early 1930s, so much that there was no prospect of selling it in a depressed international market. Warehouses sat filled with unsold bales; in the spring of 1933, a cotton crisis loomed, as nationally, unsold cotton remained at 12.5 million bales. A radical solution distressed many observers across the South: through the Agricultural Adjustment Act, cotton farmers received payment (subsidy) for destroying their own cotton crop. County extension agents speaking Spanish, Czech, and German fanned out across South Texas and the great central plains to convince cotton farmers to plow under their laden cotton plants. This dramatic and crisis-driven program was the dominant focus of an agricultural Texas world in the early 1930s: saving farms, not birds.[4]

However, in the first year of the program, 1933, the Brownsville hurricane brought the plow-up in Cameron and Hidalgo Counties to an abrupt halt. Described as one of a series of tropical storms in that year, this hurricane is yet legend in the Lower Rio Grande Valley. There were actually five hurricanes in Texas in 1933, but the winds of the September 4 Brownsville hurricane, clocked at 125 miles per hour, set it apart. Extension agents described citrus and cotton fields as swamps filled with standing water and destroyed trees. Severe flooding occurred upriver as far as Camargo in Mexico. The hurricane lasted for thirty-eight hours, wiped out 90 percent of the citrus crop in the valley, killed forty people, and destroyed all "weak buildings" in the town of Harlingen. Damage estimates were set at $12 million.

It was against the backdrop of a devastated agricultural region in recovery from a great storm and its subsequent flooding that Irby Davis and club birders voted to save the Santa Ana Groves. After the hurricane, the Lower Rio Grande Valley received government initiatives to control catastrophic flooding on the river. Birders who were hiking in the surviving woods of the riverine corridor noticed the presence of personnel from the Boundary Commission and the Army Corps of Engineers. They began to hear stories about land buy-up. To others in the highly depressed South Texas counties, the Santa Ana river frontage probably seemed just a vestige of the nineteenth century. Tangled mesquite thickets, hoary ebony groves, and hurricane-toppled trees were the last echo of an old, disappeared ranching landscape. Flood-prone river acres would finally be cleared as the Army Corps reshaped and controlled the river. Yet to the birders of the valley, these woods represented the only future for many species. When Irby Davis and other club members combed the Santa Ana woods for nests, they perceived an environment of critical value. But what was this land like in the 1930s? How had it come to be seen as expendable? Using oral accounts as well as manager perceptions, we can reconstruct what the forested acreage of Santa Ana looked like in the grim years of the 1930s.[5]

Descriptions and a few photographs from the first year of the refuge suggest a true wilderness feel to the place. Nature Club birders followed cattle trails in the steaming, miasmic heat, sensing the slippery sweat building under their binocular straps and kicking away coyote and javelina scat, vines, and brush. There was yet beauty on this tract: its tropical feel and birdsong, the clean spring skies a background for iridescent orioles in numbers unimaginable today. But this green and virile beauty was hidden away, nesting inside a brown husk of altered and degraded land. Surrounded by cleared and irrigated agricultural fields on three sides, the old forest deterred many from entering. It seemed to rise from the floodplain as a towering jungle, impenetrable and often flooded. Managers repeatedly called it "the jungle of Santa Ana" in their early reports.

Yet the edges of Santa Ana Groves were porous, threaded with many cattle and goat trails. Human use in the form of illegal border crossing and smuggling had created other footpaths. What early managers would come to call the "hoot-owl traffic" resulted in scattered campsites on the first rise above the river. Border patrols known as River Riders, eventually legalized under the Bracero Program of the 1940s, knew that unoccupied river acreage was a magnet for unsanctioned crossings. River patrols created their own horse trails in the forest, warning that people crossing at night were criminals; a manager understood from the patrol that illegal immigrants were "desperate potential and actual murderers." There is very little documentation that this was true; it likely reflects the prejudice against Mexican peoples rampant in South Texas at the time, as well as residual local fears arising from the turbulent Mexican Revolution years starting in 1910.

However, Mexican livestock also crossed the Rio Grande. Cattle broke through ill-maintained fences to ford at the Santa Ana "hot spot," bringing in fever ticks. Enormous brush piles, bulldozed ten to fifteen feet high by engineers constructing levees, left raw clearings in the woods. These pits, called borrow pits since the soil was "borrowed" for construction, filled with soupy black water after heavy rains; but because they continued to hold moisture for weeks during the dry season, they became oases for doves, red-billed pigeons, shovelers, and teals. Across the levee that still marks the entrance to the refuge forest today, immense *tepeguaje*, cedar elm, Mexican ash, and Texas ebony massed as a green wall. Almost a century earlier and in an entirely different ecosystem, the American poet Henry Wadsworth Longfellow wrote five words that have become iconic: "This is the forest primeval." He could have been writing of Santa Ana. And this forest, the enduring southern acreage of a Mexican land grant surveyed a century before, was in fact absolutely vital. It could yet attract and support such a flush of resident and migratory birds that a Harlingen-based nature club decided to act. We can envision a small group of board members sitting in a living room, sharing stories and accounts of birding and trips to natural areas such as the sabal palm forest near Brownsville. As indicated in just a few surviving letters, this club voted on preservation projects. It is no stretch of imagination to understand that the creation of the third Texas national wildlife refuge likely began with a show of hands.[6]

In the year 1940, Irby Davis conducted a nesting census of one dense tract in the heart of the Santa Ana forest. This census finally convinced J. Clark Salyer, head of the US Biological Survey and National Wildlife Refuge System, to take on a rescue. The lower Rio Grande and its thorn forest were part of the Gulf coastal flyway, providing resting, eating, and nesting resources for migrating birds coming up from the tropics. This route is much safer for birds than flying over the Gulf of Mexico. Of the 332 North American migrating species, over 80 percent "funnel along" this coastal flyway. A life-giving river, generous roosting and nesting sites, and safe skies combine to create one of the most ancient and dependable ecological relationships on the planet. But in Hidalgo County, Texas, during the Great Depression, the trees, the birds, and their river were under siege.

Three dramatic realities of the 1930s had created this crisis: accelerating game bird hunting, especially of white-winged doves and waterfowl; the destructive hurricane seasons of both 1933 and 1937 (the latter year saw more hurricane activity than any other except 2005); and finally, flood control measures in the form of dam and levee construction that were being considered and implemented by the Army Corps of Engineers. By 1939, Irby Davis was writing urgently to J. Clark Salyer: "The saving of the Santa Ana tract alone would be a very great thing." His words were specific: "The [black-bellied] Tree Ducks keep going back to the very same ponds year after year in spite of the farms crowding around them and more and more of them get shot every summer." Weekend birders had noted the duck carcasses. In addition to keeping personal life lists of birds, some club members were skilled observers who understood the key importance of specific

An early photograph of the Santa Ana National Wildlife Refuge. This is the way the Santa Ana Groves would have appeared to birders. Water fills a levee borrow pit near what is today the north refuge boundary, photographed in 1944. The forest is visible in the distance. From the National Archives.

trees to particular species, relationships that had evolved over millennia in the valley. On the roughly two thousand acres these local birders combed, some bird populations were noticeably changing. A particular case was the plain chachalaca, which one manager called the "wily Mexican pheasant."[7]

The Symbolic Chachalaca

Today at Santa Ana, the clattering, clacking, and unusually various calls of chachalacas mark every visitor's experience. But in 1940, Irby Davis's breeding census listed but a single chachalaca nest. Relentless hunting of these birds in the late nineteenth and early twentieth centuries had sent thousands to the Brownsville market. Yet another factor in their decline is their very particular nesting behavior. Chachalacas are unique among game birds in that they nest in trees—but they do not build nests. They appropriate the nests of smaller birds such as cuckoos and thrashers who create flimsy, insubstantial structures in unstable tree forks and even vines. Thus, chachalaca eggs are frequently destroyed in windstorms and are vulnerable to reptile predators. The long Texas indigo snake can coil up the trunks of cedar elm to swallow entire clutches of eggs at a time. Studies conducted in the 1970s suggest that perhaps only half of chachalaca eggs survive and that 25 percent of the losses are a result of snake predation. On Santa Ana, chachalacas most often select nests in cedar elm, huisache, and Texas ebony, and one researcher has noted that the nests are always at a certain height in these trees, above the highest floodwater levels. In conjunction with market hunting, this precision nesting threatened to remove the chachalaca forever from South Texas. As buzz saws roared through nesting habitat, chachalacas disappeared. The first refuge report of 1943 labeled this unusual, vocal bird "diminishing," but the manager also reported that a few remaining chachalacas were hiding down by the river. He had found them in sandbar willows growing on accreted portions of the Rio Grande. "Denseness and seclusion suit them," he wrote.

The 1930s birders in South Texas would have the satisfaction of seeing the chachalaca rebound. By the end of the first decade of refuge operation, the year that trails and paths were cut through Santa Ana for visitors, a report specified sixty-two "singing pairs" of chachalacas in June. It took the eyes and ears of birders and naturalists to understand what these shrieking, raucous calls meant. Earlier observers had not seen much value in the chachalaca. As late as 1910, a respected ornithologist who visited South Texas reflected this attitude. "Lo, behold!" he wrote in his field guide, "sitting not fifteen feet over my head, in a patriarchal ebony tree, were ten or more of as stupid looking aves as I ever gazed upon." These silly-looking "aves" were already uncommon in Cameron County, where the ornithologist observed them. Yet back in 1834, when the Leal family arrived on their grant, the trees of Santa Ana were likely thick with chachalacas, whose nests helped nourish the indigo snake. Today, the indigo snake is protected and listed as threatened, but the chachalaca has made a flourishing comeback and in fact can be hunted between November and February. Bird and reptile stories are intertwined, suggesting the complexity of South Texas ecology. When a species like the chachalaca disappears, in a domino effect, so go others. Today, Santa Ana preserves more threatened and endangered species than any other national wildlife refuge. The massive trees are sentinels for species survival.[8]

By the 1930s, the Santa Ana southern acreage had already claimed the title of the largest remaining thorn forest in Texas. Patches of woodland held on all along the river, niches and half-acre scraps of old land grants and porciones surviving irrigation and clear-cutting. But Santa Ana was no piecemeal remnant. Here soared nearly three miles of intact forest, a verdant, tangled, arboreal, vine-choked wilderness filled with so much life it trembled with movement on windless summer days. Despite the obvious role of riparian trees in drawing in enormous bird populations, the main focus of the day continued to be flood control. Irby Davis and his club members watched as the International Boundary Commission bought up acre after acre of these old lands, especially to the west of Santa Ana. Irby's correspondence with J. Clark Salyer reveals a sense of urgency, of impending doom for the trees and their nests. Sitting below an old military road at the southern end of a failed citrus farm, abandoned by a series of owners and left to quietly thrive on the recurring overflow of the Rio Grande, the forest was vulnerable to channelization and levee construction.

The Boundary Commission was building what Mr. Davis called "the big new levee system," with massive levees bulldozed from a series of borrow ditches on old ranch acreage. Although these borrow pits remained as miniature ponds attracting waterfowl, they were nonetheless destroyers of habitat. As machine shovels tore up the topsoil, they uprooted healthy thickets and plowed brush into dank piles. The shovels chewed deeper. Out of the pits came black, fecund earth with a strong river smell. Engineers then packed the subsoil onto the levee. A 1918 description of Alamo Tract brushland (including Santa Ana) being cleared by Mexican laborers and mules mentions vegetation so dense, rabbits could barely squirm through it. This brush first had to be burned off, producing an aromatic mesquite smoke that "permeated the air throughout the day." Extremely concerned about the habitat of ground-nesting birds such as killdeer and scaled and bobwhite quail, as well as thorn scrub nesters like sparrows, Irby Davis observed and took notes. Finally, in 1940, he sent J. Clark Salyer his nesting census for a fifteen-acre strip in the heart of the original Santa Ana grant. This census Salyer called "extraordinary."[9]

More than any other appeal, the hard data revealed in the fifteen-acre count motivated Salyer to act. Mentions of the role of riverine trees as nest habitat are rare until this census. From a published memoir, we learn that just before 1900, little Tejano girls on the old Esperanza Ranch on El Gato played with bird nests and eggs. They loved to steal a wild bird egg from the nests they could always find in "mesquite, hackberry, and huisache trees." These children routinely climbed these trees to find nests. Irby Davis's "breeding census," as he called it, identified nests in enormous elms draped with Spanish moss, in Rio Grande ash, and in hackberry and soapberry. He perceived the area as having climax vegetation, and the numbers of diverse bird nests are noteworthy. He found a beardless flycatcher nest, eleven different pairs of white-winged doves in nests, and three nesting pairs of red-billed pigeons. He wrote of the "great density of nests in these woods" and carried out other expeditions, this time with three assistants. He described in his letters "mapping" both in February and in May and June, using a hand compass and pacing distances by foot. Today, the average daily high temperature of this area in May is ninety-two degrees Fahrenheit. Irby recorded that it was "dry and hot on every census day." Yet he also saw evidence of frequent flooding, noting that a flood "was to be expected every year or two." By late May, too, a black mist of ravenous insects would already have been visible over animal scat. At times even today, the ominous hum of biting insects is audible fifty yards from the forest edge. Nonetheless, Irby Davis went in. The farm road into the tract was powdery dust. Cattle trails winding down to the river stank with soupy droppings; branches browsed and stripped by wandering goats could be whips to the hands and face. The canopy above erupted as startled birds shot up, sometimes in entire *colonias* flashing a pure yellow green on the underwing. Despite the raucous, mobile activity, Irby kept careful records. This dedicated birder noted thirty-four nesting species, with "occasional visitors": a turkey vulture, Merrill's parauque, orchard oriole, and mesquite grackle. Craning upward, he charted over 195 individual birds per census day.[10]

To carry out this fieldwork, Irby Davis drove from his home in Harlingen to the old forest, a round trip of over sixty miles. He and his wife lived in a small rental home on Polk Street, in the original downtown area of Harlingen. Anna May Davis, a Harlingen high school chemistry teacher, is noted for guiding her students in gathering data for migratory bird counts conducted by *Bird-Lore* magazine. She was encouraging Harlingen students to care about birds. In the Harlingen High School yearbooks for 1940 and 1944, she is pictured with the Bird Club as the faculty sponsor. In fact, in 1952, a charter member of the Lower Rio Grande Valley Historical Society emphasized how important Irby and Anna May Davis were to the birding movement: "Ever since the Irby Davises, expert ornithologists, arrived in Harlingen, the Audubon Christmas Bird Count in the Valley has identified far more varieties than at any other point in the United States."

In the late 1930s, the Davises were poised to watch as the town of Harlingen, founded in 1910, experienced a wild and accelerating cotton-industry boom. Despite the grinding Depression poverty, especially of the Mexican American population in South Texas, the cities in these lower valley counties were slowly recovering. By 1936, when it is possible the Rio Grande Valley Nature Club first met, Harlingen had no fewer than 288 stores supporting a valley vegetable shipping and ice production business. After the disastrous year of 1933 with its hurricanes and cotton plow-up, farmers began to see a modest improvement. In Harlingen, building permits increased sevenfold as entrepreneurs founded processing plants, two cotton oil mills, and two cotton compresses. The Davises were witnessing the daily expansion of agriculture, also evident at the edge of old Santa Ana.

On a 1939 Labor Day visit to Santa Ana Groves, a group of birders from Central and East Texas as well as the Lower Rio Grande Valley were struck full force by the reality of heavy crops. One of the birders from Alamo, Lonnie Ring, exclaimed, "You see those acres of cabbage? . . . Two years ago they were woods like those on the river. Even then we had too much cabbage . . . half of it rotting in the fields. And now we have dust storms." As the group drove west on the Military Road, Lonnie continued, "See all these cotton fields? They were woods and wild flowers. Now we have more cotton and more dust storms." By 1940, Harlingen in Cameron County claimed to be the "Winter Vegetable Capital of the World." All around Irby, Anna May, and other concerned birders, original habitat was disappearing every day. Promoters and developers saw the conversion of old riverine land for flood control as security for a remarkable future. In January 1940, an article about the proposed Falcon Dam appeared in the *Mission (TX) Times*, entitled "IBC-Endorsed Plan May Solve Lower Valley's Water Problem." At that moment, just before the government decided to buy Santa Ana, an ancient ecosystem was on its way out.

While newspapers and town boosters in South Texas were promoting land acquisition and flood control, ironically, the 1930s nationally were a time of keen interest in the acquisition of wildlife refuges. The wave of conservation and protection initiatives that developed after World War I increased through the 1930s, driven in large part by opposition to the wholesale slaughter of waterfowl by game bird hunters. In addition to a shortsighted 1924 law that permitted hunting on wildlife refuges, the 1930s Dust Bowl has been described as disastrous for birds. By 1934, bird populations were so affected that hunters began to notice the decline. "When they went out to hunt . . . the birds didn't come," one report stated. As a result, hunters themselves began to support regulations. In 1935, President Franklin Roosevelt signed legislation reducing bag limits, shortening the hunting season, and prohibiting both decoys and "baited water" shooting. In the late 1930s as well, Texas began establishing national wildlife refuges. Failed farmland was available for sale, and duck stamps provided the funding to acquire the land.[11]

Yet almost certainly, without the insistent correspondence of the Rio Grande Valley Nature Club, the federal government would not have purchased Santa Ana. Certainly local people believed this to be true. In May 1942, for example, a *Harlingen (TX) Valley Morning Star* article by Minnie Gilbert stated, "Posterity is indebted to a small group of nature lovers, with L. Irby Davis, Harlingen, as leader and principal agent, for the establishment of Santa Ana tract as a permanent wildlife sanctuary." However, J. Clark Salyer had been uncertain about it. "I would be loath to recommend the acquisition of the Santa Ana tract," he wrote, "were it not for the fact that this represents the best remaining habitat." The extreme vulnerability of that habitat in South Texas eventually motivated him to act. By 1941, he was ready to write his letter of recommendation. In it, he noted the species and nests documented by Irby Davis as well as the sheltered location of Santa Ana, lying in a right-angle bend or elbow of the International Boundary Commission levee. Irby Davis had seen the possibilities. "My idea of the best possible refuge . . . was to take all the cheap land below the levy . . . from the Donna pumping station westward to the Santa Ana tract," he urged. This "cheap land" was a thoroughfare of interrelated life forms: grasses and forbs, insects and lizards, coatimundi, jaguarundi, and birds. Most of all, birds. The trees of Santa Ana swayed with birds lifting and darting, hopping and swooping. To push through these woods was an immersion in unceasing calls and song.

Perceptions of the Forest

Yet locally, among the older residents of Hidalgo County, perceptions of Santa Ana Groves were rather dismal. Irby Davis reported making little headway with donated monies or influence. "It is really pitiful," he wrote. "Our pioneers are not conservation-minded." Indeed, those pioneers were survivors of a time in Texas history when over sixty species of birds were systematically hunted or caged for economic gain. Their use ranged broadly, from oil and eggs (brown pelican), millinery (swan, snowy egret, long-billed curlew, black skimmer), and food (American widgeon, green-winged teal, snow goose, northern bobwhite, killdeer, upland plover, greater yellowlegs, red-billed pigeon) to trap shooting (rock and white-winged dove, blackbird) and folk medicine (greater roadrunner). American robins and northern cardinals were routinely eaten in "bird pie." Woodpeckers hung upside down in rows from strung lines, choice eating in the Houston market. Crate after crate of stacked mallards on ice traveled by boxcar to Galveston and all "large towns" for the table. In the 1930s, long-lived pioneers of Hidalgo County could recall the times before the passage of the 1907 game law (a reenactment of the pivotal 1903 conservation legislation). These old-timers had lived comfortably off the land. It had nurtured them and their forebears because it was so varied an environment, seasonally abundant and intimately known in its cycles. The new, emerging ways of looking at natural resources, the scientific understanding of ecology, had few converts initially. But the Depression-era birders of Hidalgo and Cameron Counties had a grassroots passion for avian life that would characterize Audubon conservation efforts for the rest of the twentieth century.[12]

Irby and Anna May Davis, as well as other members of the Rio Grande Valley Nature Club, were awakening to crises of land fragmentation and overhunting at a time when bird species themselves were changing. One good example is the black-bellied tree or whistling duck. These were the waterfowl Irby had found shot in distressing numbers, lying along the margins of farm lakes in the 1930s. Farmers no longer tolerated them. By 1878, these large, comely ducks had come to be known by Mexicans as *patos maizal*, cornfield ducks. Their natural feeding habits had become dramatically altered by grain agriculture, turning them into crop pests. Changes to the forests of South Texas had also pressured them, however. Laying eggs on bare branches and in cavities of mature willow, live oak, ash, or ebony trees, black-bellied tree ducks may venture as much as two miles away from a river to nest. By the mid-twentieth century in Texas, very few places had riverine forest growing to that extent. (Although some treed acreage remained to the west, in what would become Bentsen–Rio Grande Valley State Park, the southern Santa Ana forest was a dramatic standout). A 1975 study found that a suitable nesting cavity occurred only once every nineteen acres in sites in South Texas. More tree cavities were available, but other factors, such as brushy undergrowth around trunks or the increasing presence of predators (feral house cats, raccoons, and opossums) made ideal nesting sites rare. So choosy are these ducks, in fact, that on Santa Ana in the 1970s, they used *only* cavities in mature cedar elms.

In the early days of the refuge, managers rejoiced at the sound of their whistling calls, knowing that the more they heard them, the more they could document recovery. In 1949, just over one hundred tree ducks migrated to Santa Ana to breed. But the manager, Luther Goldman, found them nesting in cattails as there were so few suitable tree cavities left on the refuge then, and he wondered about the possibility of building tree nesting platforms. The ducks may have been driven to lay their eggs in cattails around the inland lakes, but they were yet present, yet vocal. "The squealing calls of the black-bellied tree ducks could be heard almost anytime during the day on all of the lake areas," Goldman wrote. Only ten years earlier, these unusual tropical waterfowl were being hunted to extirpation in Hidalgo County. From 1960, the first year of Christmas Bird Counts on the refuge, until today, tree (whistling) ducks have steadily increased in number. On December 14, 2012, volunteers at Santa Ana counted 731.

In this example of a stabilized waterfowl population, we can recognize the eleventh-hour efforts of local Texas birders. These concerned residents emerge as key players in the saving of the Santa Ana thorn forest

A photograph of the West Lake during the 1944 drought. (Today on the refuge this lake is called Cattail Lake.) In 1944, only a little water remained in the old resaca bed. Note the overgrazed margins surrounding a straggling fence; for decades here before purchase by the government, cattle and goats had stripped the life-giving grass. From the National Archives.

and the birds that depend so vitally on that forest. In 1941, J. Clark Salyer finally sent a buyer to the Lower Rio Grande Valley. He began to purchase predominantly forested land between the river and the Military Road. For ten dollars an acre, the government bought parts of three contiguous 1834 grants that almost all area people saw as useless, often-flooded forest and chaparral. In a 1943 report, a refuge manager noted that the total area of the refuge was 2,200 acres. Ultimately, the Department of the Interior used a resource known as six-million-dollar funds (Duck Stamp Fund) to acquire what was described at the time as "three brush tracts on Santa Ana." The purchase price asked by the Chicago bank holding the lien was $22,414.20.[13]

Today, shifts in the flora and fauna of Santa Ana mark its known history and tie it to the twin processes of drought and flood. Changes in the land but also in the living populations form the continuum in the Santa Ana story.

For example, recent assessments show that two species of small owl have differing histories at the refuge. The elf owl is a fairly common nester there, drawn to the large cavities in massive, older trees. Another owl, the ferruginous pygmy owl, has disappeared from the old grant for long periods. A tropical species once common in the woodlands of the Lower Rio Grande Valley, this owl was last seen at Santa Ana in the early 1960s. However, staff at Bentsen–Rio Grande Valley State Park caught sight of two pygmy owls there in 2002. As habitats recover from extreme fragmentation, birds once almost extirpated may begin to return. Understanding the fluctuations of species mobility also means understanding ancient earth and water relationships. By the 1990s, environmental specialists researching in the valley could write about the impact of the Rio Grande on vegetation. Gulf storms blew in salt water that killed some species, yet floods would also deposit alluvium in new places, inviting in some plants and "carrying away" others. With protected lands providing rough natural laboratories, observers recorded the dynamic processes of the silty, muddy Rio Grande. And they found that monitoring small tracts yielded astonishing observations: yearly shifts in even the tiniest biota.

Yet in writing of this refuge historically, people have wanted to believe in its unchanging quality, to suggest a timeless endurance. "Most of its jungle-like growth has been untouched since the original grant from Spain," wrote Minnie Gilbert in a 1949 article for the *La Feria (TX) Border Scope*. In the same article, she described the way floodwaters, ending a long, five-year drought, had restored freshwater ponds and lakes at the refuge. Her words evoke the lush, aquatic feel of the place, the sounds of "plunking frogs," the "feeding flights of black terns, least terns, belted kingfishers and Derby flycatchers." Minnows and mullet were back. Wading birds explored several kinds of saturated habitats, feeding greedily on their long pole legs. The lakes again brimmed full of insects, snails, duckweed, and immense numbers of frogs. River overflow had produced a freshet of life.[14]

Sometimes that overflow arrived with startling force. In 1949, after yet another searing drought, the return of water to Santa Ana was dramatic. "The Rio went from a quiet little drip into a riproaring he-man of a river of some better than 50,000 cubic-second feet," noted Goldman. The river had begun spilling over its banks and pouring into the East Lake on the refuge on June 27. By the evening of June 30, dark, chocolate-brown water hit the North Lake. This lake had previously been a bone-dry bed, one of the oldest resacas, so long out of moisture by August 1949 that it was filled with trees in various stages of growth and height. Earlier, in 1943, an observer standing at the dried-up West Lake had called it a "wilderness of huisache." No waterfowl had visited the refuge as a result. When the drought returned in

A January 1943 photograph of a broad and lazy Rio Grande whose power is suggested by its impressive width. This may have been one of the first photographs taken of the river by staff at the newly created refuge. As such, it probably represents the first photograph ever of the river at Santa Ana. From the National Archives.

the late 1940s, refuge personnel turned to the Hidalgo Irrigation District. In early March 1948, the manager reported "squeezing" a small amount of water out of Irrigation District #2 in San Juan, the only available irrigation. This precious water poured through the old canals into the East Lake, where it soon evaporated. A heat-blown, blood-red sun burned it off within an hour.

Despite the drought, one levee borrow pit retained a little water and became an oasis for doves and ducks. And a short rain in February brought Santa Ana plants into full bloom—fresh, golden huisache, old-gold and fire-red gaillardia, primrose, and crimson-soft prickly pear blossoms. Drought-weary local visitors told the manager what being able to visit a nearby fragrant wilderness meant to them. Then the rains ceased until June. Once again, in an ancient pattern, Santa Ana was compressed between drought and flood. And then the rain returned. By August, the refuge manager had to use an inflatable life raft to make his rounds. The lakes had become inland seas.

It is precisely this see-sawing environment, this drought-flood-drought pattern, that had created and preserved the forest of Santa Ana. While we do not have consistent accounts of those earlier droughts and floods, we know that they occurred over millennia and that they shaped the thorn forest. When the first refuge manager wrote, "Santa Ana has passed into government hands," a long-evolved, irreplaceable world was saved. Santa Ana Groves had survived the Great Depression to become a national wildlife refuge. Yet the story of this rescue is the best-documented one in the old grant's entire history. In the letters and reports that flew back and forth between South Texas and Washington, DC, a glimpse of the richness of the forest emerges, of its coeval ecology and relationships. Through birders' eyes, we glean the first sense of place. We do not have any written evidence that the people who lived for decades on Santa Ana—the Leals and the Guzmáns—came to cherish their land, but we can note that their actions strongly suggest it. Throughout their shadowed yet telling history, we watch the big trees survive.

To trace and convey the endurance of the forest, an investigation like this one must rely on an assemblage of sources: accounts, maps, present-day ecological studies, documenting photographs by scientists, archaeology, genealogy, traces of landscape in western fiction, folklore, Spanish and Mexican history, and ornithology, as far back as we can find it. The story now shifts to the mid-eighteenth century, over 250 years ago. For centuries even before this, trees had reseeded and slowly attained their wild, canopied height, creating anew the forested terraces marching up from the Rio Grande. Back in the 1750s, the trees were much taller and the river much wider. Although today this can be difficult to imagine, a 1943 picture of the Rio Grande on Santa Ana suggests it: a wide, bordering river, the *Great River*, the *River of Lost Dreams*. These book titles evoke the powerful and historic Río Bravo del Norte that may have once looked like this photograph.

The land around the Rio Grande in the 1700s truly was a frontier—daunting, dangerous, unexplored. We can reconstruct the environment and suggest what it was like in the years when permanent settlers first saw it. Tracking changes on Santa Ana begins with how people from two centuries ago knew and understood it. Despite dramatic transformations of land and river, the unique beauty of Santa Ana today emerges as an unmistakable constant.[15]

CHAPTER TWO

The Original Landscape of Santa Ana

In 1834, the year that Benigno Leal received a Mexican grant for two leagues of north-bank land he called Santa Ana, Spanish settlers had been living across the Rio Grande from that land for seventy-five years. This was enough time for several generations of horsemen, explorers, ranchers, and hunters to gain intimate knowledge of the thorn forest. In considering Benigno Leal's life there, then, we must pay attention to how near he had lived to Santa Ana before acquiring it; quite likely, he knew it well. But what did he know? With what environment was he familiar? How was he prepared when he claimed his land and built a ranch homestead deep inside an ebony grove? The Leals left few written records and almost no stories, but the fact is, they persisted. They were successful, holding on to their land until the last vara was sold in 1903. They were beneficiaries of the richness and bounty of the lower Rio Grande habitat. Despite its enormous severities, the riverine corridor nonetheless shaped human lives there. Indeed, for millennia, the river had shaped every living form in the valley.

Long before Benigno and Victoria Leal chose to name their grant for Saint Anne, the land had been named and intimately known by many peoples. Yet embedded in its thousand years of known history are just two centuries of traceable narrative, from the mid-1740s to the mid-1940s, when the old grant leagues became a national wildlife refuge. And in that two-hundred-year span, the Spanish-speaking families who lived there the longest remain elusive, caught on just a few census records, legal documents, and tax rolls. Even these brief records contain more than we know about the innumerable human beings who hunted and gathered along the riverbanks of the future Santa Ana. As the river flooded and deposited soils, as hurricanes swept inland and dropped waves of salt-crusted sand onto the delta, the earth buried and buried again all traces of the earliest peoples. Archaeologists believe that packed deeply down in the silty layers of the delta are clusters of what have been termed "cultural materials." These conjectural artifacts bespeak waves of human occupancy in a paleoenvironmental era less than ten thousand years ago. From then until today, human presence proved a continuum in this rich area.[1]

By the time of first European contact in the New World, the 1492 footfall of Columbus in the West Indies, the Rio Grande delta was well known to humans. Here roamed, camped, fought, worshipped, died, and were born a multiplicity of individual Indian bands. They are generally referred to as Coahuiltecan Indians, a name derived from the northern Mexican province of Coahuila (or possibly, Coahuila derived its name from these Indians). However, similarly diverse and complex tribes were found in neighboring Nuevo León and described by Spanish observers there in the late 1600s. These accounts include as many as 150 specific groups of Indians, such as those named by Captain Alonso De León in 1686, "A List of Indian Nations That Were in Nuevo León but Have Vanished." Nuevo León and Coahuiltecan Indians named themselves as distinct tribes but were also named by Europeans, such as those nations the Spanish listed in two reports in 1747 and 1757. As more incoming people needed names for these Indians, attempts to tag them produced a confusion of referents. Living north of the Rio Grande, for instance, were the *Cootajem*, the *Pempepeum*, the *Sepinpacam*, or the *Tlanchugin*. After 1750, three Indian bands were frequently associated with Spanish missions south of the river, especially Mission San Joaquín del Monte at Reynosa, where the Leals would settle. They were the *Comecrudos* (Spanish meaning "those who eat raw food"), the *Tampacuas* ("tattooed people"), and the *Cómo se Llaman* (Spanish for "what is their name?"). The swirling mobility of these Indian peoples and their presence at different missions, settlements, military sites, and encampments over a hundred years' time, as well as their individual languages, have created formidable complexity for historians. Yet despite some tantalizing glimpses of Indian words and meanings, mostly recorded by Spanish priests, we do not know what the Indians called their land and specific places on it. They knew the Rio Grande Valley well, traveling by both land and water, for Spanish accounts before 1688 mention Indians in canoes. The Indians of South Texas provided the first identity for Santa Ana, but their names for it will remain forever unknown.[2]

Santa Ana's dense woods, teeming with rich biotic resources, yielded critical nutrition for these mobile bands of South Texas Indians. They seasonally and precisely extracted food from the great forests and river. We have only a few recorded observations of Indians hunting and gathering: a late 1600s description, for instance, mentions Indians using the mesquite bean in their diet "from the time it started to ripen until it dried." To move toward food sources, these Indians used known trails and crossings; early Spanish accounts mentioned the presence of narrow paths that Indians kept clear of thickets and brush. One of these seventeenth-century paths or "roadways" extended an entire league (about three miles) upstream from the Reynosa area on the south bank of the Rio Grande. These earliest trails that carried human traffic across Santa Ana lands have long since sunk into mire, buried beneath horse paths and pavement. Studies have definitely established, though, that bands of wandering South Texas Indians kept to the river corridor and the delta and did not much occupy the grasslands or the southern deserts. In 1747, the first estimate of their numbers was 2,500 families living mainly south of the Rio Grande. By this time, the middle of the eighteenth century, the Rio Grande delta had been explored and emphatically claimed by the Spanish Empire. From that point, geopolitical changes were rapid, driven by competing visions of who had a right to the Rio Grande resources and its powerful transportation corridor. These changes also ominously included decimation of Indian bands through disease, especially smallpox. Historians estimate the appearance of smallpox in the South Texas tribes "at least once a generation" between 1739 and 1877; sadly, there are over fourteen documented epidemics of smallpox in South Texas between 1674 and 1864.[3]

The Spanish who began arriving from the center of New Spain (present-day Mexico) finally colonized their northern frontier in the eighteenth century and immediately named it. Thus they staked their claim: Spanish labels appeared on maps. When the area was first explored and settled in the late 1740s, the Spanish settlement leader, José de Escandón, called it Nuevo Santander. In a flourish, he honored a part of Spain where he was born. In the 1820s, after Spain had let go of its North American empire and Mexico had become a country, the name Nuevo Santander changed to Tamaulipas; Mexico chose this one. The original Santa Ana land grant was Mexican, part of Tamaulipas—a wild, extraordinary, immense region. Its northern sweep was known as *Tejas*. In the late 1830s, Tejas became the Republic of Texas and then eventually the state of Texas. Yet despite human claims to dominion, the essential character of the land did not change. Shifts in flora, fauna, land, and river did occur, as those ancient, coeval processes churned slowly on despite human affairs. But the written accounts that begin to appear after 1750 use mostly the same descriptive language. Spanish soldiers on horses, long pack trains of mules and traders, then Mexican and American frontiersmen and soldiers—all were swallowed in an undulating *desierto* pushing south to meet the mountains. Life forms etched slow-moving lines against a sandy, rocky, often glittering earth. A high, heat-blown light stretched over miles of chaparral and was described in the summers as glassy, as "blasting sunlight and dust."[4]

Tamaulipas originally included the future Hidalgo County, Texas, and thus, Santa Ana. When the province was part of Spain and then Mexico, the land extended north into the South Texas Plains, stretching toward the Nueces River. The Rio Grande curved and twisted through it, creating old riverbeds (*resacas*), channeling cutoffs that moved land from one side to another (*bancos*), and sometimes even changing long stretches of its channel during lethal hurricanes. Although each spring the river flooded miles of land on either side, more often, it ran steadily southeast with a calm, muddy flow. As recurrent drought sucked the water, banks caved and rose more steeply, sometimes crashing down. Yet in some places along the southern Rio Grande, the riverbanks were pancake flat; water ran level with village streets. The original town of Reynosa, the largest Mexican city close to Santa Ana—just across the river—was laid out like this, before relentless flooding forced its relocation. In the old village, Reinosa Viejo, early residents could step out of their houses to dip river water. Accounts use words such as "treacherous" or "deceptive" in describing the placid, high summer flow of the Río Bravo del Norte, for in the space of a few days of torrential rain, the river ate villages. But as this narrative will show, the constant alternation of drought and flood was what had created this ecosystem. It has been human loss and dismay that laid down the record of a capricious river.[5]

Despite the international boundary that today divides Mexico and the United States, scientific classifications of the region include both countries. The Tamaulipan Mezquital is such a region, extending through extreme northern Mexico, across the Rio Grande, and as far into Texas as Kinney and Uvalde Counties. For two hundred miles south of the river, Tamaulipas broadens to the foothills of the Sierra Madre Oriental. Ecologists have identified subregions of plant communities in the mezquital, and the two that most likely characterized Santa Ana lands are Tamaulipan thorn scrub and the subtropical riverine forest of the floodplain. However, these are broad categories, not sharply demarcated, and they do not seem to include the rippling grasslands recorded by many observers. Today, Sonny Hinojosa, manager of Irrigation District #2 in Hidalgo County, remembers his aunt talking about the miles of pure grasses in the northern part of the county.[6]

Historical accounts of this expanse of grassland contain memorable images: "waving fields of prairie grasses broken from time to time by live oak *mottes* and occasional mesquite" or "an almost unadulterated land of trees and grasses" between the Nueces and the Rio Grande. As early as the 1820s, American observers were writing that "the whole face of the country—bottomlands, woodlands, prairie uplands—is verdant with grass." More objective assessments include references to insects: "swarms of horseflies, gad flies, ticks and Musketoes, sand flies night and day." One historian notes that descriptions of the grass being "stirrup-high" have come from American observers and not from early Spanish or Mexican sources; those

Hispanic recorders, more intimately acquainted with the lands on a daily basis, tended to see a patchy or mosaic distribution of grass communities within specific areas. The grasses of the original Tamaulipan plains varied in height depending on the availability of rainfall, springs, and rivers. It was not a uniform coverage. Yet historic observers and scientists all agree: there were miles of profuse grasses here.[7]

Three Environments

Thus, the flowing of one habitat into another on the Santa Ana grant, as understood and used by the Mexican settlers who first permanently lived there, likely included three environments. Forest coated the southern acreage and extended across the Rio Grande. Although their grants were on the north bank of the river, initially Mexican settlers traveled more often on the south side, using trails and paths linking upriver settlements like Camargo and Mier with Matamoros and the Gulf waters. This may have been because the banks were not as steep on the south side. Yet land south of the river quickly became brush and bunchgrass country, where bits of rock caught the sun, sparkling, blazing, and baking in the blindingly hot summer months. Along the Rio Grande, in places three or four miles deep on the north side, stood a broad-leaved riparian forest nourished by recurring floodwaters. Environmental scientists know that the trees of the eighteenth-century forest here were taller than those today. Then, and as late as the 1970s, the forest could be described as closed-canopy evergreen forest. On the floodplain grew Rio Grande ash, cedar elm, and sugar hackberry, a tree whose original height was especially important to red-billed pigeons. In just twenty years, the height of these trees, so important for the feeding, hunting, and breeding of birds, decreased by ten meters (over thirty feet), and the canopy became "broken." (This change occurred because of river impoundment at Falcon Lake and Amistad Reservoir). One hundred and fifty years earlier, these trees would have consistently reached their mature heights, their canopies touching and interweaving, shading the forest floor from intense sunlight. For tepeguaje, the canopy height may have been over sixty feet.

The closed-canopy forest of Santa Ana was deeply shaded, with only small, stirring patches of sun filtering down. Just as a rider on horseback would break out of the woods, he would come upon river-formed, curving lakes: the resacas. These varied in size but were capable of holding floodwaters and torrential rainfall for many weeks. We know that in the early 1880s at least, these lakes were indeed yet present on Santa Ana, for the ranch family living on the eastern league named the largest one Lake

Pechuga. As late as the 1920s, when land sales agents known as "landmen" were making their hard sell to excursion visitors, this single enormous resaca still appeared on their roughly sketched maps. It was by then commonly labeled "Santa Ana Lake." The presence of life-giving resacas—even one—would have made the leagues of this grant immensely valuable not only to a rancher but also to his family. In the 1820s and 1830s, travelers on either side of the Rio Grande observed that local people planted gardens close to resacas, which at that time were called *esteros* (estuaries). Rains could so forcefully fill esteros that they changed position and location, and the corn and bean patches moved with them. Gentler flooding happened several times a year, in spring and autumn, but the "river overflows," as they were sometimes termed, created within hours a steaming, saturated environment. Muddy river water released seeds to germinate, blooms to burst out, fish and frog eggs to hatch, waterfowl to land and feed, and grass to grow. For hundreds of feet around these esteros after rains and flooding, the margins greened up, and protein levels in the juicy stems drew deer as well as hungry cattle and sheep. The families who lived on Santa Ana after 1834 regularly witnessed these transformations and, more importantly, came to expect them. Mexican people from the Tamaulipas region knew that chachalacas would call loudly just before a thunderstorm broke, before the seasonal rains washed over the forest.[8]

Chaparral frequently opened between the trees and the rich expanse of grass. Because we have no recorded estimates of the size of the brush country as it merged into true grassland, we must surmise that it varied. Hispanic ranchers used the word *monte* to describe this land, but that term can also include some grassland; it is not exact. The use of the phrase "landscape mosaic" by many observers suggests that environments shifted into each other gradually and that brush country, or chaparral, functioned as small transition zones, microenvironments in their own right. Thickety ground cover protected upland nesting birds and cooled the soil so that reptile eggs could develop. Yet some reptiles need the high heat of sandy, unprotected soils. A good example is the Texas horned lizard, which is typically found in arid and semiarid environments and prefers a mean ground temperature of 101 degrees. It thrives in a "patchy" environment of bunchgrasses, cacti, yucca, and small mesquite trees, with edge habitat of denser thickets and trees providing protection from predators. Those predators include birds such as roadrunners, owls, hawks, and shrikes. Bobcats also eat horned lizards. These diverse species learned to hunt lizards in the chaparral, and thus the monte evolved as a significant link in the food chain habitat.

The third distinct environment on Santa Ana, nourished by water-holding resacas and the muddy acres around them, is a historic one.

Running straight north toward the South Texas Plains lay open acres of wind-combed grasses, often described as a "sea of grass." Slightly rising land north of the floodplain was still broken with forest in places, with tangled brush patches and small groves of mesquite, sometimes a live oak or two. The American Spanish name for these groves, *mottes*, remains in the languages of Texas today. But flourishing and spreading around trees and shrubs, grass survived, profuse and green many months of the year. These nutritious grasses that coated the northern half of the Santa Ana grant will never come again in such abundance to South Texas. The original grasses have left little trace—no relict or remnant stands remain to suggest presettlement species. Best guesses at which grasses grew in what would become Hidalgo County include cane bluegrass, Texas windmill grasses (*Chloris*), and species of *Bouteloua*, especially hairy bouteloua. Growing in tufts or bunches in a wide variety of soils, bouteloua or grama grasses hang their seeds to the side, where the winds catch them like pale green flags. The whirling spikes of windmill grasses move in air currents as well. Images of South Texas grasslands are replete with the terms "rippling" or "waving," words that connect to the grass species themselves. These families of grasses provide continuity: as late as the 1970s, one botanist noted that three native species of windmill grass were still common on the Santa Ana refuge, mainly in fairly open places and the floodplain.[9]

Grasses grew in association with each other and with shrubs and wildflowers. The blooms and leaves of these flowers had evolved into formidable conservers of moisture. Like all plants growing on Santa Ana today, wildflowers developed survival strategies. Competing with clumps of grass that would outshoot them as longer days unfolded, blooms appeared on the margins of old resacas and in sandy depressions where rain pooled. In parts of the Rio Grande Valley, some quite close to Santa Ana, evaporation rates have been described as extremely high. To minimize water loss, wildflowers evolved the narrowest of leaves; even their petals are often slim and minute. In selecting a single botanical species and tracing its elusive history in the woodlands of Santa Ana, we can discern how flooding has operated here over millennia.

Lessons of *Dicliptera*

The wildflower *Dicliptera vahliana*, whose slight, delicate blooms look like resting insect wings, likely once flourished near the Santa Ana resacas in presettlement days. Its twin red petals suggested an ancient insect species to the botanist who named it. Yet the first records of it on the refuge label it as rare; by the 1960s, reflecting a dramatic drop in the periodic flooding of the Rio Grande, dicliptera seldom appeared on Santa Ana. Yet amazingly, the refuge was perhaps the only remaining place in Texas to nurture it. Clumped en masse, often described as colonies, the tall, grasslike stems with reddish flowers followed one of the winding trails south to the river. This trail, long used by humans and animals on the Santa Ana grant, was even known as Dicliptera Trail in the mid-twentieth century.

The ecology of dicliptera and its importance to a range of life forms make it worth noticing. Yet dicliptera almost disappeared forever from Texas. In the 1970s, a field naturalist watched chachalacas eating dicliptera leaves in the winter months, documenting it as a food source for some birds. A recent study of South Texas plants also noted that dicliptera is host to the larval stages of three butterfly species: two crescents and a crimson patch. Other butterfly larvae, some unidentified, have been noted eagerly chewing its leaves. Yet by 1986, dicliptera was listed as an endangered plant. Upriver dams, especially the Falcon, had dramatically changed the behavior of the Rio Grande. The lack of swirling, nutrient-rich floodwaters affected many riparian plants and animals; dicliptera is but a single example. Horticulturists began to note the life cycle and preferred habitat of this red-winged flower, planting it where possible on private land. And with careful tending, dicliptera surged back. In 2010, botanist Christina Mild featured it in a natural history column, describing the aggressive, rapid spread of colonizing plants into disturbed areas, especially those recently flooded. Such patterns suggest a wildflower that evolved in tandem with persistent flooding in otherwise arid environments. Despite its meager showing in earlier decades of the twentieth century, dicliptera is back. Found in abundance during wet seasons, growing lushly on the banks of the Arroyo Colorado, a Cameron County stream, this delicate colonizer responded vigorously to the recent floods of 2010. Because of its connection to water, it is a relatively safe bet that dicliptera grew in healthy stands on Santa Ana when settlers arrived, reddening in wide half acres around the resacas.[10] (See modern photographs of dicliptera in the gallery).

Because of its proliferation after flooding, dicliptera belongs in the large group of plants and animals sensitive to the variable moisture conditions along the southern Rio Grande. "Boom-and-bust population dynamics" is a useful concept for studies of life forms in South Texas. The changes in life form in response to water are usually highly visible. This suggests that people living on the early grants looked for signs and cues to alert them to resources. They also understood dangers, to both themselves and their animals. An early-twentieth-century memoir of La Esperanza—a large ranch not too far east of the Santa Ana grant—reveals that folk culture arose from observed phenomena. Many Mexican and Tejano riddles, sayings, jokes, proverbs, and songs were connected to the natural world. A good example is "Pasa un gavilán volando." The lyrics of this riddle-song are revealing: "A hawk flies by, and seeing some doves on a branch he says, 'Goodbye, brood of one hundred doves!'" While Anglo-American tales of settling the valley—pioneer ranchers and then farmers—focus on the *presence* of wildlife, Tejano and Mexican stories often weave the *connections* between life forms and their environment. This may have evolved in some way through over 150 years of contact with indigenous Indians; one anthropologist wrote in 1917 that Indians of the "dense primeval forests of the Gulf Coast" had evolved superstitions based on trees, birds, and animals. He also noted how often Mexican Indians focused on butterflies as good or bad luck omens. Today little remains of this passed-down oral knowledge, save some expressed in the Mexican/Tejano tradition of riddling and songs; but we do know a great deal more about the natural processes operating in the Lower Rio Grande Valley.

As food resources ebbed and flowed, animals and birds located alternate and backup supplies. One commonly understood example is quail. In studying the diets of both bobwhite and scaled quail, researchers in the 1980s found an extraordinary diversity. When grasses were fresh and seed bearing, quail feasted on bristlegrass, doveweed, and panicum seeds as well as the fruits of bundleflower and *granjeno* (spiny hackberry). In fall and winter, the birds moved on to greens, and they also ate insects. This diet had evolved to strengthen quail in times of drought. Shrubs and trees had evolved mechanisms as well. The small and graceful retama, also known as paloverde, will drop all its leaves in times of drought. Yet it continues to live vitally, engaging in photosynthesis through its trunk and leafless branches. Chlorophyll rushes into the bark to turn the tree a startling green. Aboveground adaptations are matched by belowground storage of the sun's energy. Root systems of enduring brush plants are truly formidable conservers. *Guayacán*, a small, hardy evergreen tree sought by goats, has a root so tough and venerable, it has set records. Some guayacán roots are estimated to have been alive for a thousand years.[11]

Understanding the critical impact of water highs and lows has begun to clarify Santa Ana environmental history. The continuous historic observations and perceptions of aridity are now supported by objective research. Scientists have produced maps of the general climate showing the Rio Grande region as consistently deficient in rainfall. Extremes stressed the old river and its lands: horrific, hundred-year floods caused by cyclonic activity (hurricanes); annual autumn overflows; and then drought so relentless the Rio Grande itself dried up. In 1953, for instance, the entire riverbed was dry from above Laredo to the Gulf. Earlier periods of brief channel dryness have also been recorded. In 1943, record temperatures of 108 degrees Fahrenheit gripped the area from Laredo to McAllen. A year later, Santa Ana manager Earl Craven wrote of a summer drought that by August had literally scorched the refuge. He bleakly noted that the land "could hardly have presented a more burned appearance from an actual fire." This period of drought was followed by voluminous rain that led to flooding. The climate, in effect, squeezed the biome in an immense bellows of drought and flood alternation. Over millennia, these extremes produced a particular adapted environment. Grasses, flowers, trees, and shrubs became survivors of flux, as did resident birds, fish, insects, and mammals. They evolved into formidably sturdy, resilient forms.

Plants had also created distinct environments precisely suited to certain animals; in fact, the two processes were intertwined—animals also helped shape how plants survived. Soil survey maps of Hidalgo County show that the same type of soil is present on both sides of the Rio Grande, on its floodplain in both Mexico and Texas. The forests of present-day Santa Ana and the once-forested Mexican floodplain across from it contain deep, slowly permeable soils described as gently sloping. As the land of the floodplain rises, more gravel and eventually loamy concentrations appear. The place where the heavy, subtropical thorn forest ended and shrub-chaparral began indicates a shift in soil type. Especially notable were the open places described as "in prairie" by interpreters of a 1777 survey. These prairies or grasslands lay in the northwestern and southwestern portions of the future Hidalgo County. The central and eastern portions had more forest. And here flourished the trees of Santa Ana.[12]

This increase in woodland represented a greater rainfall continuum as the Rio Grande flowed toward the Gulf. The closer to the bright blue Gulf waters, with their violent storm capacity and strong inland winds, the more water fell on the earth. In "the prairies," grass roots wove through the loamier soil in hairlike, branching deltas that gripped ancient river deposits, anchoring the alluvial clay loam and conserving as nothing else could the precious moisture and nutrients. So dense was the underground mat of grass root systems that even when grazing herbivores such as white-tailed deer, antelope, and early buffalo cropped the grass stems to the ground, the grass shot back, virile, abundantly green, thick again in perhaps weeks.

The strongly regenerative capacity of the Hidalgo County grasslands was a vital feature for animal nutrition and habitat. Described today as having high rangeland potential, these once healthy grasslands originally supported myriad wild populations: predators like jaguar, coyote, and jaguarundi; foragers like javelina and nine-banded armadillo (after 1850); and upland nesting birds. Birds preferring the thorn scrub patches nested inside grassland as well as more open chaparral; these included curve-billed thrashers, cactus wrens, and Bewick's wrens. White-tipped and white-winged doves fed greedily on the seeds, fruits, and leaves of a variety of plants thriving in patches in the grasslands. Doves especially need the nutrition of native seeds such as Texas sunflower and woolly croton, a plant so preferred by white-wings it is also known as doveweed. Native seeds, far more than agricultural seeds available in the twentieth century, have been shown to prepare female doves to breed. This understanding is recent, however, and for quite a while after the refuge opened, managers talked of growing their own domestic grain supplies to encourage doves to nest at Santa Ana. In 1944, a report from Santa Ana identified key natural dove foods as pigeonberry, elbowbush, nightshade, and seeds from the prickly poppy. All grew naturally and abundantly on the refuge and probably did at the time of early settlement as well. Brush- and ground-nesting birds like quail flourished in shady, tangled, grassy borders and natural thickets. Today, although far from the one hundred thousand white-winged doves estimated in a single morning flight near McAllen in 1948, bird populations at Santa Ana are thronging and visible. It is the large mammals, the cats, that have become so critically endangered. For they must move from habitat to habitat, through a flowing landscape mosaic of hunting opportunities. When these naturally connected environments become chopped, artificially bordered and disconnected, cleared of thickets and trees, ground stalkers cannot adapt.[13]

Hunter of Flowing Habitats: The Jaguarundi

Before the arrival of domestic animals, the Santa Ana leagues hosted a relationship between birds and animals in the forest and those of the grasslands. Modern studies have supported the idea that adjacent habitats influence each other. And in centuries past, there was continual travel from one habitat to the other. The night and dusk/dawn hunters of the forest—the ocelots, bobcats, once-common jaguars, and jaguarundi—moved skillfully into high grasses on the uplands seeking the small birds and mammals that nested or lived there. One of the earliest known sketches of a jaguarundi, by Jean Louis Berlandier in the 1820s, remarkably captures the lithe, muscular outline of its body, the tree-adapted paws and claws. Like its relative the jaguar, the jaguarundi has heavy, powerful shoulders, neck, and front legs. These facilitate climbing, pouncing, and the killing of prey.

A late 1890s description of jaguarundi, the red and gray cats of the valley, vividly suggests the swift, slinking movements of these predators. F. B. Armstrong of Brownsville noted that they inhabited only the "densest thickets," where a matted underbrush of catclaw and granjeno kept out larger mammals. They wove through brush, keeping close to the ground, and with "slender bodies" and "agile movements" pursued mice, rats, birds, and rabbits. Modern-day observers of these now extremely rare cats have described long, low-to-the-earth bodies. At night, jaguarundi climb trees, dropping to the ground at dawn and then moving "in a permanent crouch." Darting in and out of brush, they hunt more during the day than any other cat of the region. Because of their small size, perhaps only ever reaching eighteen pounds, these cats can leap into the air to take birds on the wing. In 1948 a small female shot near Laguna Atascosa was found to have the bones and wing feathers of a Harris hawk in her stomach.[14]

Traces of the jaguarundi on Santa Ana are slight. In the first years of the refuge, managers reported finding jaguarundi tracks crossing dusty trails, and they occasionally saw the animals, one in a brush pile near a venerable tree called the Big Ebony. Reported as an eyra, or jaguarundi in its red phase, the words used in this long-ago report—"an elongated red beast"—evoke some of the Spanish and Mexican respect for these cats. In fact, the name of the Mexican grant to the east of Santa Ana, Agostadero del Gato, usually translated as "Pasture of the Cat," actually has a specific relationship to the jaguarundi. "Jaguarundi" is indicated in Spanish by four different terms: yaguarondi, onza, gato moro, and gato eyra. And some studies in Mexico have found that jaguarundi have a stronger tolerance and preference for pastures with thickety boundaries than for deep forest, which is

The jaguarundi (in Spanish, onza, gato moro, gato eyra). Sketched by Jean Louis Berlandier, ca. 1824, near Matamoros, and originally appearing in *Journey to Mexico during the Years 1826 to 1834*, vol. 2.

more preferred by ocelots. Moving between brushy edge habitats into more open pasture areas and then returning to a protective canopy, this weasel-like cat hunts in early morning and late evening.[15]

The trees of El Gato and Santa Ana, in fact, facilitated predation. Spanish surveyors in 1777 described the woodlands as "hid[ing] the animals that injure the livestock," specifying "tigers, lions, and wolves, and snakes." In the forest they also noted deer, javelina, antelope, hares, rabbits, and rats. When Santa Ana became a refuge, early biological inventories even listed some Mexican honey bear, or coatimundi. Daylight drew most night hunters back into the thorn forest, unless a severe drought forced them out into the open grasslands during the day. Such behavior was reported as late as the 1920s, when a pilot flying over Willacy County during a drought looked down at a tawny ring and saw "dozens of mountain lions crowd[ing] around the Old Salt Lakes." Reading through historical accounts of the Rio Grande corridor in Hidalgo, Cameron, and Willacy Counties, it does not take much imagination to conceive of these later Mexican land grants as filled with wild feline hunters.[16]

The 1830s grants like Santa Ana were surveyed using natural markers, such as distinctive trees, large boulders, and resacas, to mark property lines. But these human boundaries had no relation to edge habitats marked by animal activity. Grants sat side by side as long, ribboning rectangles on maps, but habitats defined how animals lived. Transition zones especially, the merging of one habitat into another, were porous seams of life for birds, reptiles, and insects as well as mammals. Forest birds darted out over the grasses, lured by a rising arc of insects glittering in the sun. Especially likely to hunt both forest and grassland insects were resident birds such as the green jay or kiskadee. Seasons produced layers of insect abundance, including large, "protein-rich" insects necessary for successful rearing of fledglings. One such insect was the common grasshopper, described as an insatiable eater of grasses. Birds that preferred the edge habitats of Santa Ana, the meeting of chaparral and forest where they had access to two kinds of larder, also included the passerine birds, such as orioles, warblers, and flycatchers. And the butterfly population on Santa Ana, today world renowned, is always food on the wing. In two snaps of a small, husky bill, an iridescent butterfly wing can be crumpled and then the thorax and remaining wing ingested. It can happen in a single second.

The high numbers of birds in the original thorn forest suggest an equally high insect population in certain seasons. The butterflies mentioned in early Indian superstitions were likely prolific on Santa Ana in the 1830s:

they drifted through the ecotone, that place where forest and brush met in transition. Tiny pools of water, slight declivities of mineral-laden moisture, drew them down. This water-seeking activity, known as "puddling," brought slowly fanning wings of drinking butterflies to the eyes of green jays in the canopy. The leagues of Santa Ana, especially because of adjacent habitats and corridors, were full of predation. Worldwide studies have correlated the richness of butterfly species with the diversity of birds, suggesting that many life forms on Santa Ana depend ultimately on the forest of the old grant. Yet food chain rhythms and predator-prey relationships were—and still are—so woven into an abundance of animal, bird, insect, and aquatic life that, in 2015, we yet do not know the name of every living organism on the refuge. The acreage preserves some of the original three habitats of the Santa Ana grant: forest, chaparral, and grasslands. Yet secrets and mysteries remain.[17]

CHAPTER THREE

First Changers

Hunters, Grazers, and Browsers

The documented story of the 1834 Santa Ana land grant begins at least eighty years earlier. By the late eighteenth century, a change pushed into the northern Hidalgo County grasslands that destroyed ancient rhythms: domestic animal appetite. Spanish families brought to the southern Rio Grande herds of grass eaters, the hoofed herbivores carried originally to the New World in Spanish galleons. After 1750, settlers whose livelihoods were pastoral rather than agricultural were living in the area of Reynosa, in northern New Spain. The expeditions and settlements led by José de Escandón in 1749 had anchored colonial Spain in the arid chaparral. In his initial observations of grasslands near the Gulf, however, Escandón had written of the land, "it is of good quality for all kinds of seeds and the raising of livestock. For producing the best pastures of grass I have seen in as much as I have traveled through, it maintains itself green all the year." Escandón connected the maintained "green" with the abundant rainfall he observed. Yet he had not lived through enough years in the valley nor attempted to grow crops on land farther up the river. There were no consistent abundant rainfalls to water the grasslands or forests in future Hidalgo County. There immense trees thrived on floodwaters, not rainfall. The green vigor Escandón praised was based on adaptation, deep root systems, and the ability to weather abrupt climate change.[1]

José de Escandón dreamed of Nuevo Santander farms watered by the Rio Grande. Spanish irrigation technology had worked elsewhere in New Spain and had in fact been blended with Indian irrigation practices in the El Paso and Santa Fe areas. Spanish accounts of early irrigation mention the use of ditches and "sacas de agua" (water bags). But these practices foundered on the banks of the lower Rio Grande. The sometimes high, erratically carved banks were too steep for extensive irrigation canals. The 1767 survey of land around Reynosa resulted in the awarding of specific grants for irrigation; these were called *caballerias* and measured approximately 177 acres. Yet there is little indication that these irrigation lands developed into dependable agricultural sites.[2]

Settlers attempted to import the use of ditches, or *acequias*; descriptions of their efforts at the settlement of Camargo, near the juncture of the San Juan and the Rio Grande, include the phrase "poorly developed irrigation ditches." Some irrigation was eventually successfully practiced along the San Juan River, at a place where it ran in shallow curves. Here settlers were able to grow garden vegetables—beans, melons, corn, and the squashes that were so important to their annual diet. Local Indian tribes were also described by the arriving Spanish as using the floodplains of rivers to grow small patches of "corn and other vegetables." These Indian plots were subsistence gardening, the planting often haphazard with little tending of crops. Indians had long been aware of the caprices of climate in their lands. For thousands of years before the Spanish arrived, their culture had been highly mobile. Their practice was to scatter seeds and hope that for one season, crops would survive. They would return to these casual gardens at harvest time, gleaning what may have thrived, what may have been fortuitously overlooked by birds and animals. Horticultural crops were in fact treated as backup systems to the primary hunting and gathering activities. The success of irrigation using Rio Grande waters in high-yield agriculture was 150 years in the future. For the first settlers here, it was grass that became the focus of livelihood.[3]

In the 1750s, the village of Reynosa, today opposite Hidalgo, Texas, lay initially in the floodplain of the Rio Grande. Then in 1802, after a catastrophic flood, Reynosa was moved to a more secure location twelve miles southeast of the original site. And all who lived in the vicinity—priests at San Joaquín del Monte Mission, mission Indians, ranching families, pastoral herders, day laborers, and various military personnel—accepted that their way of life would not involve extensive irrigated agriculture. Reports from the Reynosa mission describe efforts in the earliest years to cultivate large fields in order to feed mission Indians who had migrated there. These fields appeared in an area known locally as *El Desierto* (The Desert). Failure of crops can be inferred as Indians are described as having to forage for food on nearby ranches and in woodlands. Accounts of this northern Spanish settlement provide the first understanding of the environment on Santa Ana, as Reynosa was by far the closest community to the grant. Of the five early Escandón settlements, Reynosa would have the most impact on the history of Santa Ana.[4]

While the Mexican land grants to Reynosa settlers in 1834 officially carved out and defined the Santa Ana lands, the period before this, 1750–1834, must also be counted as part of the story. In the seventy years before the Leals moved onto their grant, the thorn forest and grassland were already undergoing change. Escandón's settlers came mostly from the herding province of Nuevo León, New Spain. They had been enticed

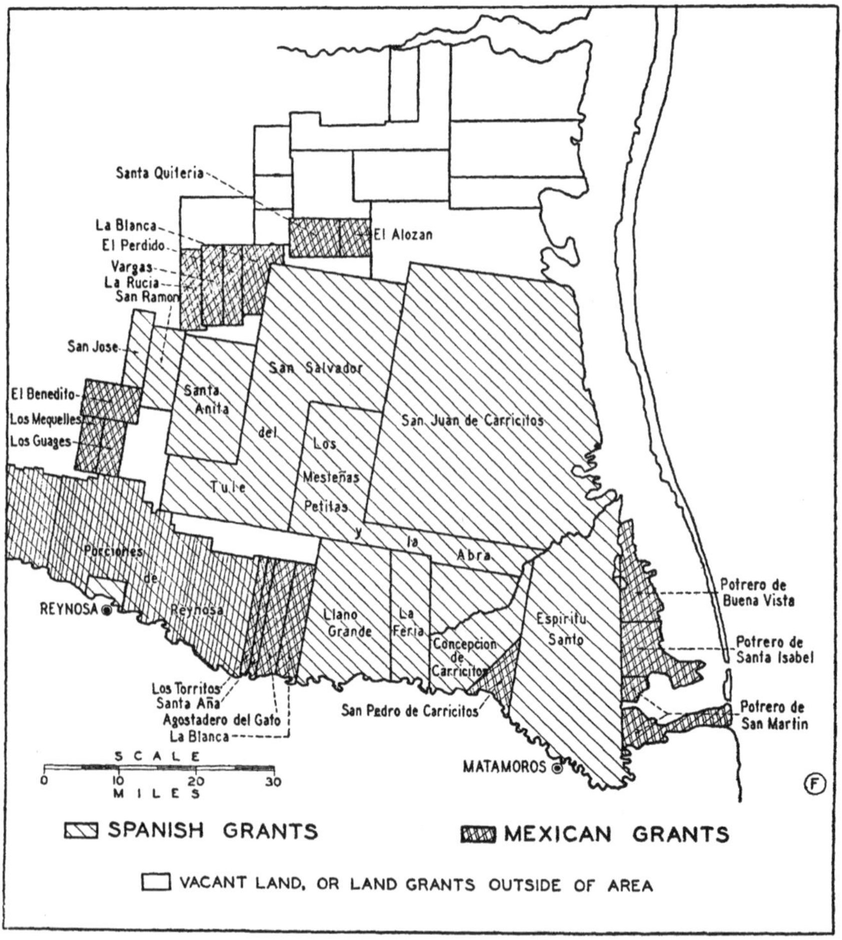

An outline map depicting the location of the second and permanent Reynosa in relation to three sets of grants: the Spanish north-bank porciones, the early Spanish land grants of the 1770s, and the final Mexican grants of the 1830s. Santa Ana is drawn carefully enough to show the protruding knob of land, the single heavily forested "point" that became two lobes after the hurricane of 1933. Map by Edwin J. Foscue, "Agricultural History of the Lower Rio Grande Valley Region."

to migrate to the unsettled northern frontier by gifts of land, tools, and exemption from taxes for ten years. The area where they built their ranches has been described variously as thorn scrub, chaparral, or grasslands. Settlements lay near forests but not in them. Both north and south of the river large swaths of woodland towered en masse, signaling a water supply for tree roots. As it is today, the understory of these woods was a tangled thicket. Early accounts often use phrases such as "interspersed with forests" in describing the mosaic quality of the land. As earth rose and fell, water levels varied. Where moisture was held longer on the uplands, the rippling grasses began to appear, and here grazed immense numbers of sheep and cattle as well as smaller goat herds. One 1820s observation from the Reynosa area mentions the color of grass in a land dip where moisture gathered. Against a landscape of "immense, untillable hills" or "waterless, arid hills," a traveler saw pools of juicy green grass "to which the herds come."[5]

New Eco-Travelers: The Lure of Resilient Grasslands

The early settlers also moved between forest and grasslands; initially, this pattern probably surfaced with hunting. As with all people in frontier zones, the taking of mammals, birds, and fish was constant, often opportunistic, a survival skill passed down from fathers to sons. Incoming Spanish from Nuevo León and Coahuila brought with them the practices of their forebears, including knowledge and use of particular kinds of firearms, knives, and traps. Hunting supplemented growing herds of domestic animals; references to the hunting of white-tailed deer and antelope are consistent in the written accounts and impressions of Europeans who crossed south across Tejas and the Rio Grande. Yet there is very little specific evidence about how Spanish settlers and, later, Mexican ranchers actually hunted. They almost certainly supported their families with game in the first decades. In the 1820s, one observer wrote about the strong preference for skunk meat. Indians such as the Comanches as well as presidio soldiers and rural Mexicans—"almost all the inhabitants of the interior states"—considered skunk a delicacy. They learned to remove the powerful musk glands and slow-roasted the meat over coals. Northern Mexicans also found armadillo to be delicious and, as reported in the mid-twentieth century, were consistently hunting it at night, throughout its range. Hunters could dig the armadillos "out of their burrows" with machetes. Northern indigenous Indians may have transferred to the incoming Spanish hunting methods such as setting net lairs or taking ducks by hand as they swam.

For larger game, Spanish and then Mexican ranchers likely used the flint-ignition hunting musket called the *escopeta*. Although these guns were manufactured in Spain, they were in short supply on the frontier. It is probable that ranchers and hunters obtained guns through trade with Indians, who had in turn obtained muskets from the French, British, and later, Americans. Ranchers kept their weapons for decades, perhaps lifetimes. The original settlers—the male heads of households—are listed on the first Reynosa census as bringing with them muskets and shields. A member of a military squad would have "all his arms." A map depicting 1754 European gun distribution through trade to Indians and sales to colonists shows Spanish arms available south of the Rio Grande and French guns circulating in Tejas. In a fluid frontier zone dominated by illegal trade—for Spain prohibited the trade or sale of guns to Indians until the 1790s—there were many opportunities to obtain weapons, even the Spanish cavalry pistols issued to military officers.[6]

The shooting and trapping of stock predators, the great cats of the valley, is well documented; their spotted and tawny hides show up on lists of skins and furs brought in to trading posts, including a successful post at San Antonio in the 1840s. And the number of deerskins shipped out of Central Texas trading posts was formidable: across a ten-year period ending in 1853, seventy-five thousand deerskins left Texas. Indian hunters likely supplied the bulk of these skins, but not all. Ranchers and hunters also profited from the trade. Yet well before 1800, hunting also supplied meat to frontier Nuevo Santander families, despite their large numbers of herd animals. Research has shown that when domestic animals arrive to a new environment, such as the much more arid chaparral of Nuevo Santander, it can take as long as thirteen years for them to adapt and begin to multiply in number. For this reason especially, the forested miles along the Rio Grande were critical for the survival of Reynosa-area *pobladores*.[7]

As domestic animals began to increase, subsistence hunting gave way to the skin and hide trade, especially, as mentioned earlier, in deerskins. Yet the changes in animal populations impacted by eighteenth-century hunting mirrored subtle changes beginning in the grasslands as well. Long before permanent residency on river land grants occurred in the 1830s, pastoral herders were driving flocks of sheep and cattle as well as goats across the Rio Grande. They were using medieval Spanish law and the customary understanding that livestock could eat grass wherever it grew on unclaimed land. Although long removed from Spain, Spanish New World herders in the northern provinces still followed European practices in making sure sheep did not graze on the same grasslands all year. This practice protected against both overstocking and overgrazing. Fording their herds in the shallowest places, crossing points that would evolve into well-known human fords and ferries, Reynosa herders headed into the broken grasslands of Hidalgo County. One history suggests that a strong draw for herders in the sandy plains north of the river was the presence of springs, *ojos* (*ojos de agua*), or "eyes," glimmering in the earth where water tables had risen. North-migrating ranchers could dig shallow wells near these ojos for their animals.[8]

The numbers provided by agricultural historians are impressive. The first Reynosa census, conducted July 21, 1750, reveals names important in the Santa Ana story: Cavazos, de la Garza, Balli (originally Vallin), and Guzmán. These settlers arrived with large herds selected for breeding. Juan Antonio Vallin brought "seventeen breeding mares and one stud horse." A Cristóbal Cano family brought in 1,140 head of sheep and goats. On this census, the phrase "equine breeding stock" appears often. Don Diego de la Garza brought 200 branded equine animals for breeding, mostly for mules. The higher numbers of horses, goats, and sheep produced substantial increase by 1757. That year, animal counts for the Reynosa area included "3,595 horses, 72 mules, 1,126 cattle, 61 burros, 7 yoke of oxen, and 13,427 goats and sheep." On earliest ranches established near present-day McAllen and Pharr, as many as 13,000 sheep and goats grazed on the rich grasses of presettlement Texas. Burros and horses that had escaped from the first Spanish expeditions had thrived and multiplied on the broad Texas plains as well. These were the days of unfenced ranges, of wild, lush grass that seemed inexhaustible—enormous leagues of grass that herders and ranchers believed would feed thousands of animals into perpetuity. In 1795, observers noted that in Nuevo Santander, "haciendas and ranches are segments of land without limits nor landmarks . . . few of the settlers have fixed boundaries, though each was assigned his own." As the Santa Ana lands stretched north toward the Texas plains, grassland appeared. The green flow of grasses punctuated by clumps of thorny brush species was particularly suited to sheep and goats.[9]

The settlers who originally came from Nuevo León, driving sheep across the Tamaulipan chaparral, well knew the strength of these animals. Despite their woolly coats, sheep are not particularly vulnerable to thirst. Studies have shown that sheep need far less water than cattle on a daily basis. Except in the blazing high heat of midsummer, sheep need water only every other day. Even on the hottest days, when a range cow may need to drink as much as ten gallons a day, a sheep can get by with a gallon. This is especially true if sheep are eating prickly pear fruits (tuna). This characteristic alone would give sheep an edge in the Lower Rio Grande Valley. In an environment such as the Hidalgo County grasslands, where surface water was not common, sheep and goats had naturally adaptive habits. Goats preferred and ate brush species, voraciously browsing and stripping leaves, blooms, buds, and seedpods. So adept were goats at choosing to eat brush species that they were always included among Spanish and Mexican herd animals. In addition to being natural leaders within small sheep herds, Spanish goats arriving with the Escandón settlers in 1749 shaped and controlled the brushy edges of pasture.[10]

These goats have become known by many names, including meat, brush, and wood goats. And the brush of Santa Ana chaparral consistently nourished goats until the mid-twentieth century. Leaves and stems of mesquite, blackbrush, *guajillo*, guayacán, Texas persimmon, and colima can form up to 50 percent of annual goat diets. Goats ate tender new spring grasses as well, grazing in that season on the bounty of the northern Santa Ana leagues. There they would have mingled with sheep for the spring, returning to evergreen shrubs like guayacán and *cenizo* in autumn and winter. Some modern studies have even suggested that goats can be instrumental in controlling the spread of trees into grazing lands—especially species of oak, hackberry, and juniper. The hardiness and browsing ability of thousands of goats north of the Rio Grande began, in fact, to blend habitats, as like all mobile domestic animals, they excreted seeds; brush flourished along their trails.[11]

Despite the numbers recorded in early Spanish counts, domestic animals raised for wool, hides, milk, meat, oil, and feast foods like young goat (*cabrito*) were not at first market economy investments. The Escandón settlements were frontier communities that could not rely on regular provisioning from the Spanish Empire. Isolationism fostered resourcefulness and cultural traits such as a strong sense of duty and respect for physical prowess, including hunting. The medium here was trade, trade and exchange, often recorded as barter. Settlers were willing to travel west to Nuevo León or south, walking or riding in enormous, formidably heavy-wheeled carts (*carretas*) pulled by oxen, or riding horses to accompany pack trains of mules laden with animal products to be exchanged in the older Spanish provinces. Commodities from the Rio Grande frontier needed to be substantial to secure important provisions in return: fabrics, blankets, weapons, snuff, tools, and utensils. Luxury items such as chocolate, silver hair combs, and ornate crucifixes also eventually traveled back to Rio Grande ranchos. There is also evidence that Spanish settlers, priests at missions, and even governors of provinces routinely traded with Indians after 1746, despite Spanish laws that forbade barter and trade with indigenous people.[12]

Nuevo Santander settlers explored a wide circumference of land around their original villages and missions. They were knowledgeable, creative, and ambitious. While priests toiled in small agricultural plots and sought Indian converts and labor, mobile ranchers on horseback learned how to extract resources. The village of Reynosa had grown and its jurisdiction had been surveyed as set out in Spanish edict—six leagues marked off around a *villa*, or settlement, in all four directions. It seems that creating villages with a central plaza was important in the surveying process. On order from the Spanish crown, all the new villages were to have plazas, as these were "vital for the distribution of land." Royal commissioners awarded land to settlers beginning in 1767. Settlers received three kinds of land: "that which could be irrigated, that which could be used for grazing, and that which could comprise the town proper." The grazing grants were enormous and spread across the Rio Grande into northern Tamaulipas. Lands held in common by villagers were called *ejidos*, and some of these were also across the river.[13]

To the settling Spanish, the Río Grande del Norte was a resource of vital water flowing through the middle of another sea of grass. It was not a border, not a boundary—that was theoretically the Nueces River, farther north. Ranchers exulted when the Spanish crown agreed to give them land grants. But settlers who had no grants were just as ambitious. They saw the value of running stock on the Tejas grasslands, and they began to rent lands on the ejidos. Despite differing kinds of land ownership, communities north of the Rio Grande formed around these ranch nuclei. Ranch settlements tended to straddle the boundaries of two adjacent grants, as settlers found safety from Indian attacks. Hidalgo County towns such as Peñitas and La Joya began their existence as 1760s rental ranches. Peñitas, "little pebbles," named for riverbank gravel, was described as a settlement with a mother city, Reynosa, across the river. A crossing trade developed, suggesting strongly that riparian forest in this area had been somewhat cleared near the water. Key tree species were extracted for wood and cleared lands hosted residences and buildings of the carrying trade in addition to ranch structures. From Peñitas, ranchers on horseback explored northeast across future Hidalgo County, eager to assess its potential. It did not take them long. Empowered by a directive from José de Escandón, they went after salt.[14]

Rock salt mined in northern Hidalgo County at La Sal del Rey proved critically important. In 1795, an inspection by Félix Calleja produced a description of this saline bounty. The Salt of the King lay in beds as "solid masses of coagulated salt." Salt miners cut large blocks, similar to quarrying stone, noting the color as "mother-of-pearl." The salt was perceived as powerful and magical. If tree branches or birds fell into the salty pools, it was believed they would be transformed within a day to salt, keeping their own outlines. Peñitas became a storage and trade site for this salt and prospered from it. Reynosa also became an important station in the salt trade. Ranchers on both sides of the river used cartloads of raw salt in the tanning and curing of hides. By the late 1790s, Spanish settlers were hunting white-tailed deer in large numbers, eating the flesh and both using and selling the skins. They bred and delivered mules to the interior provinces as well as live sheep and wool clips. This trade was the consuming economy and effort of their lives. For the single year 1795, trade statistics reveal an annual output of "4,770 loads of salt, 8,000 deer skins, 1,000 horses, 20,000 sheep, and 1,800 goats." Settlers delivered "7500 mules and 6800 loads of wool." These numbers of animals were possible because of natural increase—high reproduction—on the protein-rich grasslands. The grass thrived on violent storms and floods. The snow-fed Rio Grande, coursing to the Gulf carrying Rocky Mountain runoff, periodically delivered a nourishing inundation to its forests and grasses.[15]

For the first century after settlement, Spanish and then Mexican ranchers were the beneficiaries of an ancient system of replenishment. Animal and human populations increased, yet not all animals survived. The settlers depended wholly on their livestock, as they could not easily raise agricultural crops. Animal diet was critical for herd increase, but the farther away the herds roamed, the more vulnerable they became. Animals collapsed and died in the heat, ate poisonous leaves and berries, and succumbed to venomous snakes. Predators of the forest and thorn scrub stalked and culled weak and newborn animals. Especially troublesome for cattle and horses were mountain lion and jaguar, skilled stalkers of the forest edge that could easily hide in tall grass. Since Spanish and then Mexican herds were providing plentiful prey, the ecosystem likely began to tip toward underutilization of food resources by carnivores. It was no longer necessary for a large coyote pack to fight over a single jackrabbit and devour it to the point of marrow extraction. This inference is supported by statements of ranchers from the 1820s that predators often left half-carcasses of kills. Each week, no matter the season, Reynosa and Tejas area ranchers would come across bloated carcasses drawing in clouds of wheeling turkey and black vultures, as well as caracaras.

Like the forest predators introduced to domestic prey by the 1750s, these carrion eaters who kept the chaparral picked clean of rotting wild animal flesh also met change. They learned to eat well at Spanish ranchos. Vultures especially have been described as "once extremely abundant" in South Texas. Accounts from the 1840s include observations of entire skinned cattle carcasses reduced to skeletal remains in an hour by vultures. The presence of so many domestic animals and their frequent deaths altered the scouting patterns and survival rates of carrion birds. As pickings improved, fledglings thrived and learned new food-procurement patterns. In post–Civil War Texas, vultures were observed congregating en masse in the tallest trees surrounding slaughterhouses and butchering sites. There is no reason to think they did not also darken the branches of trees on the ranchlands of Santa Ana.[16]

One reason to believe so is the presence of black vultures on the ref-

Black vultures feeding on dead fish at Santa Ana, 1948. From the National Archives.

uge in the 1940s. When twentieth-century manager accounts became available, observations of black vultures appeared. Also known as carrion crows, these large, strong birds have a critical function along the Rio Grande, where frequent severe drought kills wildlife dependent on a watery habitat. During an almost two-year drought ending in the summer of 1948, the lakes of Santa Ana dried to a heavy, odorous mud, packed and prickly with dead plant material. Managers described deep crevices and cracks in the lake beds. The canals of the irrigation system and the old borrow pits near the levee dried first, however. There, fish perished by the hundreds and were expertly cleaned up by black vultures, who had been at it for millennia.

Even more dramatic for observers, the patrolman living on the refuge that year reported finding drowned and shot Mexicans washed up with river debris, as many as five or six. These corpses were located for him by many slowly circling black and turkey vultures. An even more gruesome report concerns a human body lodged in the river in August 1950. Before authorities could drag it out, "vultures had picked the bones clean." The river then washed the skeleton away. Large resident populations of great-tailed grackles also contributed to cleaning the habitat. In the late summer flood of 1948 on Santa Ana, thousands of tree snails drowned and lay in windrows around the lake margins, polluting the air. The manager noted the powerful, rotting stench. Then grackles came from miles around and cleaned the lake beds. Refuge staff described them as "moving in for the harvest."[17]

These cleaning processes had operated on Santa Ana land for thousands of years. But when settlers entered the ecosystem, domestic animals supported the rapidly growing human population of Nuevo Santander. Every winter to spring, new waves of colts, lambs, kids, and calves followed mature herds to the grasslands. Each ate many acres of grass the first summer of its life. Yet despite this picture, the South Texas grasslands between 1750 and 1850 could not be described as overgrazed. The land was immense and generous. Hungry animals fanned out over the miles, dots in that regenerative sea of green nutrition, able to seek the shady edges of cooler woods and thickets when the blistering summer days reached temperatures above 110 degrees Fahrenheit. In exceptionally dry years, the land took on a "naked" quality and animals resorted to stunted grasses growing in the shade of mesquite and ebony groves; the edges of the riparian forest were heavily grazed and browsed. And it is likely that in these severe drought years, Reynosa sheep, goats, and cattle released north of the river penetrated the Santa Ana forest itself, despite ravenous insects and feline predators. This was more likely to have happened when ranches were built on Santa Ana, after 1834, but for a long time, there were no fences, no demarcations. Although the final north-bank land grants were not made until the 1830s, domestic animals had been eating Santa Ana grasses, mesquite beans, and shrub leaves and fruits for decades before then. When a patch was denuded, the animals surged on. The grass next door was always greener. And grantees like Benigno Leal knew where the grass grew. Perhaps he had had his eye on Santa Ana grasslands for quite a while. It is likely he had lived most of his life in Reynosa.

Into the Forests

Land had been granted first—earlier—to Spanish ranchers on either side of the future Santa Ana land, suggesting that the four later Mexican grants—La Blanca, Agostadero del Gato, Santa Ana, and Los Toritos—were the most heavily forested. They were not claimed at the time of the granting of north-bank porciones and the larger hacienda-style grants of Llano Grande and La Feria, made in the 1770s. Spanish and Mexican land grants are often studied (and mapped) together, but over sixty years separated the occupation of north-bank porciones and large Spanish land grants from the two- to three-league Mexican grants of the 1830s. That time gap is interesting. Why did settlers from the Reynosa area not petition for leagues that included Santa Ana? Forty-three north-bank porciones were awarded out of the jurisdiction of Reynosa, yet none of these included the land of the future wildlife refuge. One explanation is surely the density of trees on the Santa Ana grant, as suggested in the Petition of 1763, by which Reynosa settlers first asked the Spanish crown for grazing land south of the river. They wished to avoid the north bank, for "these lands are of little value on account of the dense woods which exist thereon, and the plains upon which to pasture our stock being limited."[18] Below, a 1940 photograph of a moss-draped cedar elm on Santa Ana suggests just how dense those woods may have seemed to Spanish settlers.

Settlers may not initially have wanted land covered with such massive forest, but by the time north-bank grants were made, domestic animals

A 1940 photograph of a cedar elm on Santa Ana. Irby Davis, who took this photograph while conducting a nesting census, wrote, "A typical elm at side of trail." From the National Archives.

Aerial photograph of the upper part of the refuge, taken in February 1947. The ebony forest pushes right up to the clubhouse. From the National Archives.

had discovered the benefit of woodlands. Pushing into the much cooler vegetation, goats and cattle could create a new kind of edge habitat: the trail entrance. While we do not have surviving evidence that demonstrates herd animals using forests, at least one early-twentieth-century photograph captures a range cow walking comfortably on a forest path. This cattle trail winds through woods described once more as a "thorny jungle" of mesquite, spiny hackberry, and cactus. One map, showing a core Santa Ana section used for Irby Davis's nesting census in 1940, is delicately marked with cattle trails, and those trails meander in and out and across the census tract no fewer than twenty times. Yet Irby had selected this particular tract because of its dense and mature tree growth, optimal for nesting. These mapped trails communicate a message across 250 years: the understory of Santa Ana was good eating. Hoofed animals on forest soil would only pack and define trails further.

There, especially in upland tree and shrub growth along the edges of open grasslands, goats could strip tender new leaves and twigs, moving on to dried pods and husks in autumn. Cooling tree shade brought them in, day after day, along the green corridors. Although herdsmen would have tried to keep stock from roaming deep into the woodlands, in the brutally hot season, animals likely took sanctuary there. And they continued to seek forest resources for more than two centuries. In the early

1940s, ramshackle fences on the Mexican side were no deterrent to cattle and goats; they vaulted over and swam across into the refuge, using especially the main, long-established crossing. Managers described the Border Patrol—River Riders—driving wandering cattle and goats back across the Rio Grande. When settlers actually lived permanently on the Santa Ana leagues, Texas ebony and mesquite fences appeared to control stock penetration, most especially around human structures such as ranch houses and their patios, cemeteries, wells, butchering tables, and gardens. But before human occupancy, the interplay between grass and brush, shaded forest and chaparral, offered backup systems to grazers and browsers alike that kept them cooler and fed them across seasons.[19]

By the time of the 1834 Santa Ana grant, herds of sheep and cattle were flourishing on what was at the time Mexican grasses. The grants stretched north approximately twelve miles into the South Texas Plains. Because of later dramatic changes to the land involving the spread of mesquite and, in particular, its bunching into stands of taller trees, observers have tended to use terms such as "invasion" of mesquite. But mesquite was always in the South Texas Plains and always found near the Rio Grande. On Santa Ana, as elsewhere, mesquite had a keystone role. It broke out in tangled copses to entwine with other woodland trees and shrubs, especially granjeno (spiny hackberry). Granjeno often grows near and beneath mesquite, a relationship surely known and valued by ranchers and herders of the eighteenth and nineteenth centuries, as their goats browsed both trees. But there are other advantages to a thriving mesquite-granjeno understory.[20]

Modern studies have revealed that the shaded canopy of mesquite reduces the soil temperature so that granjeno seeds can germinate. Extremely high surface temperatures of unprotected soil can reach 140 degrees Fahrenheit, but granjeno seeds will begin to germinate only when the temperature falls to 104. The combined shade of mesquite and granjeno trees, as well as their fruits, leaves, and stems, provides one of the richest combinations of wildlife cover and food. These two trees were present on Santa Ana for thousands of years and nourished its birds and animals. The twisting, "curiously shaped" branches of granjeno bore orange-yellow berries each fall that Mexicans called *capul*. These berries were a critical water source for birds and small mammals such as rabbits; one 1885 inventory reported that all domestic fowl greedily ate granjeno berries. The mesquite understory stretched to the banks of the Rio Grande. Because there were ranches with large cattle herds grazing north of Santa Ana when it was granted, we surmise that riders crossing the river to Reynosa and other settlements must have known where to ford easily. One of those crossings may well have been at the protruding "point" of the Santa Ana bank. As the land sloped down toward the Rio Grande, taller trees took root, as well as water-loving black willow, which today provide the preferred nesting sites of Altamira orioles, and likely other species of oriole in earlier centuries.[21]

A striking variety of native trees, shrubs, and grasses supported wildlife and lured in domestic animals. But they also supported people. Accounts passed down through families from the Coahuila and Nuevo León regions reveal a tender and respectful knowledge of different woods and their properties. "Good wood is like a jewel," reflected a 1920s Mexican immigrant to San Antonio. A former charcoal burner from Coahuila, he knew that huisache burned fast—so fast an entire tree could be consumed by noon in an outdoor oven. But mesquite and cedar—"the noble, hard woods"—burned long, strong, and fragrant. A hundred years before the charcoal burner shared his knowledge, his forebears knew the trees of the mountain slopes, the chaparral, and the forests. Especially critical for human settlement and resource use on Santa Ana were mesquite and Texas ebony, which grew there in abundance. When the Mexican Leals arrived on their grant in the 1830s, they chose to build homes within the encircling arms of a massive ebony grove. This grove had remarkable endurance across a century; in the 1940s, an aerial photograph of part of the newly established refuge shows the ebony grove spreading south from the old clubhouse. The manager who took the photograph captioned it: "Dark foliage indicates ebony trees." The choice of location for the Leal homestead suggests considerable understanding of climate, trees, soil, and water.[22]

A chachalaca on the ground, painted in 1862 by John Cassin for an inventory of North American birds. Important in this drawing is the depiction of original South Texas habitat in the distance: a mosaic that includes woodlands. From John Cassin, *Illustrations of the Birds of California, Texas, Oregon, British and Russian America*.

An undated photograph of Irby Davis and Anna May Davis in South Texas natural habitat. From the private collection of Coralyn Davis Lundell, daughter of Irby and Anna May Davis.

Graceful mesquite overhang one of the driving and hiking roads in the western portion of Santa Ana National Wildlife Refuge. Photograph by Thomas Morgan, June 2013.

Windmill grasses catch the light on Santa Ana National Wildlife Refuge. According to plant ecologist Kimberly Wahl, many of the species of windmill grass in Texas today are nonnative; this photograph may well be of the nonnative *Chloris barbata*. Yet it can still suggest the wind-stirred movement of presettlement grasslands. Photograph by Thomas Morgan, June 1, 2013.

Dicliptera in vigorous bloom near Arroyo Colorado in Harlingen, Cameron County. Photograph by Christina Mild, March 20, 2008.

An unidentified caterpillar, possibly a member of the cloudless sulphur family, resting on dicliptera. Photograph by Christina Mild, November 30, 2008.

A jacal, photographed ca. 1915, showing the arbor or patio area linking living rooms. Easy to construct from forest resources, these homes clustered near the main ranch house on Santa Ana and numbered at least ten by 1880. Courtesy of the Blake (Robert Bruce) Papers, di_09796, Dolph Briscoe Center for American History, University of Texas at Austin.

A male and female hooded oriole, originally called Sennett's oriole, painted by naturalist John Cassin in the early 1860s. Benigno Leal and all who lived at Santa Ana saw orioles in the thousands. Painting by John Cassin, *Illustrations of the Birds of California, Texas, Oregon, British and Russian America*.

A jaguar pins a tropical bird after pouncing on a log. Jaguars stalked birds as well as mammals. Painted by Louis Agassiz Fuertes, *Wild Animals of North America*, 1918.

A sweep of water, earth, and sky near the Pintail Lakes on Santa Ana. This was Lake Pechuga to the Guzmán families, although it was a much larger, single lake then and held more water. Photograph by Thomas Morgan, May 31, 2013.

Jopoy growing at Santa Ana National Wildlife Refuge. Also known as limoncillo, jopoy, an endangered plant, is identified as limoncillo on Santa Ana. Photograph by Thomas Morgan, June 3, 2013.

This photograph was taken from the trail around the eastern Pintail Lake, a route likely well traveled by the Leals as well as by the Amado Guzmán family, who lived near here—the area they knew as Lake Pechuga—between 1882 and 1902. Photograph by Thomas Morgan, June 2013.

Author hiking into Santa Ana forest along the high banks of the Rio Grande, June 1, 2013. Photograph by Thomas Morgan.

CHAPTER FOUR

The Early Leal Years

People of the River

In 1834 Benigno Leal was twenty-seven, a young, ambitious rancher from Reynosa. His family name, Leal, places his line among the earliest settlers arriving with José Escandón. In the riverine corridor across from Mier in northeastern Tamaulipas, Juan Antonio Leal was granted Porción 55 in 1767. His land consisted of 5,783 acres stretching into future Starr County north of the Rio Grande. Another Leal, Joseph, was an original grantee in Revilla (Guerrero), receiving Porción 2. The Leals likely emigrated to Nuevo Santander from Nuevo León. The Leal name shows up extensively in census records for Monterrey and Linares. Walking or riding, into the northern province of Nuevo Santander came hundreds of Nuevo León settlers, used to a pastoral life with some modest agriculture in valleys where rainfall was more predictable. One historian who has studied the Cerralvo area in Nuevo León believes that to facilitate cattle ranching there, Spanish colonists burned the oak and pecan forests that stretched up the foothills into the mountains; thus they actively created pastureland. As a result of this deforestation, as many as twelve permanent streams flowing down out of the mountains later dried up. If this information is correct, it may have been a lesson the original Escandón ranchers carried with them into Nuevo Santander. But the mainly arid, hot, and difficult climate of Nuevo León did not change south of the Rio Grande; it was in fact intensified. The mountains the Leals may have known—the Sierra Madre Oriental—were replaced by miles of dry chaparral, a gritty drift of river delta with bright green breaking out only along rivers like the San Juan, the Salado, and the Río Bravo del Norte.[1]

The Leals of Santa Ana were originally from old families who had long lived on the southern side of that river, our Rio Grande, the vital life of all original Escandón settlements. There they had acquired decades of specific environmental knowledge. The Leals of Mier probably built their first homes, the timber and thatch housing called *jacales*, from trees of the Rio Grande forest. They cut mesquite and ebony poles, and for roof thatching, they gathered from the immense stands of river-fed grasses such as *sacahuiste* (saw grass, also known along the coast as gulf cordgrass); *carrizos* (reeds); or simply armfuls of hay and local grasses called *tule*, usually identified as bulrushes. Historians of ranch architecture believe settlers carried diverse tule seeds from central and northeastern Mexico and planted them in terraces along the rivers. In this lies a clear example of new varieties of plants entering a habitat, this time purposefully. The transported varieties thrived and proved useful. Pole and thatch jacales were open, breezy, and comfortable. Later, as more permanent homes were built, settlers ground deposits of ancient river mussels into a cementing paste used in the manufacture of lime. Fire-resistant lime paste coated the outside of homes; they were bright white until the wind threw sand against the walls, staining and chipping the mortar with river gravel.[2]

Thus, from the beginning, arriving people brought resources with them and also extracted riverine resources. In the Mier jurisdiction, the shellfish used to make lime have been described as "gigantic," some oyster shells twenty-four inches across. The snow-fed, south-running waters of the Río Bravo also nourished stands of Montezuma bald cypress growing thick in narrow woodlands. Settlers rapidly targeted cypress as a preferred resource. Cypress logs could be used as roof support beams or sawed into wide, tough planks. The wood was not only long lasting and rot resistant, it was easy to work. These cypress can grow to hoary ages and immense widths. And they must have wetlands to thrive: cypress need river overflows to germinate. The water level must be exactly right—no seeds germinate underwater, and tiny seedlings must not be drowned later. The requirements are so precise, in fact, that studies determining the effect of hurricanes on cypress regeneration have discovered stiff parameters: cypress seeds are not salt tolerant and will die if a hurricane-driven flood brings in a "tidal surge." In addition, bald cypress seeds live only a year, possibly more, in flooded areas. As most plant life is usually food for some species of animal, so with this slow-growing giant: a wide variety of waterfowl consume cypress seeds. Stands of tall, feathery cypress are in essence a code for past flood events along the river: they signal a history of Rio Grande flooding and seed survival, a sign as indisputable as a high water mark on a wall. Surveyors have even used cypress stands to settle land, boundary, and property disputes as they bespeak high water levels.[3]

Nuevo León settlers cut the abundant cypress along the Salado River and the Rio Grande to make heavy, rot-resistant doors and lintels. Bald cypress was also the preferred wood for the inner lining of the giant carts used in the salt and hide trade, the carretas. Later, after 1850, railway companies targeted it for ties and water tanks. The US Boundary Survey of 1853 listed it as "rather common" along the Rio Grande, but by 1885, it was already described as "sparse." And in the 1960s, engineers removed some of the last remaining cypress from the lower Rio Grande for channel control. Gradually, over centuries, this iconic tree was rooted out of the valley. Thus, the Escandón settlers inaugurated a use of valley resources that fit a modest population at first but gradually became extractive and threatening to some species.[4]

Frontier people used many naturally occurring building materials. From sandstone, exposed in riverbanks in long, ocher-colored shelves, settlers cut blocks for homes. These yellowish stone homes were later discovered, particularly in the Falcon Reservoir impoundment area. Many were surveyed architecturally during the 1940s before being submerged by reservoir waters. Architects have traced the square, thatched-roof homes and heavy stone wall barricades with wooden gates back to Nuevo León. The Leal families, the branching clan that soon included brothers and brothers' families, with many offspring as well as adopted Indian children, would have lived initially in settlement jacales, then stone houses. In the heat of high summer, when the sandy earth glinted nearly white hot, the bare feet of children, young women, and grandmother matriarchs slipped silently over stone floors that felt as cooling as water.[5]

Tree, shell, stone, and grass—these materials became ranch homes. Placement of the houses, traced again through archaeology, initially suggests none of the logical or orderly patterns that would become typical of relocated towns such as Revilla and Reynosa. In the early years, the pobladores looked for firm, rich soil on terraces up from the river, for timber stands to furnish firewood and breezy shade—and for water. They built the main ranch house as close as possible to water sources: rivers, wet-season resacas, rare springs, and arroyos. In this they followed ancient Indian practices. Traces of earlier Native American occupation have been documented beneath red, yellow, and blue Spanish pottery (majolica) in homesite excavations. It is clear that many peoples, in sequential occupation, stayed where high ground, trees, and water intersected. Spanish settlers like the Leals, who lived some years in jacales before building stone or handmade brick homes, learned to create vital environmental supports themselves. They planted trees to arch over their patios and outdoor cooking areas: graceful, fragrant *anacua* and *anacahuita*. They also encouraged climbing vines to weave a living arbor. Frequently, they transported seeds of the desert willow, which produced sweet, pale purple flowers to bloom around doorways and define open passageways. While desert willow did not grow at Santa Ana, other flowering trees were likely on the ranch property, near the main house, planted for shade and beauty.[6]

Always, the pobladores worked to create shady places to rest in the high heat of noonday or to sit outside in the evening air and study the skies.

Their homes, which so many Anglo observers perceived as rude, crude, and primitive, were actually highly adaptive, comfortable, and organic: sleeping and storage spaces inside opened to shadowy, windy, thatched patios where they prepared food, ate, played games and instruments, and sang. In dim patches of woven light from overhead arbors, the temperatures could drop as much as twenty degrees from places open to the direct sun. Skilled weavers and hide tanners sat cross-legged under living leaves, only their hands moving. (See the photograph of a jacal in the photo gallery.) In the 1820s in Camargo and Reynosa, a traveler wrote that "looms can be found in almost all the houses," on which women produced serapes and *colchas* (quilts). He was impressed with their complex handiwork. In extreme heat, women stayed quiet, repairing tears in wool clothing or grinding seeds and dried herbs with small pestles. To manage brutal temperatures, northern Spanish settlers had learned to economize movement, stay in the shade, and wear head coverings always. These practices were survival skills.[7]

Everything about settler homes and living was a choice based on environmental knowledge. When traveling Oblate priests visited mid-nineteenth-century Tejano ranches in Hidalgo County, they left observations attesting to a "no rhyme or reason" placement of jacales and small stone or brick homes. "Small huts, widely scattered," they noted, "some under trees, others in open fields." These priests, extolled for their hardiness and endurance, nonetheless could not read the landscape. Jacales under trees brought wind-stirred, leafy shade; jacales in fields were on high ground and often had deep freshwater wells. Priest accounts are highly selective and do not perceive the ecological relationships that their parishioners understood well. Mesquite spread all around upland jacales, in increasing thickets as well as lone trees. Ranching people understood mesquite and knew that it had "unusual powers," with burrowing roots that found crevices and snaked through them toward water. Thus, mesquite often signals water. When Americans began to leave accounts of the Nueces Strip, the land between the Nueces and the Rio Grande (also known as the *brasada*), they wrote of the "muskit tree," noting that around it, rich pasture grass, "muskit grass," always seemed to grow. Yet nowhere in the priests' accounts are words about the transient, water-driven lushness of mesquite in the spring, described by a twentieth-century writer: "[one] can never forget the beauty of the mezquite in early spring . . . the tender green leaves, then the aromatic blossoms, and the sweet gum oozing out of its rough bark." Mexican and then Tejano ranchers and farmers understood environmental relationships in the prickly, heated thorn scrub of the Rio Grande settlements, but their Spanish forebears had also brought knowledge to the area with them, an inheritance from their centuries in arid northern New Spain.[8]

Seeds carried from Nuevo León in leather pack bags on settlement train mules and horses were sown in broad, first-terrace gardens near houses. The cooks of the houses planted, tended, and harvested these gardens. Stands of corn, frijoles (beans), and squash intermingled with medicinal herbs, melons, garlic, and onions. To grow and flourish, gardens needed more water than the arid climate provided, so they were irrigated in the oldest manner known to human beings—by hand, with large pottery water urns carried between the neck and the shoulder, walked up from the river banks on the strong legs of the daughters—and eventually, from wells. For decades, it was the girls of the family who brought the water to the household and gardens. The urban water cart was in the future. The few successful acequias, or irrigation ditches, constructed from rivers like the Salado and the San Juan, flowed through small fields of crops near the rivers: corn, beans, some cotton. Because watering was so labor intensive, the settlers at Mier, as in every other Escandón settlement, became stock raisers and ranchers.[9]

Knowledge of how to live a comfortable, adaptive life using local resources passed from Nuevo León to Mier and eventually to the Reynosa area. By about 1800, branches of the Leal family had migrated downriver from Mier and settled near the old mission of San Joaquín del Monte. Perhaps they lived in newly laid-out streets, for Reynosa had been moved in 1802 and restructured. The Leals seem to have stayed in Reynosa; in 1855, a Cristoval A. Leal shows up on a census there, listed as a town scribe (*escribiente*). There is slight but suggestive evidence from census data that Benigno Leal, one of five children baptized in Reynosa, may have had some Indian ancestry. Local Indian peoples, living for decades around missions, served Spanish and then Mexican families as slaves and servants. They could be sold into Spanish families as commodities but were also treated as orphans and adopted. Female Indian servants often bore children and sometimes married into old families. As was true of many frontier settlements across North America, family lines merged and surged into the indigenous population and often ignored established religious traditions. Blended families, unmarried couples with both baptized and unbaptized children, and considerable numbers of orphaned children characterized the early Spanish and Mexican settlements. One census from Nuevo León, for example, identifies as many as twenty-three Borrego Indians included in a Leal household. As late as the 1870s in Texas, traveling priests wrote disapprovingly of the many ranch families they met living in unsanctioned marriages: "Living out of wedlock meant very little to the majority." But frontier settlements had fluid and forgiving family boundaries. The arms of these multifaceted, diverse families were wide.

The Leals and Their Neighbors: Families of the Mexican Grants

In the 1830s, the Reynosa Leals had connections to Escandón *porción* grantees and a successful lineage that included multiple households. Here was a family worthy of a land grant across the river. Benigno's parents, Cristóbal Leal and Carmen Cantú, baptized five children in the Reynosa church; Benigno was the fourth child and youngest son. There is little surviving information about his siblings, but some slight evidence suggests he may have had an older brother, Pedro, born before 1800. All five Leal children baptized by a Reynosa priest were born between 1801 and 1809: María Guadalupe, 1801; Juan de Dios, 1803; José María, 1805; José Benigno, 1807; and María Manuela, 1809. Benigno's baptismal date of 1807 would place him in his late twenties when he petitioned for land. Likely he was already a skilled horseman, rancher, and stock raiser. He and other young ranchers such as Máximo Domínguez, who received the adjacent Los Toritos grant, were actively pursuing land ownership, vital grazing leagues for their herds. Mexico, a country only thirteen years old, was eager to populate its northern provinces in the face of increasing settlement by Americans, illegal smuggling out of Matamoros, and especially, increased raiding by frontier Lipan Apache Indians. A revised Mexican colonization act passed in November 1833 allowed as many as eight *sitios* (or leagues) north of the Rio Grande to be granted to ranchers and animal breeders; unlike the directives of earlier colonization acts, this act stated that settlers who applied would receive their land for free, paying only for the survey. Interest was immediate: between 1833 and 1835, *alcaldes* in Mexican towns approved fourteen grants in the Lower Rio Grande Valley. Poised at the right time and place, José Benigno Leal received two full leagues on which to pasture his sheep and cattle.[10]

This must have seemed the smile of good fortune, the answer to many prayers and supplications. Originally, three men received a commission to survey north-bank forested land: Lino Cavazos, Francisco Balli, and Benigno Leal; eventually, two leagues went to Benigno. Just as young frontiersmen and settlers all across North America had perceived, land ownership was the route to prosperity. Benigno had married into the prestigious Balli family, choosing Victoria Balli Cavazos, whom he probably met and courted in Reynosa. Older than her husband by at least nine years, Victoria would also become heir to part of Porción 72 west of Santa Ana and to a section of Llano Grande; for original Balli lands included Llano Grande, the magnificent, generous spread of grazing land in eastern Hidalgo County awarded to the Hinojosa-Balli line in the 1770s. She may have remained unmarried as a young woman because of the deaths of many men in the

Mexican War of Independence, 1810–1821. One historian who has examined census and marriage records for the town of Laredo has found that between 1819 and 1823, the number of single young men of marriageable age declined each year by 10 percent. Similar losses may have occurred south of the river.

Victoria's early years are also of interest because of her connection to Camargo, the Escandón village founded upriver from Reynosa. Both the Cavazos and the Balli (originally Vallin) families are connected in early census and baptismal records to Camargo, although most of Victoria's siblings were baptized in Reynosa. She and her sister, Refugio, however, were not. An inference is that as the oldest children, they may have been born in or near Camargo (or possibly on Llano Grande, north of the Rio Grande). We know that the Balli family was living in Reynosa by the 1770s, as José María Balli was captain of the Reynosa militia when he married into the Hinojosa family. It is not known when the Cavazos family moved south. Yet the full name of the small village of Camargo, from where the Balli and Cavazos families originally came, was actually Villa de la Santa Ana de Camargo. Married in her late twenties to Benigno Leal, Victoria perhaps named his land grant for her ancestral village and church. In the Catholic church, Saint Anne, mother of the Virgin Mary, is a beloved patron saint for a wide range of supplicants, including horsemen, horsewomen, riders, and stable hands.

We also find Victoria's relatives obtaining land near Santa Ana, in one case, bordering it. In fact, the connections through consanguinity or marriage among the four north-bank grants of 1834 are striking. An intricate matrix of families obtained four contiguous land grants, one as large as five leagues (El Gato). Four different men petitioned for and received those grants: Lino Cavazos, Juan José Treviño, Benigno Leal, and Máximo Domínguez. But it can be argued that in truth, it was the Balli family who added to an already formidable amount of land, extending tenure along a considerable stretch of the Rio Grande. A brief overview of these family connections will demonstrate this.

The first and farthest-east grant made in 1834 went to Lino Cavazos, Victoria Leal's maternal uncle, brother to María Antonia Cavazos. Lino named his grant San Tomás de la Blanca, usually shortened to La Blanca. Directly west lay Agostadero del Gato. Although the Treviño family (Juan José Treviño, grantee) initially owned El Gato, in 1834 Juan José sold and conveyed by deed a portion of his land to Francisco Balli, Victoria's brother. Juan José Treviño himself had married Refugio, Victoria's sister. The connections between the Leals and Treviños and their side-by-side grants continued strong at least through the 1870s; in the census of 1870, Victoria's widowed niece Concepción and her four children were living in the ranch house on Santa Ana, and Victoria's adopted son, Cristóbal, had married Concepción's sister Rafaela. Concepción and Rafaela were the daughters of Refugio Balli Treviño, who died young in 1828, possibly after a difficult childbirth. In 1880, Concepción and her youngest son, Tomás, were still living on Santa Ana, but in a separate dwelling right by the main ranch house of their aunt Victoria.

The Leals also had a family connection to the Domínguez family of the Los Toritos grant to the west, for Cecilia Domínguez's name appears as the responsible party for the Santa Ana land taxes for 1848 and 1849; in addition, three Domínguez family members signed as witnesses to the Leal will drawn up in Mexico in 1859. Research reveals that Victoria Leal was a second cousin to Cecilia Domínguez; Cecilia's grandmother (María Gregoria Balli) and Victoria's father (José Manuel Balli) were siblings. This would have been considered almost an intimate family connection and once again links Victoria to another of the 1834 grants. There was also a marital tie: after the death of his first wife, Refugio, Juan José Treviño married Cecilia Domínguez, joining the original grantee families of Agostadero del Gato, Santa Ana, and Los Toritos. The Santa Anita Ranch history titled *I Would Rather Sleep in Texas: A History of the Lower Rio Grande Valley and the Santa Anita Land Grant* asserts that Cecilia Domínguez was the sister of Máximo Domínguez, grantee of Los Toritos. This does seem likely, given her association with the Leals. Cecilia and Máximo probably grew up on the Santa Anita Ranch, as their father was an heir to those lands through the Gómez family grant of 1798. Máximo would very likely have had familiarity with the forest, chaparral, and grazing lands to the south. Santa Anita, also lying wholly in what became Hidalgo County, was northwest of the land that became Los Toritos and Santa Ana. At some point, however, Máximo Domínguez relocated to Reynosa. Here he petitioned to receive a Mexican grant he called Los Toritos—the Little Bulls—perhaps because of his ranching childhood on Santa Anita. In future Hidalgo County, the 1834 grants and the earlier, larger ranches meshed into an intimate world. Stretching north from a vital river, the land was claimed by old families connected to each other in truly complex ways.

Thus, Victoria Leal had close relatives on every one of the four Mexican land grants. Her extended family—and not her husband's—bound the contiguous grants that lined the Rio Grande west from Llano Grande. This point is important when considering the breakup of the grants after the Civil War; *only* the western league of Santa Ana remained intact until 1890, preserved almost entirely through Victoria Leal's efforts. In the first decades of these grants, persistence was critically linked to family relationships. North and south of the river, Spanish and Mexican family connections spread a web of kinship, alliances, and accommodations. Because the Mexican government expected grantees to occupy their grants within six months, ranch headquarters were rapidly formed for grazing lands and stock. It is not known exactly when Benigno moved onto Santa Ana, but he would have had to show some occupancy by the mid-1830s. And what is known for sure is *where* he selected his homesite.[11]

In addition to the main ranch house, Leal structures would have included the family cemetery, outbuildings such as chicken coops, a slaughtering table, an outdoor oven (*horno*), a fenced garden, jacales for other families and laborers, fenced pastures for milk cows, and even perhaps markers or fences for the horse/foot crossing (*vado*) or boat/ferry landing on the Rio Grande. The dense thorn forest rising to the first terrace of land, often termed "the first lift," coated miles of each league. Based on the Leal family cemetery, historians agree that the small ranch community documented on Texas census returns for four decades was located "about a half mile from the river." Modern altimeter readings corroborate that the Leals selected their home and cemetery sites on the highest ground of the refuge, suggesting a long familiarity with Rio Grande flooding. A 1911 International Boundary Survey map of the area sketches in what looks to be a large brick ranch home and outbuildings directly south of the cemetery. People at the house could likely see the cemetery from some angles, a relationship consistent with observed Mexican and Tejano ranch layout. The sketch suggests that the house and its attendant structures sat on a rise facing south, toward the river. Pathways led down to the banks, winding through the forest. This home grouping was on the western league of Santa Ana, with the eastern league bordering the adjacent El Gato grant. These leagues were roughly half a mile wide, so that family members living on Santa Ana and El Gato could have easily ridden through the forest to visit each other. The location of the homestead reveals choice: the Leals constructed their ranch house and cemetery inside an old-growth ebony forest and near a resaca identified in the 1960s as "the Inland Lake." This name corresponds somewhat with the name of this ranch—Rancho Adentro, or "Inside Ranch." Building deep in the forest but also on the banks of a water source gave early ranch communities shade and protection from Indians. This was a typical pattern.[12]

Analysis of early ranch locations is possible on twentieth-century maps. In 1973, Santa Ana manager and botanist Raymond Fleetwood designed a refuge map showing the location of the cemetery. The ebony forest was still thriving at that time, encircling the Inland Lake and protecting the old crosses and *bóveda* (aboveground tomb). And there were yet three ancient trails running north from the river to the Leal enclave. Two diverged from the same site—the original river crossing where human traffic stayed steady until the 1950s. Observations in the 1940s describe how the passage of bare human feet on these trails kept them trampled and packed. The modern refuge trails very likely follow the earliest human paths leading to and from the Rio Grande.

The Trees of Santa Ana

On Santa Ana maps from almost fifty years ago, a Texas Champion ebony tree is marked. Called the Big Ebony, it grew slightly southeast of the cemetery, at the very edge of the ebony forest. Towering at forty feet above the other ebony trees, fourteen feet around, with a crown spread of forty feet as well, this venerable ebony was still a guardian of the old ranch site in the 1990s. At that time, Texas A&M University estimated it to be over three hundred years old, first taking root when Spanish settlers were clashing with Pueblo Indians in New Mexico, a century before the awarding of the first large northern Río Bravo grants such as Llano Grande and La Feria. By the time Benigno Leal first saw it, the ebony was already 140 years old; it continued to thrive during the turbulent years along the river, when traffic from raiding Comanches, outlaws from both Mexico and the Republic of Texas, Texas Rangers, US soldiers and supply wagons, and Rio Grande steamboats ended the quiet isolation of ranch communities. The roots of the Santa Ana Big Ebony snaked out into the earth of the first rise, and its endurance, straddling two different habitats, created a landmark. At some point in its history Hispanic peoples planted a mulberry and an orange tree nearby, strongly suggesting that the giant tree was part of the Leal home place. Perhaps it was reverenced, despite a marked preference of local people for its wood.[13]

In Nuevo León, the original home of most Rio Grande settlers, Texas ebony was a revered tree, widely used for furniture, handicrafts, household items such as whittled and polished spoons, log fences, and charcoal. Also called blackbean, Texas ebony naturally forms groves that make harvesting easy. It yields a "rich heartwood . . . a dark reddish-brown tinged with purple." When cut open, a split log is close grained and strong, revealing a dense and surprisingly oily wood, the most valuable wood of South Texas. Yet ebony is slow growing, often branching into multiple trunks that slowly push a broad shade crown toward the sky. The many juvenile stems forming these knotted, branching trunks signal a clear adaptation to browsing by animals over millennia. From June to August, "very fragrant" white, spiky blooms release a sweetness caught on the breeze fifty feet away. It is

The Santa Ana Big Ebony, photographed in 1949. From the National Archives.

not hard to imagine how an extensive ebony grove laden with sweet, white blooms could define an arid landscape.[14]

Yet all parts of the tree have been long prized. The seeds are notably high in crude protein, and evidence from Mexico shows that green ebony seeds are still cooked and eaten today, and dry seeds are roasted and ground like coffee. Ebony trees were also sometimes perceived ominously. In the nineteenth century, Spanish and Mexican peoples felt it was dangerous to stand under an ebony during thunderstorms; they believed the heavy resin in the branches could attract lightning. So especially tall ebony trees were avoided and often cut down. An ebony forest on the early Santa Ana grant would have been important as a resource for food, fencing, and especially firewood; ebony had been burned in ovens and campfires along the Rio Grande since the arrival of the Escandón settlers. In fact, modern studies show that it is still one of the four most heavily used timber species in northeastern Mexico. Yet in the 1830s, the Leals did not exploit the ebony forest enclosing their homestead; in particular, they did not cut down one slow-growing but massive tree marking the edge of their homestead clearing. From their patios to the south they could catch a glimpse of their cemetery, in summer ringed with the white blossoms of ebony. Since the ebony fencing surrounding the cemetery has been dated to approximately 130 years ago, it is likely that this is a second fence, erected perhaps in the early 1860s, a time corresponding to the passing of Benigno Leal. Gradually, over decades, the Leal clan would likely have enjoyed the shade-giving crown of the truly towering ebony at the edge of their clearing. Despite superstitions about lightning strikes, they preserved this tree, which remained well into the 1990s—a Texas State Champion.[15]

As soon as Benigno Leal and other men worked to clear an opening in the forest for initial ranch buildings, trails and pathways began to thread the thickets and heavy tree growth leading to the river. Leal ranch hands were perhaps the only occupants for a few years, and even then, because of outbreaks of Indian hostility and raids, these workers often lived in Reynosa for long periods. They constructed the first jacales on the high ground, upland thorn forest described as covered with "dense thickets, emergent honey mesquite and ebony trees." The presence of four thorny trees—mesquite, *retama*, *coma*, and ebony—created the interwoven, sharp thickets in which ocelots lived and hunted. As the men worked, epiphytic mosses hung in festoons above them, linking the branches. Tree limbs silhouetted against the sky held globes of ball moss; some trees bore as many as twenty globes. Mistletoe was also present, hanging in sporadic, uneven masses far heavier than the sprigs commonly sold at Christmas.

We can only surmise the way the first Leals on Santa Ana referred to their forest resources. Raymond Fleetwood, Santa Ana manager in the 1970s, mentioned in his botanical inventory that the local people of Hispanic descent had their own terms and names for many of the plants on the refuge. We cannot today know most of these names, but as the first laborers on Santa Ana, Benigno and others were familiar with what they were clearing away. As they hacked at vines and uprooted brushy growth, they sweated in patches of sun and shade. A tangled, leafy canopy reached high into the heated sky. Gaps filtered the radiant light, but gaps close quickly in a healthy forest, most often with the branches of tepeguaje, one of the fastest-growing trees in the world. Another upland shrub or tree, guayacán, can sometimes shoot to fifteen or twenty feet; known as ironwood, guayacán is exceptionally hard to saw. Perhaps the Leals saved branches and blossoms of guayacán as they worked. In northern Mexico, folk healers of the nineteenth century steamed guayacán blooms and used them to treat tuberculosis. Guayacán has known medicinal applications and also has a strong detergent quality, leading to its other name of soaptree. While it is probable that by the 1830s, Mexican women were making soap from lye, pioneers in unclaimed land were aggressive users of natural resources. Nothing would have been wasted.[16]

It is almost certain that the people clearing Santa Ana for a small ranch recognized and knew its trees. Observations from the 1940s make it possible to suggest the bird and wetland environment on early Santa Ana. If that first year of grant occupancy was a rainy one, around the resaca just west of the cemetery Benigno would have found abundant black mimosa, a small tree adapted to seasonal inundation. Mimosa can create four-foot-high tangles of prickly, recurving stems that respond quickly to rain. Plant life in these thorn forests was dynamic in both dry and wet seasons, teeming with food for hundreds of species of birds and many mammals. A twentieth-century description of plant resurgence allows us to picture that vitality. After flooding in the 1940s, a Santa Ana manager noted, "It hasn't taken long for marsh and water plants to come in since the flood . . . duckweed, pepperwort, mud plantain, water lily, bur reeds, dwarf spikerush, najas, Dallas grass, smartweed, sedges, round stem bulrushes, and dock." And when the water plants returned during that flood season of 1948, waterfowl soon followed: in a single large ash tree standing on the south shore of the West Lake, a refuge worker counted two hundred roosting white ibis.

A century earlier, there would have been even greater numbers and species of birds, their raucous cries sounding across the full resacas, whole trees shaking with their startled rising and falling. Proliferating branches held hundreds of hidden, odorous nests, some ancient of days. Here too, near the water's edge, stood the perennially lone great blue heron, his name in Spanish, *garza*, lyrically honoring the many families of Garzas whose history entwines with that of the Leals. Although the blue heron was not named for the Garza family, the connection is enjoyable. Among the first Garzas to set foot in northern Tamaulipas, then Nuevo Santander, was Nicolás de la Garza, who had built a ranch near Camargo in 1746, three years before the Escandón settlers arrived. Despite extremes of drought and flood, these earliest families prospered and spread, until nearly a century later, their descendants were chopping tangled brush and vines from northern river grants. Despite its resurgent beauty after rains, the floodplain forest was a miasmic, choking place in high summer. These were the insect- and bird-laden terraces the Reynosa grantees cleared with hand tools and a few mules, under an unrelenting sun.[17]

Yet a forest is a place of bounty as well, as is arid chaparral dotted with cactus and dusty mesquite. As late as 1895, a researcher documented how "Rio Grande Mexicans" liked to roast the young central shoot of the Spanish bayonet (Spanish dagger, a variety of yucca); the taste of this shoot, when baked on hot coals, was not unlike that of a sweet potato. Once they had moved onto their land, perhaps Benigno and Victoria began to perceive the richness of their two leagues. On their initial explorations, they may have found the chili pequin pepper growing wild, its red heat free for the taking. A description of how twentieth-century Mexican ranchers in Coahuila sought this plant reveals its pungent lure. Ranchers sometimes cut huge bundles of pequin branches, "speckled with gemlike chilies, the peppery smell of the capsaicin fill[ing] the air around us." These branches would be hung to dry in the open-air patios, along with other wild herbs and ropes of garlic. Women also gathered and dried the leaves of cenizo, or purple sage, boiling them to make a tea infusion for congestion. (Later, American settlers on the Alamo Tract adopted this remedy from Tejanos; they reported that steeping cenizo leaves smelled "like a wet dog . . . but [you should] drink it morning, noon, and night.") The Santa Ana forest was a natural storehouse. It furnished a range of resources, from the tiny pepper to heavy black Texas ebony logs driven deep into the earth to create a vertical fence; from mesquite beans that fed cattle, goats, and deer to succulent white-winged doves spit-roasted over outside fires; and from herbal and medicinal roots and leaves to the occasional treat of a sweet, pink-red prickly-pear tuna.[18]

Forests as well as rivers have nourished and supported frontier families in all areas of North America. Spanish and then Mexican settlers learned to read the vegetative and animal environment and to extract from it a range of spicy, sweet, liquid-laden, or mealy fruits and leaves. The Leals, following practices in Tamaulipas, may have planted anacua trees near their ranch house, as anacua berries furnished chicken feed, and the creamy white blooms of the tree scented the air. The multiple branching trunks of anacua created a large umbrella-like patch of shade for women, whose day included long hours of food production. They may also have planted or used anacahuita, Mexican olive. Almost all parts of this spreading tree of medium height—leaves, seeds, even bark—are highly aromatic and were once commonly used to treat bronchial and lung ailments. In 1885, an observer found anacahuita extract being sold in local drugstores along the southern Rio Grande.[19]

In addition to planting trees and vines around their homesite, Mexican ranchers hunted the forests for animal skins, especially those of coyote, deer, and ocelot. These were used as rugs in frontier homes. But perhaps more important, the cash income from the hide trade allowed early ranchers to keep solvent in the cyclical drought years that came as regularly to the valley as flood. Hides of "lions" (mountain lion or puma) and "tigers" (jaguar) from the valley were shipped out of Matamoros. In the earliest available records, from 1825, "tiger hides" and otter skins (possibly a transcription error for "ocelot") appear on lists of exports from Matamoros. In 1827, 44 tiger skins and 336 otter/ocelot skins left the port. The hide and deer trade continued through the nineteenth century, with deerskins making up a portion of exports as late as 1878. Just before 1900, American settlers on the La Blanca and El Gato grants were reported avidly hunting deer and setting traps at night for fur-bearing animals such as raccoons, skunks, coyotes, and foxes; they were selling these skins in Brownsville. Finally, observations from the nineteenth and twentieth centuries indicate that javelina, antelope, white-tailed deer, turkey, dove, and quail were critical supplemental foods on the early porciones and grants. Studies of hunting in northern Mexican provinces as late as the 1950s show that even the big cats, especially the cougar, were "eaten with relish." Ranch workers required steady protein sources, and while young goats were often butchered and barbecued, daily meat probably came from the Santa Ana forests.[20]

The Leals certainly produced food as well; all ranch communities had gardens. It is not known exactly where the Rancho Adentro vegetable plots were located, but there is evidence that these plots would have been around the resaca or near the river, on the first riparian terrace, for access to ready (hand-dipped) irrigation water. Histories of other Hidalgo County ranchos document gardens of corn, beans, squash, garlic, onions, and small green calabaza squash planted near the Rio Grande. In the first two decades of Leal occupancy, 1834–54, the family almost certainly raised only subsistence-level produce. The dense forest along the Rio Grande would have had to be cleared; the riverbanks at the crossing and well along the south border were often flooded and frequented by the big hunting cats; people were staying away from Santa Ana and other north-bank ranches because of Indian raids; and, most important, census data establish that the Leal ranch did not have many people living on it in the early years.

The census of 1850, the first recorded trace of people in households on Santa Ana, lists five people in the Leal home: Benigno Leal, age forty; Victoria Leal, forty; Cristóbal Leal, twenty-three; Pedro Leal, twenty-one; and José Angel Garza, forty-five (likely a ranch hand). Benigno and Victoria gave their ages to the census taker, but these were expedient estimates, for baptismal and genealogy records clearly show that in 1850, Benigno was forty-three and Victoria was likely fifty-two. Cristóbal Leal was their adopted son, and Pedro was probably a Leal nephew. Benigno and Victoria were living and working on Santa Ana without many children, but they may have had some additional help. While exact household relationships are not verifiable from this census, a second household is listed next to Benigno's, that of a forty-one-year-old woman, Francisca Garza, and four children: Miblesa, twenty-three; Estéfana, twenty; Raman [Román], fifteen; and Elario, nine. Because José and Francisca Garza are not recorded as living together, it is possible that Francisca was the widowed sister of the ranch hand, José Angel Garza. Hispanic household communities were formed in this way, with relations being cared for and all contributing to the work of the ranch. Thus there were at least four adult women on Santa Ana by 1850, but this number was quite low compared to that on other Hispanic ranch communities, some of which reached village size. The excavated ranch community of El Capote on Porción 69, to the west of Santa Ana, is a good example of a village ranch. By 1850, on the southern acreage of Porción 69, a ranch community was in place known as El Capote (The Cape). Many homesteads, described as "scattered," stood on the river varas of this porción, crowding almost to Porción 70. Thirty years later, El Capote had burgeoned into what researchers describe as a typical, mature ranch community—families, homes, school, church, cemetery, public ferry, and brickyard.[21]

A House of Handmade Bricks

El Capote Ranch is important in the history of Santa Ana, as it is the likely source of the handmade bricks used to build the Leals' main ranch house, sketched on the International Boundary Survey map of 1911. The key to this probable connection is the presence of the Garza family on Santa Ana. Records have been confused in many ways, through both census and genealogy errors. The Garza family certainly has a connection to El Capote Ranch;

in the history of a later ranch on Santa Ana, that of the Guzmán family, the matriarch, Estéfana Guzmán, is identified in one source as originally being Estéfana Garza from the El Capote Ranch community. However, this information directly conflicts with marriage and baptismal records of the Guzmán family in Reynosa; most records show that Estéfana Guzmán's maiden name was Guzmán as well. It is likely, though, that the Garza family is indeed entwined with the Guzmáns, and possibly with the Leals; at least in 1850, there were Garzas living on Santa Ana. One interpretation is that the Garzas moved to Santa Ana from El Capote after the death of Francisca's husband. While living in El Capote, they would have daily seen the *ladrillera* (brickyard) and its master brick maker. Studies of the master brick makers of Mexico establish that the era of ranch brick masons began around 1840 and produced some extraordinary artisans. Both Reynosa and Laredo were centers of brick making in the nineteenth century; by 1910, Laredo had fifty-five brickyard workers. The connection between Reynosa and Hidalgo County—a continuous washing back and forth of people, families, day laborers, traders, artisans, outlaws, and military personnel—is also strong in the sharing of brick culture. Master artisans passed on to their sons the knowledge of how to make beautiful handmade bricks from Rio Grande clays—how to mold them, fire them in a kiln, and stack and store them. These masters often crossed the river and shared knowledge with Mexican and Tejano residents. Historic buildings in the town of Hidalgo are reported to be built of "brick burned in the vicinity." Most important, the archaeological excavation of the Guajardo-Vela site on El Capote has uncovered a small ladrillera and evidence of an old kiln. This brick-making site operated in at least the second half of the nineteenth century, and probably earlier.[22]

The kiln at El Capote, like all brick kilns in the area, was wood fired. The preferred wood was mesquite, easily found, gathered, and chopped. Its abundance made it the most likely choice. The firing process required a significant supply of wood that had been stacked and seasoned for several months. While producing a run of bricks, brick makers needed a cord of firewood for every two thousand bricks, and some skilled brick makers have been documented producing as many as three thousand bricks a day. A late-twentieth-century photograph shows an enormous mound, perhaps over fifteen feet high, of mesquite wood stacked near an operating Mexican kiln. Handmade bricks must be fired for at least three days, with the fires burning hot and steady, fed by loads of mesquite and other local woods, including ebony. The clearing of forested areas south of porciones around El Capote may have been due in part to the continuous operation of the El Capote ladrillera across at least fifty years. Because of the warm, semitropical climate of the lower Rio Grande Valley, it has been easy to overlook the use of Rio Grande timber for firewood, but a ladrillera is a key piece of evidence.[23]

These locally made bricks had a distinctive appearance. When the green bricks were released from brick molds and turned out onto the sandy dirt of a riverine brickyard, they took the imprint of the earth. Handmade brick faces have been described as "rough," a soft, natural, rustic look much prized even today in the architecture of South Texas. And they are extraordinarily durable. Made for a climate of steady heat, little rain, and few freezes, these bricks have lasted for over one hundred years in the buildings of Hidalgo. Weathering to a creamy gray-white and ocher, the brick house of Rancho Adentro lasted until the 1920s. Because of the possible El Capote connection through the Garza family on Santa Ana, it is probable the bricks were made and transported from the ladrillera at El Capote. It would be by far the closest source of bricks for the new home Benigno built for his family, probably in the 1840s when he still owned both leagues of Santa Ana. Floating the heavy bricks downstream to the river crossing into Santa Ana would have been far more practical than hauling them overland.[24]

Francisca Garza's name on the 1850 census, showing her living close to the brick ranch house with her children, allows us to make plausible guesses at connections among these early Mexican ranches. Yet there is truly scant trace of the women of Santa Ana, aside from their names in census and deed records. But whether they were honored matriarchs, like Victoria, or poor kin finding sanctuary on a relative's ranch, isolated rural women worked long hours. These were the days of exceptionally labor-intensive food preparation. Women used mortar and pestle grinders, called *molcajetes*, to grind spices and herbs; for corn, they used *metates*, stone basins on three legs. The first mechanical grinder, the masa mill, did not arrive until the 1880s, when the coffee mill was introduced as well. Preserving food, and especially guarding against spoilage in the intense heat of the summer months, required a complex knowledge of procedures for smoking, salting, and drying all forms of vegetables, especially corn and beans, as well as the safe handling of meats.

Ranch women at Santa Ana, described by the census taker as "keeping house," probably continuously tended the domed, outdoor stone horno. Stoves did not appear in ranch kitchens until the 1880s. Women were responsible for managing the heating of the house during colder winter months, when the horno produced coals that could be brought inside. There may also have been an outdoor kitchen at Santa Ana, a special, small jacal fitted with a stone fireplace raised from the floor at least three feet. While this made it possible to cook while standing, the heat inside this jacal during the extended summer months of the valley could be intense, described even as "unbearable" at times. Cooking in volume depended on heavy metal implements, including copper pots and iron skillets, which cooks had to hoist down from hooks on the walls. They often set beans to simmer all day in fire-blackened cauldrons. Inside the open kitchen, despite the breezes, smoke hung thick. On some days, sounds of the metate and stone-on-stone rasping never ceased. Stewing and searing, scouring and grinding, skinning, smoking, slapping moistened cornmeal into thin tortillas for quick cooking—the mothers, wives, and daughters of ranch workers carried out these activities unceasingly. It was *in perpetua*, an activity of precise, strong, sun-reddened hands that can only be imagined from accounts a century later. At Santa Ana in 1850, we glimpse these workers through a single census entry: Victoria, Francisca, Miblesa, and Estéfana.[25]

Women had many other responsibilities besides the creation and preservation of family food. They also carded wool, weaving and tinting it from native dyes; made clothing; washed clothing in the river; and continually repaired tears and seams in leather, wool, and cotton cloth. They also prepared medicinal herbs, pastes, and tinctures, and they brewed plant teas. The tradition of the *curandero* in Mexican culture—the village healer, often a female with proven medical skill and spiritual, frequently occult, knowledge—was transported to the north-bank ranches. As late as 1907, a curandero in the Lower Rio Grande Valley, Don Pedrito Jaramillo, was widely sought for his healing powers; his practice has been documented in books and newspaper articles of the late twentieth century. Described as using "folklore medicine," the neighborhood healers of Mexico and Texas remain critical resources yet today; even in the 1970s these skilled men and women helped maintain a health standard in isolated rural communities. Curanderas in central Mexico were observed in the 1930s to still be prescribing many ritualistic and superstitious cures; at the same time, these women made "considerable use of herbs, leaves, and roots." Their knowledge was handed down, learned from observation and oral instruction. For example, curanderas used the herb *gordo lobo*, or "fat wolf," as an expectorant and allergy treatment. They gathered small branches and leaves of the *fresno* tree (Rio Grande ash) and made tinctures for skin infections and hair loss. One curandera relied on mountain lion grease to massage rheumatic limbs. The Texas bull-nettle, or *mala mujer*, was used to treat venereal disease, and mistletoe berries could ease the pains of childbirth. As late as 1952, a speaker described how "*Corazon huisache*" (the heart of the huisache tree) was used "by native herb women to dissolve kidney and gall stones and to heal internal bruises and abscesses."

But not every village or ranch could summon a curandero or curandera, especially if he or she lived across the Rio Grande in Mexico. Expert immediate treatment was necessary for injuries sustained in handling domestic animals or in encounters with the snakes, big cats, and javelinas of the forest; and for women, practical knowledge of midwifery was critical. A midwife, known as *la partera*, could also be a curandera. Historians describe Tejanas, women in the Spanish colonial period and in the Texas settlement era, as "exclusively responsible" for medical care. The heirs to the knowledge of these women eventually became part of the "constant, two-way border crossings . . . playing a role in Mexican-American health." The links among families living on the Los Toritos, Santa Ana, and El Gato grants would have provided support in illness, childbirth, and emergencies; even relations farther away, on the El Capote or La Blanca ranches, were vital resources. These human connections were critical in the persistence of frontier ranches between 1834 and 1850.[26]

The Santa Ana treed acreage was an immense resource for herbal healers, yet the woods were also threatening. Early Spanish accounts of the Hidalgo County lands make frequent use of the word "dangerous." A 1794 map by a Nuevo Santander surveyor traces the route from Reynosa through the San Salvador del Tule Grant, passing near El Sal del Rey, the salt lake northeast of Santa Ana. Near the trail is the notation "Tigers, Lions, Wolves, and Snakes." Poisonous snakes included the heavy western rattlesnake and the slender coral snake with its bands of yellow and red, still frequently seen in the 1940s on the Santa Ana refuge after flooding. Animal and snake bites required immediate attention. Because of the importance of Mexican women in healing and emergency medicine, it is unlikely that men would have lived alone on a forest ranch for any extensive time. And because the census of 1850 shows only two families living on the Santa Ana grant, an inference is that the Leals may have taken up permanent residence on their grant only within a few years prior to the Mexican War.[27]

Mounted Raiders in South Texas

The years between 1834 and 1850 were ones of uncertainty and fear for Mexican ranchers and their families. Even before 1834, there is evidence that southern Comanches and Lipan Apaches were fighting among themselves for access to ranch cattle and, especially, domestic and feral horses. The Texas Revolution of 1836 seemed to "encourage" Indian attacks on settlements of the lower Rio Grande. One researcher noted that by 1837, Indian raids occurred with every full moon. In West Texas, where the moon indeed rose with enormous brilliance, Comanche raiders relied on its blanching light. "The most dangerous time was during that period in the month when the moon gave light at night," wrote an early observer. He explained that Indians would approach stealthily down from the north on foot, seeking settler reserves of horses. In 1842, these raids were concentrated in the Austin area, but they were reported as well for the lower valley, especially in the late 1830s. Under that ominous and warning full moon, through a landscape of shadows and starkly lit, plain-as-day trails, southern Comanches and some Lipan Apaches expertly raided stock farms along the river.[28]

The Comanches, described as "master spirits of the prairie," were also master hunters. Still using bow and arrow as well as trade rifles for big game, they ate wild horse meat regularly. In 1849, a special agent for Texas Indians estimated southern Comanche numbers at twenty thousand, with four thousand warriors. Lipan Apaches were the second most feared tribe, even with much smaller numbers—perhaps five hundred, with only one hundred warriors. They were known for attacks against competing Indian tribes as well as ranchers. In the fifteen years before the Civil War, histories report that the frontier line lay just west of San Antonio and Austin. Yet this frontier line represented the advance of American settlers from the east; the Mexican ranchers along the southern Rio Grande had been there much longer. Perhaps this long-term occupancy had created too much familiarity between Mexicans and the Comanches. In 1837, testimony given in the Senate Standing Committee on Indian Affairs reported that "Comanches . . . [are] the natural enemies of the Mexicans—they [the Indians] call them 'stock keepers.'" The committee described the Comanches as "roving Indians" with many horses.[29]

Benigno and Victoria Leal, like other north-bank settlers, almost certainly abandoned their stock, fields, and garden at times to return to Reynosa. In 1838, for instance, on the San Antonio de los Esteros Ranch east of Santa Ana on Llano Grande, Victoria's brother and family were threatened. They "fled across the Rio Grande" because of Indian raids. On the San Juan de Carricitos Ranch, the Cavazos family was forced off their grant "until 1850." Indian raids in South Texas spread eastward as well. A single observation from this period tells the story: "The left bank of the river en route from Brazo to Santiago had only three or four ranches in 1829 and none by 1837." Comanches were much feared; in the 1830s and 1840s, ranchos were fairly isolated, and protection was believed to lie in the towns. Yet it was not always safe even across the river. In the mid-1830s, Lipan Apaches and Comanches were raiding Reynosa so frequently it was reported to be "in misery." The raiders were now picking through the south side of the river after having exhausted the north-bank ranches. Unfortunately for the reconstruction of northern Mexican provincial history, the forum for reporting Indian attacks and Mexican deaths was not consistently public, as it would be with the advent of Texas newspapers. Accounts of Indian raids along the Rio Grande do appear in the early Matamoros newspaper, but the focus is on the area nearest to Matamoros. More typically, the alcalde of a village would send a letter to the provincial governor describing outrages and begging for military support. The new government of Mexico lay hundreds of miles to the south, across central mountain ranges, in equally mountainous Mexico City. Authorization to employ large protective military force could be slow in coming, although the Mexican general at Matamoros did send out a small, almost useless force against Comanches in the area.[30]

At one point, the Reynosa alcalde mobilized the town men to engage Comanche raiders who had previously burned and looted ranches and killed over nine hundred animals around the town. Reynosa volunteers found four hundred mounted Indians south of the village with a "great herd of horses they had gathered." There is no way to know whether the Leals participated in the fighting south of the Rio Grande, but since many Leals are listed on Mexican censuses, they may well have. Once northern Tamaulipas became part of the United States, the documenting of "Indian outrages" became much more consistent, but the records focus on white American settlers as victims. The proliferation of Spanish-language newspapers in the Lower Rio Grande Valley did not occur until 1849, with the founding of *El Centinela / Rio Grande Sentinel* in Brownsville. And while other bilingual newspapers were published straight through Reconstruction years into the 1870s, there is a noticeable lack of documentary evidence about Comanche depredations on the Tejano ranches of the first-formed Cameron County. The evidence is obscured, like so much of the history of Santa Ana; we guess but cannot know the interactions between Mexican and Tejano ranchers and Indians, those face-to-face hostilities—or just conversations—occurring on the old land grants of the Rio Grande.[31]

However, the significance of the Rio Grande forests during this time is clear. A nineteenth-century history reported that settlers had learned "never to enter the timber" at the point where Indian watchers might expect them to. Ambush and murder inside groves of trees were common outcomes for single travelers; an undocumented oral account states that Benigno Leal was killed in this way, ambushed by Indians on his own land in retribution for having killed a single Indian earlier. Since one of the last traces of the grantee is his signature on a document in Reynosa in 1859, the attack probably occurred in the early 1860s, when Benigno was in his fifties. In the Reynosa, Mexico, civil records, a Spanish-language death record, called a *defunción*, contains information that Benigno died June 5, 1861, but gives no cause. Tax roll information for

Hidalgo County is unfortunately missing for the years 1858–64; in 1865, however, Benigno's adopted son, Cristóbal, appears as the owner and taxpayer for the western league of Santa Ana, evidence that Benigno had died.

Indians were yet appearing in the lower valley before, during, and after the Civil War years. In 1859, in the hill country of Uvalde County, a settler was killed while gathering pecans on the Frio River; another was killed while crossing Hondo Creek; yet another in the same year on Sabinal Creek; and earlier, in 1856, a local rancher was also murdered on Sabinal Creek after running off "a party of Indians" (possibly Lipan Apaches) attempting to steal a *caballada* (a herd of "fine horses"), just rounded up and corralled. In these accounts of the ambush and killing of single family men, or men and their teenage sons in western Texas, the pattern is suggestive: victims were commonly found, pierced with arrows and mutilated, in timbered regions along creeks and rivers.[32]

As late as 1871, historians describe a "most conspicuous year," a dark period in western Texas history in which murders and Indian massacres were frequent. While studies find that the main violence after 1850 was north of Laredo, the strong anecdotal belief persists that Benigno Leal died at Indian hands in the early 1860s. He was, after all, one of the stock keepers despised by the Comanches; he probably ventured alone into the forests of Santa Ana, and as a frontiersman, he would not have hesitated to kill an Indian who might be waiting to steal his horses. There is no marked grave for Benigno in the Santa Ana cemetery, and it is not certain where he lies. The decade of the 1850s provides the last hard evidence that both Benigno and Victoria were at times living on their grant together.[33]

In the spring of 1848, just before rapid change swept through the valley, it is probable that Benigno Leal paid a visit to Santa Ana from Reynosa. The tax rolls for Cameron County in 1848 and 1849 record that Benigno paid land taxes then, and also that he was assessed both years on thirty cattle and ten horses. The Mexican War was ending, but probably, in addition to paying taxes, he would have wanted to make frequent checks on his homestead. If he rode across to Rancho Adentro after the spring rains, he would have witnessed seasonal revitalization. Between the Rio Grande and the military trail that had been laid down during the war, the forest steamed in a moist heat, just replenished by floodwaters. Cedar elm, tepeguaje, and ash likely held many oriole nests, guarded by darting, circling birds. The canopy above flashed with gold, cerulean blue, and orange. These nesting traditions continued without ceasing, binding avian life to the forest. Sennett oriole nests were still appearing by the hundreds in the mid-twentieth century. Documented by the Santa Ana manager in 1948, over *one thousand* Sennett orioles, now termed hooded orioles, built nests in the Spanish moss draping the oldest trees on the refuge. These orioles rarely nest on Santa Ana today. But they were first observed in the riparian forests in 1878 by George A. Sennett, for whom they were initially named. Sennett noted that the nests were invariably built in the "hanging trusses" of Spanish moss. Orioles prized the "curly dry hair," as he called it, weaving it expertly into long, supple pouches. The twentieth-century manager who casually wrote of a thousand Sennett orioles left a word picture that functions like a shutter through time. Although it may be that the species most prevalent on Santa Ana in the 1840s was Audubon's oriole, orioles—including hooded and orchard orioles—were nesting there in numbers we can barely imagine. In that spring of 1848, perhaps Benigno Leal was crossing the river on his horse, threading his way up through the woodland terraces toward his brick ranch house. This was his land, this wilderness of epiphytic mosses and towering thorn trees. Overhead through the gray-green festoons darted hundreds of slender orange and yellow orioles. The owner of Santa Ana could gaze up into a sun-drenched kaleidoscope of color and form. In Spanish, he would have termed these bright nesting birds, the tropical orioles, *oropendula*.[34]

CHAPTER FIVE

The World Outside Comes to Santa Ana

In the first years of occupancy of Santa Ana, animals changed more of the environment than people did. But this shifted as the American nation became interested in the territory between the Nueces River and the Rio Grande. As a war brought soldiers into the area of the old porciones and newer Mexican grants, the river was initially the conduit. In the summer of 1846, the Rio Grande was high, at flood stage. General Zachary Taylor was preparing to move an army upriver from Matamoros to Camargo. In May, fighting had broken out between American and Mexican forces at Palo Alto, near Brownsville, and the Mexican-American War was under way. After two short years of hot, bitter fighting, troop exhaustion, and disease, the territory of the United States would dramatically increase. All the ranches and small farms north of the Rio Grande would become part of the expanding American nation under the Treaty of Guadalupe Hidalgo. The boundary between two adverse nations was specified as the Rio Grande, not the Nueces River. And while these geopolitical shifts would engender rapid changes in the lives of Tejano peoples, the river was also changing.

It is in the years of the Mexican War that we can begin to document how the Rio Grande and its banks were affected. The war increased human and animal populations, and significant irrigation far upriver around El Paso and in New Mexico affected water levels downriver. Along the southern Rio Grande, steamboats were requiring a staggering fuel load, extracted from the chaparral and riparian forests. These processes of land and river alteration and of military conflict were happening simultaneously. But the nature of war obscures slower, more insidious shifts, hides changes in the earth of battlefields or the rivers of military landings. War on foreign soil creates an illusion of land as a stage, a combat arena. Locations and outcomes of fighting become critically important, while firsthand observations carry a sense of static land and mobile human beings. In truth, both are dynamic.

A national border war far to the south required the transport of men, munitions, and food supplies. Artillery, such as the cannon that had blown a Mexican regimental marching band to bloody smithereens on the Palo Alto battlefield, had to be hauled far into Mexico from its arrival point by sea at Brazos Santiago. By August, a massive buildup of troops and weaponry at Matamoros signaled to the valley that all ranches lay in a war zone. General Taylor determined that his men should travel by both river and land, as the steamboats were light, shallow draft ships not suited to the numbers of infantry, horses, artillery, and supply wagons—an ominously waiting tent city described as an "invasion force." The river was difficult enough, filled with snags and sandbars and immense fallen trees from caved-in banks. One soldier moving upriver left a pointed account of its serpentine loops: "Still winding our way to Camargo, it is most emphatically a winding way for no river in the world is more tortuous than the Rio Grande."[1]

Using both approaches, General Taylor sent a march overland, on the south side of the Rio Grande, following a long-established trail, and he, his staff, and some officers traveled up the Rio Grande by boat. Thus began the troop movement of the war, described often with this phrase. Troop movement brought a wave of people and animals straight through and near the borders of Santa Ana. Two military transport steamboats powered upriver in July and early August 1846: the *J. E. Roberts* and the *Hatchee Eagle*, carrying General Taylor. The boats made the trip in four days, but it took the "heavy movement by road" eight days. Soldiers on that eight-day march experienced the new world of the Rio Grande corridor as onerous, stifling, mud- and filth-laden, and dramatically filled with exotic animal and bird life. The old trail along the south bank, variously described as a road, a route, or an Indian trail, was flooded in many places. Mexican cattle stood in the shoreline "ponds" desperate for relief from the miasmic, soupy heat; they fouled the water and their dung attracted heavy curtains of insects. Soldiers reported startling bands of wild horses. Clouds of tropical birds lifted from the tree canopy as the toiling columns of marchers approached. Like the engineers who would travel the same route conducting the Boundary Survey in 1853, infantry likely saw scissor-tailed flycatchers "rising from the top branch of some acacia . . . seem[ing] to float rather than fly." Abundant caracaras left stick nests "low in the trees"; chachalacas "[sat] around in gangs" in the densest chaparral; and now and then the lines of men passed an "always solitary" blue heron standing in the water. The recent flooding made the 1846 march especially raw and exacting. It was so debilitating, in fact, with 130 miles of blazing sun; black, malodorous floodwaters; bloated animal carcasses on debris-laden banks; heat exhaustion; and "blasting dust," that eventually steamboats took over entirely.[2]

At least twenty steam transports were employed in the US war effort, appearing on the Rio Grande at a time of summer flooding. These boats fought their way upriver against a high, heavy current. Their design, with long, low, flat hulls, was probably the same as that of the shallow steam vessels beginning to ply the lower Missouri River at the time: boilers were "fueled and stoked from the bow." There, deckhands stacked cords of wood, and in South Texas, the wood was usually the abundant green mesquite, described as a slow fuel. The crew loaded mesquite each night, but often steamers ran out of power in the middle of the day and had to pull over to the banks to be reloaded. After the mesquite began to burn, the boat sat with burners firing, a load of steam building, until finally, pistons pounded powerfully enough to push the keel into the thick brown current. When flooding occurred, obtaining dry fuel was an ongoing problem. After reaching its crest, the river receded slowly. It had swirled over the banks in many places, soaking the available brushy wood. The reports of those first months of war described the Rio Grande at "high water" all summer, from Camargo to the sea. This meant that for months, riparian forests along the Rio Grande at El Gato, Santa Ana, and Los Toritos were standing in many feet of water. River runoff sloshed against the immense trunks of venerable bald cypress, Mexican ash, and cedar elm. Where matted forest undergrowth had once created a safe travel zone for many small birds and mammals, an inland sea emerged. The steamer crews cursed the miles of saturated wood. But, for the forest, the microbe-infested, silty water that stood slowly heating that summer was bathwater of incalculable value.[3]

Hard for People, Good for Trees

We can strengthen our understanding of this flooded war landscape through accounts from later decades. Mentions of men in boats on inundated farmland are consistent in the records of the valley. The memories of the Nathaniel Jackson family, for instance, an extended multiracial family who bought old Porción 72 in 1857, include boat searches. A newspaper account describes how, "during flood times," neighborhood families near the Jackson Ranch ventured out in rowboats to find stranded livestock. Nearly a century later, in the 1940s, a flood at Santa Ana Wildlife Refuge sent the manager, Luther Goldman, poling silently through the watery woods in an inflatable raft. In 2010, Hurricane Alex drove torrential rains upriver to flood the refuge again. Information posted on the Santa Ana Web site noted refuge personnel canoeing through parts of the refuge they had rarely seen before. A year later, in assessing the effects of this flood, refuge manager Jennifer Owen-White noted that change had been noticeable and swift. The soil was so saturated on the refuge that it was easy to push a six-foot pole straight down until it disappeared. A day after the waters peaked, staff had seen cottontail rabbits up in the trees. Some plant populations had been wiped out—yuccas had died, and anacua had not proven tolerant. But the tall, riverine tepeguaje trees had survived. There had also been a big boom in amphibians: a large population of spadefoot toads had been noted along Bobcat Trail near the resaca. And with the amphibians had come waterfowl. The Christmas Bird Count of 2010 noted many more cormorants, anhingas, grebes, and wood ducks. Only fourteen wood ducks had been seen at the refuge since 2000, but at least five flew in that December day to the giant inland lake forming from the overflowing resacas. In 2010, as had occurred for millennia, life in many forms pulsed back, out of the floodwaters.[4]

In the last twenty years, the science of river ecology has given rise to valuable short-term studies that provide keyhole glimpses into the environment of the past. In 1997, an experiment in artificial flooding at Santa Ana revealed a virile resurgence of life as well as the disappearance of some species. Back in 1950, only a decade after the first managers wrote assessments of severe drought, the federal government provided funds for the installation of a turbine, diesel-operated well-pump, set up just south of the old clubhouse and the Military Road. Staff pumped water into the bone-dry resacas, but a manager noted, "Cracks of the lake bed were so wide and deep, it was several days before the results of pumping became really noticeable." Since then, pumping river water into resacas on Santa Ana has at times been critically important for plant (and animal) survival. Managed pumping can also allow researchers and students to study the effect of water suddenly arriving in a drought-stressed location. After flooding Owl Trail Resaca, a selected transect, the 1997 researcher found a temporary disappearance of quite a few plants along flooded trails and lake edges, yet new plants also arrived. As the water receded, grasses were the first to show green on the mud-dredged banks. Then water clover surged back. A tall, slender willow, commonly known as barrenground willow, and a wildflower, coastal germander, formed extensive, dominant patches. Neither had been noted in the area before flooding. In another small study area, cat brier and common balloon vine appeared for the first time. But two grasses, including a variety of dropseed, did not return at all after inundation. In this small study of the late twentieth century, carried out on a patch of Santa Ana earth carefully staked and measured, we find the evidence: historic Rio Grande flooding brought ripples of healthy and conserving change to riparian forests. River water did much more than hydrate dying plants; it swept in a load of new seeds, redistributing species; water also drowned out some kinds of plants that may have dominated a tiny area.[5]

The increase in birds after a trial flooding of the Owl Trail Resaca was dramatic. Only a few days after flooding, the first aquatic birds skimmed in for a landing on the fresh water. Researcher Charles David Castillo counted a peak of 230 birds in May, compared to only 60 seen along the Resaca Trail, an unflooded area. The species diversity was also higher near the Owl Trail Resaca, with about 30 species noted, compared to 16 in an unflooded area. Words observers used to describe these birds—the black-bellied whistling duck, mottled duck, blue-winged teal, little blue heron, green heron, ringed kingfisher—include "visiting, foraging, foraging for small fish brought in by the floodwaters, flying over and investigating, standing in the water." A controlled pulse of artificial flooding created an avian theater of vital action and interest. Of significance in Castillo's thesis is his belief that the "best remaining Resaca/flood forest . . . in southern Texas is located west of the Old Cemetery on Santa Ana National Wildlife Refuge." The Leal homestead was the heart of the most ecologically rich and preserved "riparian woodland biotic community" anywhere in Texas.[6]

Thus, the yearly flooding of the Rio Grande was the primary regenerative force of the woodlands, bringing hundreds of cubic feet of seed- and spore-laden water into the Santa Ana forest. Flooding also deposited earth; in one mid-twentieth-century flood, a manager saw the "southernmost point" of the refuge built up by nearly ten feet, a deposit stretching for two hundred yards. One hundred years earlier, after the Mexican War had given a new nationality to Santa Ana, the flood pulse of the Rio Grande was probably even more vibrant. It nourished the riverbank trees, inviting the easy taking of firewood. So wooded were the banks of the lower river that the supply of steamboat fuel seemed inexhaustible. In that year, 1850, a US military wife left an account of gathering wood for fuel. Helen Chapman wrote of her trip up the Rio Grande: "We came in a steamboat as the roads are impassable on account of the high state of the river. There are little Mexican settlements along the river called 'ranchos,' a little group of huts at which they collect wood for the use of the steamers. It lies piled up along the shore in the same way as along a railroad line." People of the river provided firewood for steamboats regularly. At least two ranch histories of Hidalgo County mention that workers were engaged in operating a wood yard for the steamers. The end of the war only accelerated steamboating on the river. In 1850, a new partnership formed, of men pivotal to Texas history—Mifflin Kenedy, Richard King, a Mr. O'Donnell, and Charles Stillman. They brought twenty-six steamboats to the lower river and took in huge profits right through the Civil War. Despite that war and its human and economic devastation, this company continued in "profitable operation," slightly reorganized, until 1882. With so many steamboats on the Rio Grande, passengers and crew passed by Santa Ana regularly. The shape of the southern grant boundary is even recorded in an incident from 1852, when gunfire from the south bank of the river hit the steamboat *Comanche*, piloted by Richard King himself. A testimonial published in the *Rio Bravo*, and eventually in the *New York Times*, stated that the gunfire occurred near "a point" known as Santa Ana Rancho.

The stripping of wood from the lower Rio Grande banks during the forty-year steamboat era caused intermittent erosion, undercutting and caving in of banks, and tree loss. There is no comparative data available to pin down the degree of loss, but the effect on rivers was complex. When mature plants are removed from stream banks, seepage erosion occurs. While stream or river flow is a part of this erosion, another factor has to do with a process called evapotranspiration. In summer months, trees remove a formidable amount of moisture from the soil; the subsequent drying out of riverbanks strengthens the earth and provides key structural support, actually more than root systems. Without mature trees wicking the moisture from banks, seepage erosion sets in and continues.[7]

Today, the banks of the Rio Grande at the southern edge of Santa Ana are very steep. There is no evidence that anyone living on Santa Ana participated in chopping fuel for steamboats, but the number of workers there was lower than on surrounding ranches. In addition, the ranch house itself, as well as outbuildings and worker jacales, sat at least half a mile up, on the first rise, hidden from view by tall, flourishing trees. Steamboats signaled their arrival and docking for fuel with whistles and bells, and those sounds would have carried through the woods, also signaling a new era for ranchers. Reliable transportation had arrived in the valley. Several miles above the Leal ranch house, an old Indian trail running from Brownsville to Hidalgo began to be used for overland supply trains heading for Ringgold Barracks. The route does not appear to have been in much use during the Mexican War, but it became much more heavily traveled in the 1850s as the population of South Texas rapidly increased. This trail, known as the Military Road or the Military Telegraph Trail, became US Highway 281, the quiet paved road that today leads visitors into Santa Ana Wildlife Refuge.[8]

Horses on Santa Ana

In the winter months, the Military Road near Santa Ana is flanked by fields of cotton, swiss chard, and cabbage. To the south of high-yield rows stands the riparian forest, protected by its federal status. In the 1850s, however, this scene featured a dusty horse and wagon trail beating through a mixed chaparral-upland forest, crossing the two leagues of Santa Ana and paralleling the river. As Texas republic and statehood history enters the record, a narrative emerges filled with riders: cattle rustlers, insurgents, outlaws,

Texas Rangers, and eventually, Civil War soldiers. Many more hoofed animals passed over the Santa Ana grant. The number of mounted people in the Lower Rio Grande Valley was legion. Everyone rode.

We find the passion for horses reflected in the original Reynosa Census of 1750, when horses and equine stock for breeding dominated domestic animal counts (see chapter 3). Observers from the 1820s on noted the Mexican preference for riding. Horsemanship had evolved in the herding and ranching culture, just as it became symbolic of Texas cattle drives in later decades. Mexican ranchers and militia sometimes hunted even wild turkeys on horseback, lassoing them expertly as they ran in weaving paths across the chaparral. Tales from Texas Rangers camped at Reynosa in 1846 describe riding contests held on June 24, the Feast of Saint John. A single Texan would try to outrun "the entire body of Mexicans" on horses, while carrying a live chicken. These horsemen operated at "breakneck speed" through the chaparral, churning up clouds of sparkling dust and gravel. In the years before the Mexican War began, horse patrols appeared along the Rio Grande. Texas Rangers rode along both sides of the river, frequently using the main trail on the south bank of the Rio Grande, especially for scouting expeditions. In 1842, for instance, forty horsemen under the command of Ranger Ben McCulloch rode from Matamoros to Reynosa on the old Indian trail. They would have passed near Santa Ana and its fording place. The local people of the Reynosa area as well as Mexican ranchers on both sides of the river preferred to ride rather than walk even a short distance. Observers watching the crowds of riders galloping past in the enveloping dust saw Mexican women as well as men commanding sweating animals. And north of the river, the number of horses and mules, serving different populations—Indians, ranchers, Texas Rangers, military convoys, herders and vaqueros, and smugglers with long pack trains—had created purposeful trails long before the Military Road snaked its way toward Ringgold Barracks. Many accounts of Indian raids underscore that Comanches, especially, were after horses. But by 1852, armed bands of both Indians and Mexicans were involved in "river piracy" up and down the Rio Grande. They were stealing horses as well as cattle. Small displaced groups of Lipan Apaches, Kickapoos, and Seminoles who crossed in night raids from the south to the north bank of the river also plundered stock.[9]

The involvement of Mexican raiders has its roots in the reorganization of government following the creation of Mexico in 1821. In December 1823, in an effort to regulate the fluid access to feral animals in northern Tamaulipas, Mexico passed a law controlling the holding of *corridas de caballada*. These were exuberant, specialized parties leading to the capture of escaped stock and feral horses (mustangs). The illegal roundups grew out of ranching culture, enhancing and celebrating the horseback skills of the raiders. Some of these horse raiders grew to legendary status. Despite the law, bands called *mesteñeros* roamed the arid country between the Nueces and the Rio Grande, especially in the years before the Texas Revolution and the Mexican War. They operated concurrently with a rising market in cattle hides, which were sent out of the valley by sea from Matamoros and Corpus Christi. Soon the rancheros of the valley also found a market for horses and mules in the United States. It is impossible to calculate how many of these horses were stolen from river ranches, captured wild on the Nueces strip, or bred. The horse trade was vast and, for the most part, undocumented; one historian has termed South Texas "the great horse funnel." Both Hispanic peoples and southern Plains Indians were likely supplying mustangs to northern Plains Indian tribes whose horses perished in the bitter winters. The demand for fresh horses in the written record is palpable.[10]

Horseflesh was cheap in South Texas, but herds were not being carefully managed by the populations that depended on them, especially Indian herds. In 1834, Colonel Juan Almonte surveyed the Texas region for the Mexican government. His findings, in the *Statistical Report on Texas (1835)*, mention that wild horses were so common on the Texas plains that they had little value beyond twenty *reales*. A section of northern Hidalgo County became known as Wild Horse Desert for the long, streaming herds of "shaggy beasts" seeking the grass that grew more abundantly there. Wild horses were seen by many as a free and inexhaustible supply. By the early nineteenth century, a Spanish official estimated that a thousand mustangs a month were entering the United States through East Texas, herded by raiders into Louisiana. Like the proliferating herds of sheep and cattle south and north of the Rio Grande, these horse herds represented a strong force of change in the specific ecoregions where they were concentrated. Just as the first-arriving domestic herds from Nuevo León in the 1750s had changed predator-prey relationships, the thousands of feral horses in South Texas began to lure the big cats.[11]

Jaguars and Horses

By 1800, wild and domestic horses had become a prime food for the consummate feline hunter of the tropical borderlands: the jaguar. Reported for centuries as stalking and pursuing the javelina (and in Central America, the peccary), by the time of consistent accounts in the early 1800s, jaguars had learned to prefer horseflesh. In South Texas, their traditional diet included turtles and their eggs, deer, fish, turkeys, and increasingly, "cattle and wild horses." Mexican ranchers near Reynosa in the 1820s complained to the traveler and writer Jean Louis Berlandier that they were continually losing colts and young horses to jaguars and cougars, *animales de uña* (animals with claws). This preference was also reported in Central America, where in 1895, the jaguar was described as "a ferocious animal causing great destruction among horses and asses." By 1850, a mammalogist traveling with the US Boundary Survey noted that the wild-running herds of cattle, mustangs, and feral mules formed a "rich support" for what he termed a vast number of pumas and jaguars in the Lower Rio Grande Valley. The formidable jaws of the jaguar deliver the strongest, most brutal snap of all felines. Jaguars have been documented crushing the skulls of javelina and some unfortunate humans, snapping the legs of galloping horses, and breaking the necks of young horses instantly.[12]

These are the dramatic stories, however, and most accounts of jaguars in Texas stress their elusive quality and their rare sightings. Yet they often did leave behind half-eaten carcasses of colts, calves, or small horses. Ranchers learned to distinguish the kills of jaguars from the kills of mountain lions. Jaguars often consumed only the front parts of an animal, leaving the body beyond the ribs intact. Careful modern studies have verified that jaguar kills will show a bite at the base of the throat, behind the ears, or at the base of the skull—or there will be a fractured neck, from a bite so powerful it leaves "the head turned around facing backwards." Jaguars targeted large mammal prey and could stalk it long distances. The heavy forests on the southern portion of Santa Ana would only have facilitated jaguar hunting, allowing them shade and cover during the blistering hot days and access to grasslands in the dusk and night hours. Dense forests and river corridors were their natural environment; these places in Texas, Mexico, and Central and South America are usually termed "their haunts," suggesting the scientific reality of considerable jaguar migration and mobility. Hidden in a lush understory, they waited for prey to come warily down to drink at the Rio Grande in places like the Santa Ana crossing. The narrow, shallower parts of the river, selected by humans for centuries for easy wading, also lured javelina, deer, mustangs, or stray domestic animals. Far into the twentieth century, in fact, animals from Mexico continued to come to the old Santa Ana vado. This pattern was an ancient one. The Boundary Survey naturalist of 1850 confirmed jaguars lying in wait for mustangs and deer at "the watering places" of the river bottoms. Jaguars also killed large birds on forest floors.[13]

Early Spanish accounts use the word *tigre* for the broad, lethal head of a jaguar crouching in tall grass, for its camouflage of light and dark spots.

The coat is mimetic, looking like dappled sunlight falling through small leaves as the animal lies still upon a log or rise of earth. (See jaguar photo in gallery.)

Thus, the jaguar's coat itself suggests a long evolutionary relationship with the forest. Jaguars were fluid travelers of the borderlands, as they were also confident swimmers, powerful enough in leg and paw to plunge into a turbulent river. Eventually, they learned to prey on domestic horses as well as the managed herds of mustangs of the South Texas Plains, bred for hefty profit by both Mexicans and Tejano ranchers in the antebellum years. Packs of jaguar skins, each spread out broadly for six to eight feet, appear on Brownsville and Matamoros trade lists from as early as 1827 (see chapter 4). Although there is no way to tell where jaguar skins originated, eyewitness reports of later years, including those of General Sam Houston and John James Audubon, suggest that these striking feline hunters had been drawn across the Rio Grande, into its forests and well beyond, by the presence of feral horse herds. This migration would have happened in the early 1700s, as escaped Spanish horses—never gelded—found the abundant nutrition of South Texas grasslands and multiplied. As the high-protein yield of horseflesh began to boost female jaguar fertility, cat populations climbed to numbers well able to cull domestic horse herds, despite aggressive hunting by ranchers.[14]

Yet even though jaguar numbers in South Texas probably increased throughout the eighteenth century, wild horses increased even more dramatically, breeding freely on the Texas plains. So many had proliferated between Corpus Christi and the Rio Grande that by 1846, as he marched south with the US Army, Lieutenant Ulysses Grant described the herd as the size of the state of Delaware. Ten years earlier, Colonel Almonte had noted that there was not enough water and pasture for horses when Comanche raiding parties traveled across Texas, so Indians took hundreds of horses with them. "No Comanche goes on the warpath with less than three horses." Some of the raiding groups numbered one thousand mounted warriors. The passage of these war parties with their horse reserves would have seemed an immense hoofed wave beating down the sea of grass. The arid climate, burning heat, and constant mobility strongly affected horse reproduction and colt survival. Healthy foals from managed Indian herds did not often spread out through the lush grasses, proliferating as did the wild cattle; only the feral mustangs, free to move into ungrazed grasslands, saw herd increase. Even among domestic horse herds, ranchers reported that "a large number" died in the pastures during the summer droughts.[15]

They also died moving, stumbling in the searing noonday hours. Horses were ridden hard and daily; night was cooler, but without broad moonlight, dangerous. There are accounts of thunderous chases on horseback in the high heat of the day but also night raids where riders swam their horses across rivers. The droughty climate in which forage could never be predicted took a heavy toll on large animals. In 1860, Colonel Robert E. Lee was in San Antonio, considering crossing the river into Mexico. He wanted more troops on the "outposts of the Rio Grande" to secure the border against Comanche depredations. Yet he knew a crossing of the frontier was impossible without better horses. The horses of the northern posts were described as "poor, worn down, and underfed," without good access to forage. Modern studies have shown that healthy horses need to eat 1 to 2 percent of their body weight daily, perhaps ten to twenty pounds of forage. Young grazing horses may need to eat for as many as fifteen hours a day to meet developmental needs. Although there is a historical tradition celebrating the richness of the South Texas grasslands, by the 1850s, one hundred years after domestic animals multiplied north of the Rio Grande, grass was already impacted. The continual raiding for horse replacement suggests that animals died young, collapsing from thirst and malnutrition. Horses of all ages grew gaunt and skeletal in the months when the grass lay dry and yellow brown. Horses and cattle, in fact, have similar dietary needs. Studies of these two competing populations in other desert areas of the country have found a strong dietary overlap—as much as 72 percent during the summer and 84 percent in winter. Overlap means grazing competition. Because historical illustrations and film have depicted lone cowboys riding horses in a churning, red-brown river of moving cattle, it is easy to overlook the numbers of horses competing with cattle for grass in South Texas.[16]

International conflict brought in more horses. Throughout the 1830s and 1840s, the region was a theater for four wars: the Texas Revolution, 1835–36; the Federalist Wars, 1838–40; the Texas-Mexican War, 1842–44; and the Mexican-American War, 1846–48. In 1836, the number of men moving into Texas toward San Antonio under the command of Mexican general Santa Ana may have been close to three thousand, with at least three cavalry units of three hundred horses each. These international conflicts have been described as raging "back and forth along the Rio Grande." Because there are no records in these war years firmly locating Benigno and Victoria Leal on their Santa Ana ranch, the impact of decades of conflict must be inferred: slow and halting economic growth of north-bank ranches. It was just too unpredictable and dangerous to live north of the river. Although by the 1860s, entrepreneurial Mexican Americans had begun to breed horses on river ranches, in the early years of the Los Toritos, Santa Ana, El Gato, and La Blanca grants, records reveal small numbers of stock.[17]

All the South Texas river ranches bred their own horses, but not many, and not at first, and horse numbers do not show steady increase. Throughout the 1850s, when only two tax roll entries reveal Benigno Leal paying a tax on stock, he owned few horses: five in 1855. Yet with these horses, he was managing eighty cattle. In 1860, on the Antonio Balli ranch, a census taker counted twenty milk cows, twenty-four grazing cattle, and four horses. By 1860, west of this ranch on Santa Ana, the Leals had twenty milk cows and twenty "other cattle," but only two horses. Gradually, over the next thirty years, the number of horses counted by census takers at Santa Ana increased, no matter who owned the land. In 1870, Cristóbal Leal was pasturing thirty-seven horses on the western league. Because of national events and the use of the Military Road, horses traveled over the land of Santa Ana in increasing numbers after 1850.

The presence of water-filled resacas fairly close to the trail would have invited frequent watering of horses and mules, and there they would also graze and browse. Early observations of richer, greener grass near mesquite trees (called "muskit grass" by one Anglo observer) also support the inference of vigorous equine grazing and then browsing from pod-laden branches. Although there is no way to determine the origin of generally held folk beliefs about plants and animals, we can note that an award-winning author of western fiction drew on such beliefs in a 1975 novel: "In this country [Texas], mesquite was nearly always a sign that water was near, for only wild mustangs ate the beans, and if they weren't bothered they'd rarely get more than three miles from water. Mesquite mostly grew from horse droppings."

After 1850, increasing numbers of horses digested and spread mesquite seeds. Seeds that are scarified by passing through the digestive tracts of sheep, cattle, and horses are much more likely to germinate, perhaps two to three times more likely. In addition, studies in the mid-twentieth century have shown that mesquite seeds from the dung of horses, especially, have a strikingly high germination rate of 82 percent. Estimates are that horses "effectively disperse" nearly 80 percent of the seeds they consume; for cattle, the dispersal rate is 55 percent. These numbers suggest a connection to the widely observed spread of mesquite in the ranching landscape of the river tracts; the ranchers on many of them, Santa Ana included, bred and sold more and more horses as the decades passed.

Modern findings like these help explain the impact that both wild and domestic horses had on South Texas. In addition to spreading mesquite and other brushy species, horses, with their powerful, sharp-edged hooves, damaged and changed microcommunities of plants. The passage of horses even ridden at a trot creates trampling effects that alter plant resilience.

Research today can only suggest the true environmental effects of horses as well as cattle, but on the Santa Ana leagues, in combination with twentieth-century overgrazing, some land became degraded, much of it the grassland stretching north of the Military Road. By the 1920s, only small goat herds grazed there, often wandering to browse the edges of the forest. A large citrus farm had failed in the midst of patchy, irrigated farms, most abandoned by 1930. Yet rising majestically to the south, out of the altered landscape, stood the flood-replenished Santa Ana trees. "On the banks of the Rio Bravo are large plains covered with dense forests," wrote Berlandier of the area in the 1820s. Those trees and their descendants survived. Almost 130 years later, refuge managers would describe them as "the jungle."[18]

Losing and Gaining Santa Ana

When the Mexican ranches north of the river became part of the United States, the ranchers and their families feared they would lose their land. Land was everything to them, anchoring them in a shared history with forebears who had crossed the river from the Escandón settlements, who had created the nascent ranching landscape there. This history was predominantly unwritten, yet it was vital, a surging blend of Catholicism, folk custom, family story, music and ballad, genealogy, and powerful, still perceived connections to Spain.

The Balli family, for example, was careful to record the word "Spanish" on the Reynosa Census of 1750. They cherished the Balli family coat of arms. Spanish and Tejano land grants were named with tenderness and panache, and these names persisted for years after the original families left the area. These old families felt their land to be so entwined with their personal identity that loss to Americans would be unbearable. Americans did not always understand this very well, at least as expressed in the correspondence of the Texas General Land Office (GLO): "The situation of these [original] settlers is Peculiar," noted an early commissioners' report. However, both the federal government and the state of Texas respected the meaning of original title. To establish and secure title under American law, the governor of Texas, P. H. Bell, created a commission to take documentary evidence and testimony from landholders. The result would be the recertification of lands to the original landholders. The commission became known as the Bourland and Miller Commission, named for the two men who sat long hours in morbidly hot, tiny wooden rooms listening to halting translators and witnesses.[19]

Did Benigno and Victoria Leal testify before the Bourland and Miller

Commission and secure title to the two leagues of Santa Ana? Yes. But the story is more painful and more complex: before they regained Santa Ana, they lost it. And their case is all the more poignant because it seems to have resulted from an error that may well have been subterfuge. Between the end of the Mexican War and 1850, a mere two years, a swarm of men described as "die-hard speculators willing to gamble" arrived in South Texas. The gamble was that the United States would not award title to the original Spanish and Mexican landholders; and lawyers, entrepreneurs, and men with money to invest began to acquire old Mexican and Spanish lands. They used a variety of pressures, levers, and spurious means of acquisition, but a common approach was to tell Hispanic owners they had not paid land taxes to the United States for 1848 and 1849, that they were in arrears. A tax auction would be organized. Old, mature ranchos filled with cattle, goats, milk cows, horses, and acres of improved land were auctioned away from impoverished owners. In 1850, two Brownsville lawyers, Elisha Basse and Robert H. Hord, acting as land agents for potential and absentee buyers, got hold of Santa Ana in this manner. To understand the raw, entrepreneurial climate of the day, consider this description of Brownsville in the early 1850s, the town from which Basse and Hord operated: "Bankrupts, escaped criminals, deserters from the armies of the recent war, gamblers and swindlers set the tone. Barrooms were fighting pits. Pistol duels added style to murder. Murderers and other offenders were lynched at the town shambles by hanging from the timbers on which beeves were butchered . . . the sheriff—a huge man of great strength and brutal force—usually killed the men he set out to arrest. Bloodhounds guarded the gate of his jail." This fledgling border town, whipped by river winds and sprayed with its gritty sand, nonetheless attracted rich Americans. The Texas Census of 1850 described Basse and Hord as personally being worth $10,000, and they were acting for much wealthier men. Santa Ana and other north-bank grants, such as Los Toritos and El Gato, would have seemed plums ripe for the picking at tax auction. At a time when, ironically, Mexicans "outnumbered Americans 10 to one," the financial predators along the lower Rio Grande had much success. The following entry in the *New Guide to Spanish and Mexican Land Grants in South Texas* is actually contradicted by the available documents: "Conveyance (assessor's deed) in file, stating 4,428 acres sold August 16, 1850 at public auction to Elisha Basse and Robert H. Hord because of failure of Cecilia Domínguez to pay taxes for the years 1848 and 1849."[20]

The mystery of Cecilia Domínguez as taxpayer for the Santa Ana leagues can finally be understood as an error that may have been highly convenient. The Texas GLO file for Santa Ana contains a receipt showing that the land taxes for 1848 and 1849 were paid. Victoria's brother Isidro Balli came forward to pay $27.80 for "Don Benigno Leal." Once again, Victoria's family connections provided the means to hold on to the land. Yet somehow, the record of Cecilia Domínguez, showing her to be in arrears on El Gato taxes, was used to place Santa Ana on the auction block. Of the four 1834 Mexican land grants, Santa Ana had by far the most available groundwater. To American entrepreneurs, its rich grazing lands were lucrative real estate, dotted with rippling *esteros* in the rainy season that could nourish "vast" cattle herds. The auctioning of a league of Santa Ana could well have been a deliberate step. One detail that supports this interpretation is the name of the tax assessor and collector: Adolphus Glavecke. This man had a history of corruption as a suspected cattle rustler. When he was also elected alderman, the city council of Brownsville tried to have him removed. According to the historian Jerry Thompson, Glavecke had a working relationship with Elisha Basse, one of the men who bid on and acquired Santa Ana. It is a fair assumption that Glavecke lumped one league of Santa Ana with El Gato to be auctioned and disregarded the tax payment by Isidro Balli. The presence of the tax receipt for Santa Ana, still available along with Cecilia Domínguez's arrears statement, strongly suggests that this happened.

Cecilia Domínguez did have a family connection to the Leals. The Domínguez family had originally owned the Los Toritos (Little Bulls) grant to the west of Santa Ana; for a short time, they shared a dense riparian forested boundary with the Leals, on the southern portion of their land. Although the genealogy is complex, the Domínguez and Leal families were related both through consanguinity and a marital connection by 1848. Cecilia Domínguez, baptized María Agapita Cecilia in Reynosa, 1804, was Victoria Leal's second cousin (see chapter 4 for this connection). Cecilia was roughly the same age as Benigno Leal. Her father, Estanislao (sometimes written Estanislado) Domínguez, is identified in private records of the McAllen Santa Anita Ranch; these same records identify Cecilia's brother as Máximo Domínguez, so she was a direct relative, a sibling, of the Los Toritos grantee. A lawsuit filed in 1966 to establish the original survey of Los Toritos mentions that the old grant was "confirmed by decree of the District Court of Hidalgo County" in May 1860. This suit also provides the important detail that Don Benigno Leal and Victoria's brother Don Francisco Balli were "present and of assistance" in the original 1834 survey of the two leagues of Los Toritos. The survey as well as the lawsuit suggests the ways these young, ambitious Mexican ranchers acted together on the northern frontier, revealing their keen interest in land and legal boundaries. The 1834 survey also provides evidence that Benigno and Máximo knew each other, probably well. Yet while Benigno Leal was carving a homestead rancho from his southern forest, Máximo could not pay the survey and application fees for his grant, and a Domínguez ranch never materialized. In fact, the Texas GLO file for Los Toritos indicates that Máximo Domínguez sold his grant less than six weeks after acquiring it. The purchaser was the older and shrewder Juan José Treviño, grantee of Agostadero del Gato to the east.

Yet from the beginning, Los Toritos seemed to present problems for ranchers. The New England sea captain who lived on Los Toritos, Sanforth Kidder, never owned more than seven cattle, suggesting that water remained in short supply, especially on the northern part of the grant—the grazing lands. It is clear from early maps that Los Toritos did not have the number of resacas that had formed on Santa Ana. On the Leal grant, in the early part of the nineteenth century, people and animals alike could rely on at least two generous, seasonal lakes, one supporting the Rancho Adentro homestead. In addition, the tip of Santa Ana's western league protruded into the Rio Grande, narrowing the distance required to cross it on foot and on horses. The Rio Grande channel changed so often, bringing floodwaters closer to inland depressions and also washing them farther away, that tracking the presence of small resacas is difficult. The 1852 Boundary Survey map depicting the grants does not show resacas on Los Toritos. Perhaps old lake beds were dry and filled with trees at that time; on early-twentieth-century maps, a crescent-shaped lake does appear. Today on the refuge, this wetland area is known as the Cattail Lakes, but it is not likely to have been a ready water source for people and livestock when Máximo Domínguez obtained Los Toritos. And in the northern part of the grant—the grasslands—only a small, curving end of a resaca known as "Resaca del Gato" stretched across into the eastern league of Los Toritos. Taken with the density of its southern forest, the grant may not have proven good ranching land. Juan Treviño may have decided this early on: he made a significant profit by selling Los Toritos in 1838, after owning it only four years. Yet, known locally as "El Toro," the leagues have nonetheless retained their original Mexican grant name for nearly 180 years, regardless of who owned it. The name persists in common reference, as do the Santa Ana and El Gato titles. The land and its identity endure, but the identity of many of the people who shaped the history of the land remains in shadow.

However, Cecilia Domínguez was surely well acquainted with the Leal, Balli, and Treviño families who owned the partially forested grants, for before the Mexican land grants ever materialized, she had become the second, younger wife of Juan José Treviño. Juan Treviño had been Victoria Leal's brother-in-law, first marrying her sister Refugio. In 1831, Cecilia married Juan Treviño in Matamoros, and by 1850, she may have been living there as a widow. She would have been just across the river from Brownsville, the place where land taxes were paid for the extensive Cameron County. Yet she apparently did not pay taxes on the portion of the large, five-league grant she had inherited. And her tax arrears document appears in the Santa Ana GLO file. As discussed earlier, the 1850 census has verified only five persons living at Santa Ana, suggesting a scant workforce and little profit from the selling of stock (it is possible that there were other families living on Santa Ana in 1850; the census cannot be used to determine exactly where families were located). In the end, however, the tax assessment, as demanded of the Domínguez and Leal families, was too high. Used to thinking in Spanish terms such as *vara*, *sitio*, and the Spanish league, these landowners watched as their grants were assessed by the acre, and Santa Ana was 8,856 acres.

Although Isidro Balli paid the taxes for Santa Ana, the two leagues were somehow grouped together with El Gato, and both land grants, or portions of them, were scheduled to be sold to bidders. However, the El Gato grant was never auctioned. A tax receipt exists showing that a month after 4,428 acres of Santa Ana were sold, an agent for Cecilia Domínguez, an Anglo-American man recorded as H. Sission [or Sisson] showed up to pay the back taxes on El Gato, about thirty-five dollars. The receivers of those taxes, the parties listed as owners of El Gato, are none other than Elisha Basse and Robert Hord. These sharp-eyed land agents thus had obtained El Gato somehow; why El Gato did not go up for auction on the courthouse steps in August remains a mystery that we cannot solve. Perhaps Benigno Leal or Isidro Balli protested that Santa Ana was wrongly being auctioned; if so, we have no record.[21]

The public sale of Santa Ana on August 16, 1850, was held in Brownsville, then the county seat of the immense Cameron County. However, the auctions of old porciones and grants were almost certainly publicized in the settlement known as La Habitación, future town of Hidalgo and then for a short time, known as Edinburg. In this river-crossing village, buyers would have been quite close to the grants and north-bank porciones they wished to buy and would have been able to personally ride across land going up on the auction block. The lush grasslands of these grants, stretching north for ten miles, could have been verdantly green from seasonal August rains. The resacas would have been full and overflowing, supporting wild ducks and geese as the banks were greening up. American speculators could not have failed to see the fertility or the grazing potential. By 1852, when the town of Habitación/Hidalgo changed its name officially to Edinburg for a short time, one of the Anglo-Americans living there was a tax assessor and future commissioner, Dr. Eli T. Merriman; his signature appears on the receipts for taxes paid on Santa Ana in 1852. It is not difficult to surmise that in his capacity as tax assessor, he saw the potential in the grant.

Described originally as a "small village," La Habitación may have been growing slowly as a river crossing as early as 1774. This tiny place, a cluster of jacales, a few brick buildings, stock corrals, and a muddy landing, looked across to the Mexican town of Reynosa. The clearing of timber along the banks had probably been ongoing since the early Escandón settlements. Perhaps there was a trading post or small store as well. All early histories emphasize that this riverine village was for years the only town in the newly formed county of Hidalgo, created from Cameron County in 1852. Tax auctions, sheriff sales, public hangings, rudimentary jail facilities, and the tamer civic business of elections or the granting of licenses or registering of cattle brands—Hidalgo eventually saw it all. Within a few years of becoming part of the United States, this area of the valley had changed dramatically. The brisk trade of an American river town, the legal infrastructure supporting settlement growth, and many arriving settlers all increased the traffic into this border village. Here in 1850, the eyes of incoming Americans turned to Santa Ana.

To obtain it, buyers had to be present in Brownsville, where half of the grant was auctioned off, likely with other Mexican grants and Spanish porciones. The 1877 GLO file for Santa Ana states simply that the auction was held on the steps "of the courthouse" and that Basse and Hord bid on a league of the old grant successfully. Yet from this point on, sociopolitical change rolled into South Texas and began to alter the landscape. By 1851, the American entrepreneur John Young had obtained a ferry license to cross the Rio Grande between La Habitación and Mexico. The McAllen ranch history *I Would Rather Sleep in Texas* pinpoints this ferry as eventually operating on the old La Blanca grant just east of Santa Ana. Elections in Hidalgo County were held for county commissioners, and the name Edinburg was tried out for the new county seat, replacing Hidalgo; yet as this legal machinery began to operate, the Bourland and Miller Commission also met with ranchers to certify their holdings.[22]

While Santa Ana was sold to Basse and Hord in Brownsville, it would have been westward, at Rio Grande City, that Benigno and Victoria Leal reclaimed their grant. Much of the knowledge of how to apply to the commission was passed orally, through word of mouth. The commission posted notices in English, tacking them to the wooden walls of the few prominent buildings. The notices were also posted in Mexico. Petitioners traveled to the city where Bourland and Miller heard testimony. Their petitions had to be in English and had to prove that their land had been continuously occupied since it was granted, that it had been improved, and that the owners had been and were raising stock. In addition to any supporting documents, witnesses came forward to testify with sworn statements. Sometimes, of course, there were no documents and only witnesses. And as a shipwreck destroyed a cache of original documents linking owners to their grants and porciones, what remains, unfortunately, are only witness statements. In the Bourland and Miller Commission report, the witnesses for Benigno and Victoria Leal's claim to Santa Ana are not identified. Yet Benigno, who was literate, was the applicant in the recertification for Porción 72, owned by both Victoria and her brother Ignacio Balli. It may be, then, that some of the Balli and Treviño family members served as witnesses for the Santa Ana claim. Their application was recommended by the commission, and in 1852, Santa Ana was recertified to Benigno and Victoria Leal.

The Bourland and Miller Report reveals a hard truth about the financial state of Mexican land grants in the early 1850s: of the four north-bank grants, all bearing a family connection to Victoria Leal Balli, *only* Santa Ana was recertified to the original owners. To either side, on the Los Toritos and El Gato grants, the original grantees were not living on their land. Los Toritos had been sold several times, ending up in the hands of the Kidder family. However, no witnesses could be found for any improvements or occupation of the Domínguez land on Los Toritos, and it took until 1860 for Benjamin Kidder to obtain legal title. Because of this family's presence there across several decades, the area had become known as "Kidder Ranch." To the east of Santa Ana, on Agostadero del Gato, John Young and others applied for the "five leagues of pastureland" originally granted to Juan José Treviño. Witnesses stated that the Treviños had occupied their land since 1836, but no Treviños stepped forward to ask for recertification. Change in land ownership was occurring rapidly; in fact, Anglo-American John Young already owned part of El Gato. Cecilia Domínguez held on to two leagues, but she sold them quickly, in 1853, to John Ferdinand Webber. This enterprising American also bought two leagues of land on La Blanca a few years later, and he proved to be the only rancher on La Blanca who was able to consistently pay taxes on his land. Without a ranch income, it certainly would have been a formidable challenge for the Treviño sisters, Concepción and Rafaela, or Cecilia Domínguez, widow of the original grantee, to pay American land taxes as they came due. When Cecilia sold her land, Benigno Leal was present as a witness. Perhaps standing by as support for Victoria's nieces, Benigno was also witnessing an early sign of Anglo-American ascendance in South Texas. It is impossible to know, really, why or how portions of these land grants changed hands in the chaotic years of the early 1850s. We can only surmise human motivations. Original Hispanic owners selling to Anglo-Americans was a pattern that also occurred on La Blanca, the first of the 1834 Mexican grants to have been awarded. As was the case with Los Toritos and El Gato, La Blanca was not recertified to Lino Cavazos. For some time, he had probably been selling small portions of his land to others, including possibly Antonio Balli. Thus, Benigno and Victoria Leal were the *only* 1834 grantees who held on to some of their land after the Mexican War. Their tenacity and refusal to sell the alluvial earth of Rancho Adentro, their ebony-fenced family cemetery, at least three large resacas, and a mature, graceful ebony grove must be counted as significant in the survival of the Santa Ana forest. This perseverance is all the more impressive in the face of the likely fraud perpetrated on Santa Ana to auction it in 1850.

Yet all was not well for this old Reynosa family. They must have been extremely cash poor by 1852, for in that same year they did sell the entire eastern league of Santa Ana, 4,428 acres, to Dr. Eli T. Merriman, the entrepreneurial physician, rancher, tax assessor, and commissioner; however, Merriman soon relocated to Banquete, Texas. Official accounts from the Santa Ana refuge Web site describe this sale in the passive voice: "and a vast cattle ranch was planned." There is little evidence that a "vast," successful ranch developed on this league, despite the registering of a Merriman cattle brand and the identification of Santa Ana as "Merryman's Ranch" or "Merryman's Banco" on International Boundary Commission river maps from the 1850s. The profits and final size of the Merriman Ranch are not known. In 1853, Elizabeth Merriman, Dr. Merriman's wife, purchased the western league of El Gato, an acquisition that would have significantly increased the ranch. Yet by 1854, she had sold half of it again, to Henry E. Merriman, her stepson. Portions of these grants were being sold and resold within families, suggesting that profits from cattle ranching were not steady. In addition, Dr. Merriman and his family had left Hidalgo County in the early 1850s, so his ranch was managed by others. He and then his wife were absentee landlords, not an uncommon practice. The Leals continued to live in their ranch house on the western league while running their own stock on the land to which they still held title. Significantly, this league was the more heavily forested. The Leals stayed on as custodians of the trees.[23]

Although geopolitical change had been dramatic for the entire area of the original Tamaulipan Mezquital—the ecosystem that spread from northern Mexico into southern Texas—visible change now erupted. In the decades of the 1850s and 1860s, people, animals, and new structures began to imprint the landscape and the habitat of the old Mexican ranching world of the north bank. The Jackson Ranch community church organized and became a magnet, a social institution for river people. Citizens organized to improve roads. One new road was laid out "along the north bank of the river," stretching east from Hidalgo. The old salt road running diagonally northeast across the county saw improvement as well. Tejano landowners and incoming Americans both saw advantages to clearing and improving land for roads. Horses, cattle, and sheep thronged through the old grants, multiplying without fences and without much management from herders or stock overseers. As the decade built toward the Civil War, more people on horseback, more mule teams pulling wagons and carts, and increasing numbers of military personnel passed over Santa Ana on what was being called the Military Telegraph Road. In 1859, during the Cortina Uprising (also called the Cortina War), the regular army, with a division of cavalry as well as Texas Rangers, pursued Juan Nepomuceno Cortina, champion for Tejano justice, along the Military Road as far as Rio Grande City. Santa Ana was crisscrossed with galloping, mounted soldiers.[24]

These are the incidents that have been verified in the written record. It takes historical imagination to envision a countryside that in just a year had "been laid waste, the citizens driven out, their horses and cattle herded across the Rio Grande into Mexico." Historians have noted the impact of the Cortina War of 1860 on the ranches of the Rio Grande; in the history of the McAllen Santa Anita Ranch, the authors state that South Texas suffered "inestimable damage." It is probable that Benigno and Victoria Leal were among those ranchers who fled, once again, across the Rio Grande to Reynosa. In the will they drew up in Reynosa, possibly as early as 1859, Benigno and Victoria were described as "citizens of this town." They had obviously moved to Reynosa for a time. The north-bank grants were filled with soldiers, often requisitioning food or demanding forage for their animals. Cattle rustling had escalated, sometimes with dramatic numbers. On Rancho Relámpago, east of Santa Ana, thirty-five men described as *Cortinistas* stole seventeen cattle, thirteen horses, and at least ninety goats. On La Blanca grant, the young widow of John Young, Salomé Balli, reported losing as many as eight hundred cattle. Gardens, fields, chicken coops, and even beehives were often burned. The revealing census of 1860 tells this story of a depopulated countryside. This census does record a family living at Santa Ana Rancho. Yet when the census taker rode down the forested trail on July 23, 1860, whom did he find? A Benigno Leal came out into the high heat of midsummer, perhaps leaning on the ebony fence as he talked to the "government man" with a leather notebook. Yet this Benigno was not the original grantee, José Benigno Leal.[25]

The Leal Fortunes

In 1860, the census taker recorded a vacant landscape along the river in Hidalgo County. Although three people were recorded living at Santa Ana Ranch, the previous twelve dwellings visited by the census taker were unoccupied. Just to the west of the Santa Ana ranch house, the census taker found four occupied homes; he then progressed upriver through a startlingly vacant ranchland: nineteen homes were empty of people. It is possible that some of these abandoned jacales and houses were yet on the western league of Santa Ana; there is no way to verify location. At the main ranch house, the census taker found a Benigno Leal, age thirty-six, occupation farmer; Josefina Leal, age twenty-nine; and Antonio Leal, age nine; all three were born in Mexico. They were living on thirty acres of improved land with four thousand acres of unimproved land, a combination of riverine forest, thorn scrub, and grasslands to the north. These three people, perhaps with the help of day laborers crossing from Mexico or from other ranches, had raised 550 bushels of Indian corn. They owned ten milk cows and ran about twenty head of range cattle. The ranch size, with its small distribution of horses, cows, and improved acreage, corresponds well to other ranch holdings of the time. Yet it is uncertain how many people were being supported, fed, and clothed from Santa Ana Ranch on the western league. The Benigno listed on the census was almost certainly a relative of the original grantee, living there while the senior owners, Benigno and Victoria, were away in Reynosa. It is even possible that he gave his name as Benigno Leal fictitiously, to appear to be the grantee living on his land. Legal documents with the real owners' signatures place them in Mexico in 1859. In 1862, their will was registered in Texas in English. Both the will and the formal 1859 adoption of Cristóbal Peña, a twenty-six-year-old relative of Benigno and Victoria, are significant. They are indicators of the Leal fortunes and family size, as well as familial relationships and feelings.[26]

Cristóbal Peña, born in 1833 in Mexico, was likely the son of Victoria's brother José Isidro Balli and an unknown woman who probably had the surname Peña. This connection is expressed in a Balli genealogy as a "strong family tradition[al] belief." As recorded in the adoption papers, Cristóbal Peña, living with Benigno and Victoria from the age of seven months, had become "as a son to us." It appears that the Leals faced a prospect of dying without heirs; their family line was scant in comparison to that of other ranch families in the area. The Balli family, for instance, produced eight children, including Victoria Balli Leal, who grew up to become the powerful surviving matriarch of Santa Ana. On the Zacatal Ranch of the Llano Grande grant, the Hinojosa family healthily multiplied, becoming "the largest settlement of the Hinojosas." Marriages between Americans such as Thomas James Handy, of the Fourth Wisconsin Cavalry during the Civil War, and Tejano women (in this case, Angelita Cavazos) also produced families of seven and eight children. The Leal family was an exception to the pattern; as will be seen, their failure to multiply and produce significant heirs probably contributed to the survival of the Santa Ana forests. Like Benigno, the adoptee Cristóbal had become a skilled rancher, ready to assume the heirship of the remaining Santa Ana league. Ten years later, successfully settling and working on Santa Ana, he had developed the ranch stock to seventy milk cows, one hundred range cattle, and thirty-seven horses. He had married Rafaela Treviño, Victoria's niece (listed on the 1870 census as "keeping house"), and he had a fifteen-year-old son, also named Cristóbal. When Cristóbal (Peña) Leal was adopted, his son was about four years old; church records show that grandson Cristóbal Leal was baptized in Reynosa on October 7, 1855. Through a legal adoption, Benigno and Victoria were ensuring that Santa Ana would eventually pass to their grandson.[27]

In the world of Santa Ana in Texas, demographic change was occurring so rapidly that Benigno and Victoria may have worried about preserving their grant. Both the 1870 and 1880 censuses reveal a steady influx of diverse people who continued to create a multicultural landscape. Living near the Leals by 1880 was an American, George Kidder, son of old Sanforth Kidder, the Connecticut sea captain who eventually obtained the Los Toritos grant. George was possibly renting a house and some land on the Santa Ana western league from Victoria Leal; at the time, he was a deputy inspector of hides in Hidalgo County. As reported by many census takers, acreage not planted with corn or beans and not listed as grassland was noted as "unimproved woodland." It is therefore probable the Kidders lived on the southern, forested part of the league, near the river. They formed part of the astonishingly diverse cultural landscape of southern Hidalgo County during these years, which included African American farmers such as Eli and Columbus Jackson; white settlers married to African American women (William G. T. Brewster and Minerva Singleterry, or John Ferdinand Webber and Sylvia Hector, his former slave); both Union and Confederate soldiers who became ranchers (Thomas Handy and Lina Helen Box); blended Tejano American families (such as George and Jesusa Kidder or Thomas Handy and Angelita Cavazos); and a high population of strong, vital Hispanic peoples born in both Mexico and Texas. Many of these Mexican peoples were of Indian lineage.[28]

In keeping with their desires to hold on to the remaining league of their land, Benigno and Victoria drew up their will as well in 1859. During the second year of the American Civil War, the will was legalized in the (Confederate) state of Texas, making adoptee Cristóbal Leal the Santa Ana heir. A motivation for registering this will in Texas is not difficult to find: the American Civil War was raging, and Cristóbal had decided to enlist in a Ranger unit connected to the Texas Confederacy. On December 8, 1862, he was mustered into Captain William A. Thomas's Company of Partisan Rangers. His service records, entered with the spelling "Cristoval," indicate he brought with him a better than average horse, worth one hundred dollars, and "equipment"—saddle, canteen, possibly a rifle—worth fifty dollars. Like almost all young men on the river ranches, Cristóbal was a skilled horseman, for a hundred-dollar horse was above middle range at the time. Thomas's Rangers were but one group of mounted soldiers from a host of such units in the area; records show small guerrilla-like Ranger bands forming with names such as Nolan's Mounted Cavalry, Ragsdale's Company, Treviño's Squad, and Upton's Company. These units were primarily protective, as ranches continued to be in jeopardy from different groups of raiders. The area was mobilized at the local level, and the units were all cavalry, many of them loyal Texans like Cristóbal. There is strong evidence that Thomas's Rangers had formed in response to raids by Cortinistas. The historian Jerry Thompson has found that in 1861, the town of Edinburg (originally Hidalgo) was thought to be at particular risk for raids, and partisan Ranger groups defended it "night and day." Most of the population living around the town had retreated across the river to Reynosa. At the time, Santa Ana lay about eight miles to the east.[29]

Although he served only four months between 1862 and 1863, did not appear to see military action, and did not reenlist, it is an obvious inference that Cristóbal's adopted family was concerned he might be killed. In formally leaving Santa Ana to him, the Leals were securing their land to their family line, in this case to their grandson, Cristóbal Leal, who was at that time seven years old. Benigno's signature on this 1862 document (likely first executed in 1859) is the last legal trace of the Leal patriarch and original grantee. Victoria had never learned to read or write; she asked that her brother Francisco Balli sign for her. The other witnesses' signatures on this will, many of them from the Domínguez family, all reveal the flourishing, decorative embellishment of the final letter of each surname, a characteristic of formal Mexican penmanship. And Benigno Leal's clear, firm signature also remains, testament to his determination to preserve Santa Ana. He had sold the eastern league and had lived long enough to see it become known locally as "Merryman's Ranch." This change had occurred early, within a year of the sale. A tragedy

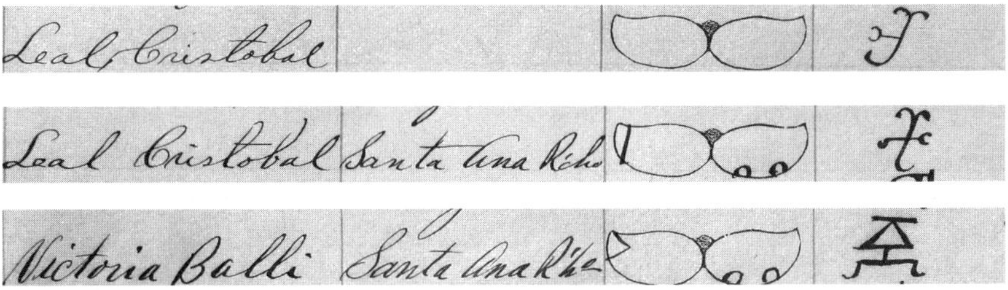

The livestock ear marks and brands registered by Cristóbal Leal in 1858 and by Victoria and her grandson Cristóbal Leal in 1874. From the Hidalgo County Marks and Brands.

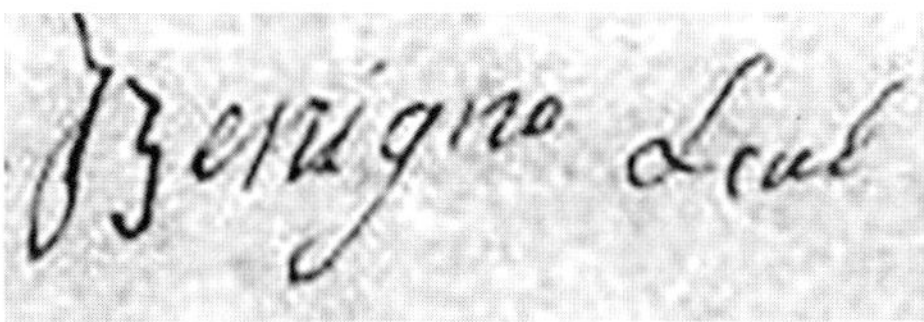

Benigno Leal's signature as a witness appears on the sale document of two leagues of El Gato land, by Cecilia Domínguez to John Webber in 1853. From the Texas General Land Office file for El Gato (Juan José Treviño).

on the river near Santa Ana helps verify local referents. In 1853, a member of the International Boundary Commission drowned while surveying the lower river. On July 23, Thomas Walter Jones died when his skiff overturned in the Rio Grande; he is described in the Santa Ana Ranch history as being buried "at Dr. Merryman's rancheria." Santa Ana—the Mexican riverine land grant honoring Saint Anne—had rapidly taken the name of an American rancher who had owned it for only one year.[30]

For ten years, Benigno would have watched as part of his grant gradually took on the personality and local reputation of the incoming and prominent Americans. This pattern is distinct as early as the 1850s and it is revealed ever more strongly after the Civil War as landholding and employment opportunities swung to the dominant Anglo-American settlers. We see the first traces of their ambitions developing after the Boundary Survey of 1850. Under the direction of Major Emory, survey markers appeared delineating the channel, the international boundary, between Mexico and the United States. By 1861, the Hidalgo County Commissioner's Court had granted a license to Dr. Merriman to operate a ferry across the river at the southern edge of his ranch. Yet Merriman, who had been elected as one of the county's first commissioners back in 1852, had long since relocated. His ferry and ranch were operated by others.

Nonetheless, the structures of growth and change were visible. Riders and pedestrians were likely using the hard-beaten paths through the old grant to reach the ferry. By 1885, local people of Protestant faith attended the Jackson Ranch Methodist Church to the west of Santa Ana, built on old Porción 71. Methodists and Catholics alike used the Military Road and well-known bridle paths crisscrossing the ranches. In earlier years, beginning in 1849, the traveling priests of the valley had come to river ranches, using the winding Oblate Trail that connected river settlements. A re-created hand-drawn map in a 1975 publication shows Santa Ana Ranch marked as a stop on the Oblate Trail. This map includes four crosses perhaps indicating residences. These may have been gathering places in larger ranch homes; one of the crosses is in the correct place for the brick home of Benigno and Victoria Leal. Here, frontier priests on horseback, picking their way from Brownsville or Rio Grande City (and later, La Lomita Mission), stopped to administer the sacraments: Mass and communion, baptisms of infants (often many at once), marriages, anointing of the sick, and especially, confessions. In February 1875, Cristóbal and Rafaela Leal were witnesses to the marriage of Lauriano Ysaquirre and María Reyes Rubalcaba at Santa Ana; Father Louis Pitoye officiated and signed the marriage certificate. It has not been possible to discover evidence of funeral Masses performed at Santa Ana, despite the somber crosses on over thirty marked graves in the Leal cemetery. Perhaps some of these graves are those of newborn children, or of people who perished in epidemics and who had to be buried quickly; perhaps some represent deaths by violence. We have no evidence aside from a general belief that most of the burials are of ranch laborers.

Significantly, although it appears to be a synthesis over time, the Oblate Trail map emphasizes the presence of Santa Ana as a permanent community: it is the only ranch of the original four 1834 grants marked on the trail. Ranch homes of Santa Ana are shown to the south, in the forest. Perhaps this is the area referred to by the author of a sketch titled "The Oblate Trail," which stated, "The territory of 100 by 150 miles was a territory of grandeur and heat mirages, yet very real in soils both rich and poor, with areas of almost impassable vegetation."

For thirty years before the 1878–79 construction of the first nearby Catholic church in Edinburg, a frame building first known as the Chapel at Edinburg, priests had visited river ranch communities. Through their committed ministration, they bound isolated ranches to the Catholic faith, bringing news from other ranches and enriching the landscape of shared experience. Once the Chapel at Edinburg, built from many local subscriptions and donations, was consecrated, baptisms, marriages, and funerals shifted from scattered ranches into a single, permanent structure. In 1879, in one of the first marriages celebrated in the chapel, Victoria's grandson, Cristóbal Leal, married Ascensión Ozuna of Reynosa. Given the number of Leal, Balli, Cavazos, Treviño, and Domínguez relatives in South Texas by then, guests at a wedding celebration may have numbered into the hundreds. As recorded in many ranch histories, weddings could span two days, and the traveling Oblate priest often stayed the night. Nuptials were commonly performed before dawn to allow time for an extended wedding feast and dance. We have no records of such day-long ceremonies at Rancho Adentro on Santa Ana, but they may well have occurred.[31]

By the time of Cristóbal and Ascensión's marriage in 1879, the threat of violence from Indians, river raiders, cattle rustlers, and independent factions was diminishing. Yet in earlier decades of American statehood, continuous residence on the river ranches was marked by day-to-day hardship and danger. Benigno and Victoria had lived in their Santa Ana brick ranch house on and off through the 1850s, and for two of those years at least, 1855 and 1857, Benigno paid taxes on his land and stock. We also have tax records for the initial, undivided Cameron County showing that he was living on Santa Ana and paying land and stock taxes in the late 1840s. Yet Benigno and Victoria were not there in 1860 when the census taker came by, and by the 1870 census, although Victoria was still living, their adopted son, Cristóbal, is listed as owner, occupying the ranch house "as agent, owner, or manager." Benigno fades completely from the record, perhaps killed by Indians in the early 1860s. However, he had planned for a successful ranching enterprise: he had registered a brand for his cattle in Hidalgo County. The marks and brands record book that contained his original brand has disappeared. Yet there is a similar core shape to the brands of his adopted son and grandson that followed it, suggesting an original and enduring Leal design. Victoria Balli Leal's brand is distinctly different.

It cannot be proven that one of the thirty unidentified graves in the Santa Ana cemetery is that of José Benigno Leal, original 1834 grantee of Santa Ana. Yet his probable brand design, his signature, and, most dramatically—his forest—endure.[32]

CHAPTER SIX

Fire, Water, and Goats on Santa Ana

The Guzmán Dream

In the years after the Civil War, the great shapers of the Lower Rio Grande Valley ecosystem, fire and flood, changed in frequency and severity. Fires decreased; floods increased. On Santa Ana, there were no recorders of this shift. Small ranching communities are pinned at few points into the historical record, mainly through legal documents such as wills, tax rolls, and deeds. Agricultural census data begin to be important by 1870. But tracking environmental change, especially on local, individual tracts, is a slow and elusive process; it must be inferred from both animal and human history. Larger events in towns are recorded, such as the destruction of the first Catholic church in Edinburg in a catastrophic 1889 flood. And we know that between 1865 and 1887, when Victoria Leal died, a second Hispanic family bought and moved onto the eastern league. Their management of field and forest primarily preserved those habitats until 1905. Environmental shifts surely occurred on both leagues of Santa Ana, primarily because of the rise of human population in South Texas. While much of the story of the Leals and the Guzmáns during these decades is in shadow, we can learn from the history of even a single mammal now commonly seen on the Santa Ana refuge: the nine-banded armadillo. Hikers on the trails today may catch sight of one, moving with slow, trundling gait just off the path, where it keeps to thickets and snuffles into the dirt for insects. Yet it is quite certain that the Leals did not see armadillos on Santa Ana before the Civil War.

The Traveling Armadillo

Modern researchers have pinpointed successful migration of the nine-banded armadillo into the United States across the Mexican-Texan border, but only after 1850. In 1854, Audubon first documented the armadillo in "extreme South Texas." Across well over a century, this immediately recognizable mammal has moved steadily east and north. By the late 1990s, the armadillo was noted in Nebraska. Like many species brought into new territories through human movement, the armadillo found a means to expand its range. With greatly increased human traffic—more migration, more raiding and smuggling, and more frequent military crossings—armadillos were able to cross the Rio Grande, possibly as stowaways or as trophy captures and exotics brought back by US soldiers. Arriving in a habitat undergoing change, this species found advantages. Its successful implantation in South Texas suggests those changes. The ranching boom after 1860 resulted in accelerated human hunting of the armadillo's predators as well as a critically important activity for its habitat: partial clearing of woodlands, often followed by grassland erosion. Mesquite brush country is much more inviting to the armadillo than heavy forests or dense grasslands. Thicket and brush foragers, digging for subsoil insects by night, armadillos could also swim rivers (or ford at shallow areas by submerging and wading on the bottom); they may have begun crossing the low-stage Rio Grande more consistently. Accounts from old-timers in the 1880s establish that by that decade, the armadillo had reached the Nueces River. By 1891, a cowboy saw an armadillo come out of a thicket near the center of Padre Island, and armadillos were described as commonly occurring north of Brownsville. The Rio Grande Valley began to be described as their primary home.[1]

By the late nineteenth century, so many armadillos were living in South Texas that local peoples were making baskets from armadillo shells and marketing them as ornamental cultural items. This practice is documented especially in Hidalgo and Cameron Counties in the decades after the Civil War. Increasing armadillo populations suggest environmental shifts as well as a more populated ranching region. With the increase in

Louis Agassiz Fuertes sketched the nine-banded armadillo in northern Mexico in the early twentieth century. Painting by Louis Agassiz Fuertes, *Wild Animals of North America*, 1918.

fenced boundaries came more buildings, roads, and wells. Most especially, growing cattle herds changed natural processes as well as the land itself. As herds increased to what historian Armando Alonzo identifies as Class 4—more than three hundred animals—their protection mandated control of fire. Sweeping grassland fires began to decrease. Prevention of fire became a new priority, and the drop in fire frequency especially impacted South Texas grasslands.[2]

The Way of Fire

Many historians describe the post–Civil War years as a desperate time: in addition to a cattle rustling fever that drew bands of Mexican outlaws across the river, real yellow fever and cholera epidemics swept through the river systems. These illnesses may have been driven by a "severe storm" in 1867. The origin of this storm is not known—perhaps a hurricane, perhaps a torrential, incendiary thunderstorm originating on the South Texas Plains. Studies of lightning strikes on drought-dry grasses there have concluded that such strikes were legion; in fact, South Texas has been designated a "lightning-fire region." Leagues of amber grass exploded into a flaming mass whose core heat killed brush. Prairie fires that consumed thousands, perhaps millions, of acres appear in the historical record as late as the 1880s, and the frequency of historical fires in this area has been calculated as every five to ten years. Travelers such as Frederick Olmstead, passing through the South Texas Plains in 1857, reported "charred grasslands" and a swollen sun slowly sinking in the distance, inflamed with the heat and acrid smoke of a prairie fire. From the supercharged layers above the earth, lightning spears smoked the flammable grasses. After the advent of barbed wire in the 1870s, extensive fencing and enclosed fields mandated ranch homes and structures. Controlled burning was extremely risky, as it could so easily become uncontrolled. Humans were fearful of fire and fought it. Prairie fires were viewed as lethal, lightning as a devastating act of God.[3]

It had not always been so. Early Indians of South Texas were recorded as setting fires to drive lizards from the grasses; they also used fire to encircle large deer herds. Spanish settlers in the Americas have been described as early as 1534 as setting fires "everywhere . . . to clear brush and renew grasses." From the combined histories of both Indians and Spanish peoples, it is likely that the northern Nuevo Santander settlers employed carefully set brush fires to rid their grazing lands of small, tough trees. In 1846, Zachary Taylor's troops marching from Corpus Christi reported evidence of burning by the Mexicans ahead of them. Firing the land was well known, but once grazing animals appeared in enormous numbers on the South Texas ranches, as happened after the Civil War, fire lost its potency. It could no longer roar through heavy, tangled grasses where proliferating mesquite and cactus could hide. The grasses had been the fuel load, the key to the cycle of burn-off. Immense, tinder-dry clumps of nearly bone-white grass had stoked prairie fires to a raging heat, strong enough to char the underground roots of mesquite. Deep down in the dark soil stretched root systems laden with many nodes, the source of life for the ubiquitous mesquite. Unless the fires destroyed these nodes, mesquite would reappear. Lightning fires in this region have been endemic across a sweep of time unfathomable to most humans—millennia, perhaps eons, of virile, racing flames. But those millennial fires imperceptibly shaped trees and shrubs like mesquite and blackbrush to evolve protective mechanisms to survive. From the beginning of this ecosystem, lost in geologic time, fire and drought created the hardihood of vegetative seeds. Modern researchers note the resilience of mesquite in particular: in one herbarium, a mesquite tree has been grown from seeds over forty-four years old.[4]

There is no way to verify whether ranchers like Benigno and Cristóbal Leal ever touched a flaming stick to patches where mesquite had pushed into their grasslands. In the mid-twentieth century, refuge managers described a small field deep in the woods as an "internal pasture," but the northern part of the grant was the main grazing acreage. On the long, narrow grants stretching toward the South Texas Plains, lightning fires may have routinely consumed and also protected the grass. And the number of domestic animals grazing on Santa Ana—cattle, horses, and goats—was never consistently high. By 1880, Cristóbal and Victoria Leal were recorded as raising jointly thirty-five horses, eight oxen, fifty milk cows, and three hundred head of cattle, the largest herds ever to graze on the western league. This league had 4,400 acres described by census takers as "unimproved land." Except for the southernmost forest, most of this was grazing pasturage. Approximately four hundred pasturing animals on perhaps 3,500 acres is a sustainable ratio. The number of cattle being raised and grazed on the eastern league, once envisioned as the "vast" cattle ranch of Dr. Merriman, cannot easily be ascertained. After 1905, that acreage passed through a series of owners, all of whom kept stock and grazed some cattle and goats. So it is not surprising that by the time incoming refuge managers first assessed Santa Ana in the early 1940s, they perceived it as significantly overgrazed. This is particularly true of the eight hundred acres of pastureland located inside the refuge, where grazing leases had been issued indiscriminately to many cattle owners.[5]

The Eating of the Grass: Clues in the Twentieth Century

Because of the keen eyes of the first refuge managers, we have a striking case study of overgrazing and recovery on a precisely defined acreage. Within six months of acquiring permanent title, in the spring of 1944, Santa Ana manager Earl Craven wrote a report about grazing on the refuge. He noted that a large percentage of the area carried a weed cover, with only a few specific patches near the river and trails showing a reappearance of nutritious grass. Through grazing leases, decades of heavy cattle and goat use had so stripped the refuge grass that the animals would move on, searching out "the fruits, browse, and seeds of wildlife food plants." The wildlife critically depending on those fruits, leaves, and seeds then lost out. Local estimates for the number of acres per head of cattle grazed—the optimal ratio—had been given as ten to fifteen acres per animal. Earl Craven strongly felt that for Santa Ana and its degraded fields, the minimum should be thirty acres per grazer. In all the early reports from the newly established refuge, managers advise against issuing any new grazing rights, calling the refuge overgrazing "severe." The last lease had put four hundred cattle, owned by sixteen different people, on the internal pasture, which may have been less than five hundred acres by this time. Managers felt the number of animals should never exceed one hundred and called the situation "deplorable," especially the efforts needed to manage the dipping of these animals for fever-tick eradication. Throughout the 1940s, assessments of available food and cover for birds used the term "recovery." Without abundant grass—nest sites, shelter from predators, and a stunning variety of nourishing seeds—many bird species were deprived. Across the river in Mexico, drought and overgrazing conditions were also so critical that by 1947, a manager reported a unique form of poaching. Mexican farmers were wading across the Rio Grande at night to steal large armfuls of grass from ungrazed sites near the river. They stuffed hand-torn Santa Ana grass into "large, homemade sacks" and carried it back across the Rio Grande to feed their cattle. Whether the grass was eaten or stolen, the birds on Santa Ana still lost out.[6]

"Overgrazing" is a blanket term, difficult to precisely define for specific areas; each grass type and its association of plants seem to respond differently to overgrazing. However, ranch personnel know it when they see it. Range managers have described it as grass chewed down to subsoil level; a crumbly, sterile earth; or poverty grass and weeds clumped in a patchy cover. The "choked" quality of pastures filled with cactus colonies has been well documented. Although dramatically visible by the mid-twentieth century, this change began in the decades of the great cattle ranches and accelerated straight through the Great Depression. Yet overgrazing is not an isolated factor; it works in tandem with another. The boom in South Texas livestock grazed, herded, bred, sold, and shipped out to distant ports after the Civil War inaugurated a process made worse through a corresponding drop in high-intensity, seasonal fires. The assumption that fires dropped significantly between 1865 and 1885 is based on ranch expansion.[7]

Local ranch histories on small holdings near Santa Ana indicate that many Tejano ranchers began to raise and sell stock then, joining the burgeoning American market economy. On nearby Santa Anita Ranch, Macedonio Vela bought a square league of land from John McAllen and Salomé Balli and named it Laguna Seca, "Dry Lake Ranch." In the ten years after the Civil War, Vela and his sons raised mules and horses; they also sold and shipped donkeys to Cuba. This was the decade of the massive King Ranch herds, the overland cattle drives, and a general population boom in Hidalgo County, and especially in Cameron County, as migrating postwar populations poured in. During these cattle drive years, smaller ranches like Santa Ana would sell cattle to a dealer who organized the immense herds for cattle drives. By 1870, three cattle drive routes had evolved out of South Texas: straight east to Corpus Christi and then by steamer to New Orleans; by cattle trail north to shipping points on the Red River; and then north again, on a blisteringly hot, dust-blown trail, all the way to Kansas. South Texas cattle then traveled via railroad to Chicago. These cattle drive trails had a distinct look: "many narrow grooves side by side," reflecting thousands of regulated hooves keeping to a strict formation. With three trails leading from the valley and massive herds moving along those trails, overgrazing as a postwar phenomenon set in. During the Civil War itself, despite extreme political and military conflict, sales of hides and skins from the Lower Rio Grande Valley to New York City totaled almost $32,000. This trend only accelerated in the recovering markets of the Reconstruction Era.[8]

Between 1865 and 1885, the Lower Rio Grande Valley swarmed with people and animals. Cameron County jumped from 6,028 persons to almost 15,000. Hidalgo County gained over 3,000 residents. Despite this rise due to relocating Americans, most of the owners of domestic animals in Hidalgo County remained Tejano or Mexican-born ranchers. In the 1870s, 231 cattle owners grazed over 14,000 cattle in the county. Between 1880 and 1885, that number jumped to 615 owners grazing 38,467 cattle; and over 90 percent of the owners were still Hispanic. In Hidalgo County, between the Rio Grande and the South Texas Plains, the reality seems to have been not vast ranches, not thousands of acres of grazing cattle, but a cumulative effect of small to medium cattle herds on modest ranches. Most ranches were Class 1 (up to 24 animals) or Class 2 (24 to 99). Victoria Leal's Class 4 cattle herd placed her among only a few large-scale stock raisers in Hidalgo County.

Victoria Leal had lived on Santa Ana for five decades. The widow of the original Santa Ana grantee was an unusual and interesting woman. Born probably around 1797, she was celebrating eighty-three years of life in 1880. Marrying a younger man, she had probably longed for children, but none came. It is easy to understand why, in 1836, when she was almost forty, she consented to take into her home a seven-month-old male infant and raise him as her own. By 1880, she had lived long enough to witness the early deaths of her husband and adopted son; to have made repeated trips across the river to Reynosa for refuge; to have lived through three national wars and the devastating Cortina War; and to have endured droughts, floods, epidemics, and the deaths of relatives and laborers on her ranch. (As noted in chapter 5, the Leal cemetery at Santa Ana today contains at least thirty unmarked graves.) Yet stock on Victoria's land had increased from twenty range cattle in 1860 to an impressive Class 4 herd in 1880.

After she was widowed in the early 1860s, Victoria likely depended on her adopted son, Cristóbal (and eventually on her grandson), other male relations, and hired workers for much of the physical labor needed to develop a ranch; but it was Victoria who owned and retained the land. Perhaps she looked to Rosa María Hinojosa de Balli, her great-aunt. The sister of Victoria's maternal grandmother, Rosa María became a formidable Balli family matriarch also known as "La Patrona." Her success as a widow in the 1790s, when she bought and managed herds of cattle, horses, sheep, and goats on her many ranchos in South Texas, has become legendary. She may in fact have owned over a million acres. Because of her successes, Rosa María is known today as the First Texas Cattle Queen. At the end of her life, she gave much money to support Catholic village churches, including Nuestra Señora de Santa Ana Church in Camargo, from which the Santa Ana land grant most probably took its name. It is tempting to imagine that Victoria Balli Leal, also a widow, saw herself in some way as carrying on the legacy of Doña Rosa María. Despite changing family circumstances, La Patrona had held on tightly to her family land. Victoria Leal did the same. Yet as she kept and lived on the western league of her husband's 1834 grant, she did not build up her cattle herds to numbers that seriously compromised the grass of Santa Ana. Even the bare records of tax roll data can suggest a mind astute, strong, and provident.[9]

Victoria's long life spanned decades of highly visible change in her world. When she arrived on Santa Ana, the forest and grasslands around her stretched for miles, unpopulated and often completely silent except for birdsong and the sound of wind in the trees and grasses. What happened to those grasses has been the focus of many environmental studies in the past decades. People, cattle, railroads, towns: human expansion is the story. Gradually, as the century rolled toward 1900, human-set fires on grasslands decreased, human-built structures increased, and railroads arrived to replace overland cattle drives. Although there had been a downswing in cattle numbers, reflected in the census of 1880, the jump afterward in the number of cattle in Hidalgo County is likely connected to the opportunities afforded by rail transport into Corpus Christi from Brownsville. The doubling of the cattle population in such a short period, coinciding with a drought in the late 1880s, would have most seriously begun to impact grass yield. Studies in heavily grazed grasslands of the United States have found that in some cases, there was a "complete elimination" of fires because of intense, concentrated grazing. There simply was not enough grass to burn. Without fire, small trees, shrubs, cacti, and brush can take quick, avid foothold. Just as important, the doubled number of Hidalgo County cattle spread double the number of seeds as, ambling slowly between woodland and chaparral, cows digested and dropped plant seeds in their dung. Where thirsty cattle congregated around water holes, rain-filled resacas, and stock ponds, they spread blackbrush and mesquite in observable circles.

Yet, as with all recurring processes in the natural world, such changes can also have positive effects. The increasing presence of brush has shifted bird populations in interesting ways. The South Texas Wintering Birds Program in Kingsville has noted a significant expansion of brushland birds. Such birds include the Harris hawk, white-tipped dove, greater kiskadee, green jay, long-billed thrasher, and Audubon's oriole. The aggravating, expanding brush country has actually begun to function as a food and thicket bridge, enticing birds farther north. Such a corridor is working in tandem with climate change to shape the arrival and disappearance of different species. Rare, raging wildfires do break out, such as the fire in March 2008 that burned over 95 percent of the fifteen-thousand-acre Chaparral Wildlife Management Area. Birds such as the loggerhead shrike and American kestrel were observed to benefit from this fire, and predictions are that over time, quail will do better as well. The fire thinned out the brush, providing a better ratio of nesting cover and open land. Birds respond sensitively to fire, to flood, and to increased or decreased cover, and such change can be charted. What improves the habitat for some species will drive out others. During the time the Leals lived on Santa Ana, such natural flux and flow in avian population certainly occurred. The ornithologist Timothy Brush has suggested that in those years, "forest birds such as Red-billed pigeon, Tropical Parula, and Audubon's Oriole" appeared more commonly.

We must make best guesses based on our understanding of avian habitat in the presettlement and early settlement years.[10]

The only evidence of fire on Santa Ana itself is found in a report from 1945. Two separate July and August fires, both breaking out on the banks of the river, burned twenty acres each. The second fire was hot enough to consume large willows. These fires occurred near the old river crossing still steadily used by Mexicans at night (thus designated "hoot-owl traffic" in reports), so managers suspected that people had set the fires. Neither fire burned very far up the slope into the interior of the old grant. In this lies a lesson. The absence of a high load of grass on the refuge prevented the fires from becoming hot enough to burn through the tall riverine forest. Even during the severe drought conditions of 1945, decades of repeated overgrazing on the refuge ironically protected it. But Texas grasses are profoundly resilient. After only one and a half years of recovery management, with all cattle and goats off the land, manager Earl Craven wrote that the improvement of ground cover on Santa Ana was "a startling feature." He noted fresh, juicy grasses returning and saw that grass had begun to grow thickly again along the river, concluding, "We are strongly in favor of allowing this area to follow Nature's course."[11]

Today on Santa Ana, there are limited prescribed burns, but the internal pasture has long since filled in with semitropical tree growth. In 1945, the manager at the refuge wrote that huisache had almost covered the site of the old pasture. Conceiving this small, fragrant tree as a nuisance, he called its rapid spread a "phenomenal growth." Trees were reestablishing, but in the 1920s, evidence of Leal ranch life had begun to disappear. The brick home of Victoria Leal and her assorted ranch outbuildings, outdoor oven (horno), slaughtering site, arbors, and what remained of other family jacales were torn down. To stand today on a trail next to the original pasture and ranch home location is to be overwhelmed and overshadowed by "the jungle." Mexican ash and cedar elm festooned by ball and Spanish mosses have created a density that suggests a literal arboreal wall. Once off the trails in the heart of Santa Ana, there is a silence in which bird calls are piercing and immediate. The woven living barricades of vines and branches and the dimming, green-humid light eerily re-create the first conditions of settlement. In the understory, small mesquite and retama strive for sun. Occasionally, prickly pear colonies break out at the thicket edge. Since prickly pear tuna and fat, spine-studded pads are the prized food of javelina, it seems that nature's course provides. But nature's course in its purest sense would involve an occasional catastrophic fire, mean and hot enough to get at the roots of that persistent mesquite. Those fires may never come regularly again to South Texas. Their absence by 1880 on Santa Ana was primarily a result of the increased number of people.[12]

Santa Ana in 1880

When Victoria Leal celebrated her eighty-third birthday, the census revealed a definite community of people living on "Santa Ana Rancho." Victoria was surrounded by family and neighbors, all of whom knew and probably revered her. In 1880, forty-seven people were making a living on the western league of Santa Ana. For the first time in its history, the old grant was supporting a true ranch community, yet in comparison to the other ranches surrounding it, Santa Ana still had the lowest population. La Blanca Ranch to the east had 232 people; Relámpago Rancho on the old Llano Grande grant, 157; Agua Negra had 174, and the large, busy, El Capote Ranch community numbered 229. Even the smaller ranches owned by multiracial Americans, such as the Webber and Jackson ranches, had more people. Dwellers on Santa Ana lived in ten households, likely expanded jacales sitting near the brick ranch house with access to a resaca (once called the Inland Lake) and an internal pasture. The census taker described five farmers, one herder, and the stock owner, Victoria Leal, matriarch of the Leal family across almost fifty years on Santa Ana. She was living in the brick ranch house with Matías Leal (seventy), a servant; and living near her were a mother and son, Concepción Cavazos (forty-five) and Tomás (fifteen). As noted earlier, Concepción was Victoria's niece. Also on Santa Ana in this year lived and worked Rafaela Leal (forty-nine), the widow of the Leals' adopted son, Cristóbal. Her son and only offspring, also named Cristóbal, was twenty-four at the time and lived nearby. At least three generations of Leals were therefore present on the land. Yet this census also reveals a curious pattern.[13]

One of the farmers whose dwelling was near the main ranch house was Santo [Santos] Rubalcaba (forty-eight). His wife, Andrea, two teenage sons, a twelve-year-old daughter, and a two-year-old grandson also lived with him. This household is also shown as being quite near the Leals on the 1870 census, one of the few continuities of residents. One suggestive fact may explain this: Santos Rubalcaba had consumption (tuberculosis). The inference is that Victoria allowed him and his family, who may have been distant relations, to live on Santa Ana and make a living through helping on the ranch. The ranch would have needed all the willing hands it could muster, for the mean age of the seven "laborers" identified on the census was under seventeen. The farm and ranch hands were all young boys. The combined cattle herds of the two stock owners, Victoria and Cristóbal Leal, numbered three hundred animals. Cristóbal also pastured thirty horses, and together, they owned fifty milk cows. From the scant census data in this year, an interesting picture emerges of ranch food production. For 1879, Victoria and her grandson Cristóbal reported they had sold seventy-nine cattle and slaughtered twenty-two. The census taker reported no sheep or swine on the ranch; however, he carefully noted an extensive outlay of poultry. Over fifty hens scavenged and pecked near Rancho Adentro, and those hens had produced over five hundred dozen eggs in a single year. Because of the low number of people on the ranch, it is probable that the Leals were selling eggs locally.[14]

Exactly where they marketed eggs is unclear. The nearest town was still Hidalgo/Edinburg (old Habitación), but some ranches had stores. This is documented in an 1875 incident at a locale known as Fulton's Store on the adjoining Los Toritos grant to the west. "Twelve or fifteen armed Mexicans" had crossed the river; in a robbery, they attacked and killed the store owner, George W. Fulton, and his clerk, Mauricio Leal (this clerk has also been identified as Mauricio Villanueva). Perhaps Mauricio was the link between Santa Ana and Fulton's Store; perhaps this store sold the Leal eggs. Fulton's Store seems to have been important in the neighborhood, for the American rancher Lina Helen Box, giving testimony about the violence and criminal activity along the river in the 1870s, mentioned it. Joseph Fulton himself had been both a surveyor and a justice of the peace in Hidalgo County. He had purchased land known as "Fulton's Strip" from B. F. Kidder in 1870; the Kidders had long occupied the southern portion of Los Toritos. To the west of Fulton's Store, on old Porción 71, also flourished the considerable Jackson Ranch (ninety-eight people) as well as the start-up farms and ranches of newcomer Americans. El Sauz Ranch, the next ranch west of Santa Ana, had a blended population of black, mulatto, Mexican, and white residents, including some male Leals. At Webber Ranch, immediately to the east of Santa Ana, a multicultural marriage had produced a thriving family and employed Mexican and Tejano workers. The mean age of the laborers on John Ferdinand Webber's ranch was about forty-two, and on El Sauz, thirty-five. Perhaps Victoria sold eggs to these ranches as well, although most ranch owners also reported chicken and egg production on the census. The workforce was generally mature on most ranches, and dietary requirements were high.[15]

The ranch landscape of Hidalgo County in 1880 was busy and populated. Stores, chapels, and schools developed in larger ranch communities. The "Capote Rancho" had grown so much it almost touched the edge of Hidalgo/Edinburg, as both communities lay close to the Rio Grande.

Working at El Capote in 1880 was an impressive range of artisans, including a silversmith, a shoemaker, a saddler, four carpenters, and even a professional musician, Francisco Leal. In many jacales lived servants, shepherds, herders, and a considerable number of farmers. No such diversely skilled workforce, school, stores, or private chapels have ever been noted for Santa Ana. There, a small group of people, mostly related and dominated by teenage boys, must have faced a life of formidable physical labor. The daily care of over thirty horses included making sure they were pastured on available grass with access to water. It also meant guarding them from predators and horse thieves. Milking the cows without calves twice a day would also have been necessary. Yet in addition to caring for this number of animals and a Class 4 ranch herd, Victoria and her grandson had produced 450 bushels of Indian corn and 18 bushels of beans. This crop was almost certainly for their own consumption. On the census, both Victoria and Cristóbal reported that they paid seasonal laborers wages of $150 and $100 per year, respectively. Cristóbal stated he employed laborers fifty-two weeks a year; perhaps some of the families living on Santa Ana were included in this statement.[16]

On the western league where Rancho Adentro lay, production was modest and probably still tied in some basic ways to forest resources. Despite slaughtering cattle, goats, and chickens, Tejano people evidently routinely hunted and ate some wildlife, especially deer and javelina. As late as the 1930s, ranchers in the area testified that Mexicans "widely" hunted javelina and that ranch laborers crossing the border ate javelina as an important part of their diet. Wild animals were likely still important in 1880 when the census taker estimated the value of Santa Ana "farm produce" at $450. When available, some dried, pounded, and cracked corn was probably tossed to the chickens, but many ranch studies mention that free-roaming chickens consumed anacua and granjeno berries eagerly. Owners often planted the encircling land around their houses with anacua trees. Chickens would have been left to forage and peck in the thin grasses at the edge of the forest, but they too would have been fenced out of the woods. Not only mammalian predators stalked chickens, such as the cat species of the night forest, the day-hunting jaguarundi, and, as on almost all chicken enterprises anywhere, the raccoons that stealthily appeared after dark. Hawks and falcons also watched for chicks, and snakes came after eggs. Some of the outbuildings on Santa Ana must have been chicken coops.[17]

From published memoirs of pre-1900 life on ranches near the river, we can imagine similar experiences on Rancho Adentro. Before dawn on a June day in 1880, the ranch community was stirring. Perhaps some mechanical corn grinders were now in operation, as well as the old metates rasping out the ancient and long familiar grinding and pounding. As herd dogs barked at cattle and goats being slowly moved out to pasture, the few young girls carried water to the ranch house, possibly from a well; both boys and girls also broke sticks and took wood to the outdoor kitchen fires. Cows and goats were also being milked. Domestic and animal noises echoed across the large household clearing, mingling with abundant birdsong in the encircling forest. In contrast to many other ranches of Hidalgo County, Rancho Adentro sat in the middle of truly giant trees, thick with birds.

Vocal at first light, they flew overhead, crossing the clearing on their way to the river, streaks of bright green, yellow, and orange. Because of its surrounding trees, the ranch house a half mile from the Rio Grande was perpetually shaded and breezy. Although it was hot that June morning, fires for the first meal had been lit early by the women of Santa Ana. Their names as rendered by an American census taker those many years ago hint at family connections: Louisa Gutierez, Genoveva Anaya, Rosalia Cortes, Femina Avila, and Ascención Leal, the seventeen-year-old wife of Cristóbal Leal, Victoria's grandson. In a separate home, also cooking breakfast, was Jesusa Kidder, the Mexican-born wife of George Kidder, the deputy inspector of hides living on Santa Ana. Jesusa had been a widow when she married George Kidder; she had three children then, but together, the Kidders had five more. And out of the entire population of children at Santa Ana, only James Kidder, age eight, was going to school. Perhaps that school was the one at Relámpago Rancho, where the census taker noted a schoolteacher in 1880, B. F. Kidder, brother to George. The Kidder family had long been in the area, as the patriarch, Sanforth Kidder, had been living on Los Toritos possibly since 1839.[18]

As brief as its entries are, the 1880 census provides a poignant look at literacy and the availability of schools. In 1880, James Kidder could read and was learning to write. Interestingly, the census notes that most of the other Kidder children could both read and write, as could their mother, Jesusa. Perhaps George had taught his wife and family English. None of the other children on Santa Ana were literate, and few of the senior members were. Victoria Leal, providing for all of these families through her land and stock, could not sign her name. Significantly, however, her grandson Cristóbal could. He could both read and write, and he owned and managed a considerable number of the animals on the western league. This fact should be balanced against the many anecdotal accounts of Cristóbal being "weak-minded" or dissolute. The undocumented story that Santa Ana, or a part of it, was "once traded for a violin and a suit of clothes" is thought to pertain to Cristóbal Leal's disposal of the last of his land in the early 1900s. This did happen, as will be seen, but there is no trace of a trade or barter in the last transaction involving the Santa Ana heir. No violin or clothes appear in any record. And in 1880, the forces that were about to change the ranchlands of South Texas forever were over a decade away.[19]

There is some evidence that Victoria and her grandson were close. In 1874, two years before adopted Cristóbal Leal died, grandmother and grandson went in together and registered separate brands in Hidalgo/Edinburg on the same day. We can imagine them walking on the dusty streets in the high heat, Victoria with her head covered in the shawl always worn in public by Mexican and Tejana women. She and Cristóbal each had separate livestock herds grazing shared pasture on the western league of Santa Ana, and they each designed a personal brand (shown in chapter 5). In 1887, Victoria made a will, leaving her land and property entirely to her grandson Cristóbal. Perhaps she knew she was ill, for she died on May 5, 1887, within two months of drawing up the will in her brick home on Santa Ana. The language strongly suggests an attempt to forestall any other relatives from contesting the will on the grounds that Cristóbal's father was adopted. Victoria states, "Since his infancy we raised him and gave him our surname and for his [loyal?] services rendered to us as a true son." She made a clear attempt to legitimize Cristóbal's father in the Leal line: "I name as my universal heir Cristóbal Leal, legitimate son of the late Cristóbal Leal Balli and Rafaela Treviño."

Cristóbal Leal Balli had originally been Cristóbal Peña, adopted in 1859 and, as noted earlier, believed to be the son of Victoria's brother, José Isidro Balli. Victoria was creating a legal inheritance for her adopted son and then her grandson. The patterns in Tejano culture of adoptions, both formal and informal, and of raising orphaned children, frequently resulted in relatives contesting wills and inheritance. As Benigno had done twenty-five years earlier, Victoria acted to keep her league of Santa Ana firmly in the family. The great southern forest and the grasslands to the north—this land was paramount. Victoria also stated in her will a desire for simple burial: "After my decease let my body be shrouded and buried in the Cemetery without ostentation." Because the probate file for her will states that it was drawn up and witnessed in Hidalgo County, in her ranch house in fact, Victoria almost certainly died at home on Santa Ana. We do not know which cemetery she refers to in her will, but surely we can believe she meant the ebony-fenced Leal family cemetery visible from the main house. This is the closest we get to having verification that the original grantee and/or his wife lie in the earth of their land.[20]

Although the census of 1880 provides a vivid picture of the small family-based community on Santa Ana, it must be remembered that these households were on the western league of the original grant. The fortunes on the eastern league had changed abruptly in the late 1870s, when the Merriman ranch failed. In 1878, Dr. Merriman's widow, Elizabeth, sold the ranch and the eastern league at a tax auction. Her husband had died in the yellow fever epidemic of 1867, and by 1878, having lived in Corpus Christi for many years, she was running a successful and popular boarding house. Perhaps she simply could not oversee ranch operations well enough to make a profit. And in fact, Dr. Merriman himself had divested himself of the eastern league after only nine years of ownership. In 1861 he sold three-fourths of it to Henry T. Merriman, his son from a first marriage, and one-fourth to John Fusselman, Elizabeth's brother. These sales suggest that Dr. Merriman himself was no longer interested in a ranch operation. Perhaps Henry Merriman and John Fusselman jointly attempted to oversee a cattle ranch or granted leases, but these family members did not keep their Santa Ana land either. Fusselman sold his fourth to his sister Elizabeth almost immediately in 1861, and it is possible that the majority of the league owned by Henry Merriman passed to Elizabeth because of his death.

It is not clear exactly what happened with this ranch venture, nor is it possible to know whether any Merriman family members ever lived on Santa Ana. On May 7, 1878, Elizabeth Merriman sold the entire league at tax auction, 4,428 acres, to William J. T. G. Brewster. And just a year later, Dr. Brewster sold the league back into the Merriman family, to a legal representative, Josiah W. Turner. The inference is that Elizabeth Merriman was attempting to hold on to the eastern league and sell it at a profit. There are thus striking differences in land ownership between the eastern and western leagues of Santa Ana. A single Hispanic family, the original grantees, owned the western league and lived there from 1834 until 1890. The eastern league, owned by the Leals until 1852, was parceled and sold in pieces, back and forth, among Merriman family members until 1882. Although Dr. Merriman registered an austere, diamond-shaped cattle brand, Hidalgo County tax rolls show no taxes ever being paid on stock grazed there. Only a few years indicate any land taxes paid at all by the Merrimans, such as 1868, when Henry Merriman was taxed on his league—but he owned no livestock. The Mexican and Tejano owners of Santa Ana's rich grassland are the ones who are recorded as not only paying taxes on both property and animals but as living year to year on the land.[21]

By the time Elizabeth Merriman sold her league, the fortunes of cattle ranchers in South Texas were in a period of flux. In 1880, the number of cattle in the region south of the Nueces River had fallen off almost 50 percent. For Hidalgo County, the three-decade cattle counts show this clearly: in 1860, 6,468 cattle grazed there; in 1870, at the peak of the post–Civil War cattle boom, the number had risen to 13,141; but in 1880, only 8,268 cattle are listed on the agricultural census. The most significant reason for this drop was the competition from the northern Great Plains cattle herds, rapidly developing in that region with the arrival of the railroads across Kansas. Then in 1880–81 came a "humid, cold winter" with sleet storms and blizzards that killed lambs and calves as well as vulnerable mature cattle. Perhaps this was the last straw for Elizabeth Merriman; in 1882, her agent, Josiah Turner, once again sold the eastern league. The buyer this time was an ambitious and shrewd Tejano rancher named Julio Guzmán.[22]

The Dream of La Pechuga

For the next twenty years, the Guzmáns, at least two of their grown children, and many grandchildren lived on Santa Ana, building a ranch complex they named La Pechuga. This phrase signifies the breast of a bird, a symbol of valor. Very little direct information exists about La Pechuga Ranch. From the 1880 census, taken two years before Julio Guzmán bought his Santa Ana land, we find the extensive Guzmán family living on a rented ranch that he had also named La Pechuga. This ranch was part of a much larger community the census taker named "Derramadero Rancho," carved out from the immense Llano Grande grant to the east of Santa Ana. Julio and his sons, Amado and Julio Jr., as well as his wife and five daughters, were farmers, herders, and "house keepers" on this ranch land. They managed domestic animal numbers that demand awe for the human labor required to care for them: 8 oxen, 25 milk cows, 167 "other cattle," 50 sheep, 10 swine, 20 chickens, and 70 horses. The horse count especially suggests that Julio was making money from horse breeding and sales; only two years later he was able to buy his own ranch.

The new La Pechuga Ranch on Santa Ana eventually included a cemetery with eight graves, which in 1988 were still visible. In that year, surveyors noted the presence of fresh decorations on four areas of mounded earth. They also found homemade concrete headstones, a stone angel, and the remains of a brick headstone. Julio and Estéfana Guzmán are very likely buried in this small, long-disappeared place, but there is no way to ascertain this. Today, the town of Alamo has expanded south over the old Santa Ana grasslands, over La Pechuga Ranch, and over the cemetery. Like Cristóbal and Rafaela Leal, and probably Benigno and Victoria, Julio and Estéfana likely wished to remain with their land. We know more about how Julio Guzmán acquired his land than what his ranch looked like, where the main house sat, or even whether any of the Guzmáns had interaction with the Leals. Yet land acquisition by Mexican American ranchers during these decades reflects what one historian has termed "the continuing importance of land [to Tejano ranchers] and their determination to earn a decent living from their own endeavors." All too soon, as the increasing Anglo-American population began to dominate business institutions, ranching, farming, and schools, Mexican Americans found themselves marginalized and segregated. This happened especially after Tejanos had given up land ownership, forced out in the tide of irrigated farming ventures that replaced ranches. Land ownership continued to be a critical goal for Tejanos in the postbellum years, however, as the two ranching family histories of Santa Ana demonstrate.[23]

In 1883, with a clear eye to a future as a successful rancher, Julio purchased more land: an adjoining half league of the old El Gato grant, including 762 varas of river frontage. The Guzmáns now owned this riverfront forest as well as the entire eastern league of the original Santa Ana grant, described in records by this time as "lands of Elizabeth T. Merriman." The eastern league also included 946 varas on the Rio Grande, riverine earth still dense with tropical thorn trees and occasional evergreen giants, with waterfowl, bright resident nesters, and, in the spring, migratory raptors. These life-packed portions of the old grants were often awash with flooding, the great nourishment of the forest and a blessing to stock raisers

This photograph was taken from the trail around the eastern Pintail Lake, a route likely well traveled by the Leals as well as by the Amado Guzmán family, who lived near here—the area they knew as Lake Pechuga—between 1882 and 1902. Photograph by Thomas Morgan, June 2013.

whose animals drank from overflowing resacas. Flooding also changed the southern boundary of Santa Ana during this time. Thanks to a 1909 lawsuit brought by Titus Merriman, the son of Dr. Eli T. Merriman, against Peter Ebenezer Blalock, we have some intriguing evidence about the Guzmáns' use of land and how they adapted to its changes. Quite early in their tenure, the Rio Grande undercut the steep southern banks. Described as "erosion and caving in of the river banks forming the southern boundary," flood-driven collapse ate away between a half mile and a full mile of land. Julio may have decided to create his internal pasture at this time, as bank collapse softened the river edge. The description of Julio's ranch operations mentions herds of horses and cattle as well as sheep and goats. The energy and ambition of this rancher are palpable in the legal account of his acquisition of Santa Ana.[24]

Directly countering entrenched Anglo-American beliefs about Tejanos as "an indolent people," Hidalgo County tax rolls reveal that Julio probably sold every animal he owned to buy Santa Ana. In 1881, he was assessed on 70 horses, 70 cattle, 40 sheep, and 40 goats—but on no land. He was still a renter. Yet in 1882, Julio paid taxes on 4,725 acres of land: the eastern league of Santa Ana. (He had also inherited 111 acres through his wife, Estéfana.) In that year, he owned land but no animals. The next year, 1883, he still owned no stock. It may have taken him three years to be able to purchase start-up livestock once more. By 1884, he was able to buy part of El Gato—but still owned no animals. By 1885, he paid Hidalgo County taxes on considerable stock: 80 horses, 350 cattle, 80 sheep, and 20 goats. This small, nearly buried story reveals a shrewd Hispanic rancher's calculated risk: to sell off all his stock in order to obtain title.

It also bespeaks a passion for land that had characterized Mexican settlers long before the 1830s. After he bought his league of Santa Ana, Julio Guzmán, at that time close to fifty years old, accompanied the legal surveyor recording the boundary of his purchase. Riding on old but well-known horse trails, Julio knew exactly where "the line" was. That line was the long, patchily wooded eastern boundary, originally surveyed in 1834. Because he had raised and sold horses for decades on land to the east, Julio had familiarized himself with Santa Ana. He knew the forest and its trails, the resacas, the nearly three thousand acres of grassland. In the earliest accounts of Santa Ana as a refuge, a manager mentions a dirt road and gate entering the woods from the east, which was soon blocked to prevent illegal access. This was a ranch track that had evolved during the decades of Guzmán ownership. Because it passed over high, open ground, it may well have been in use much earlier as a horse trail crossing east into the El Gato grant: a neighborhood path that Victoria or her nieces would have used, riding over to visit her brother Francisco. He lived on a ranch on El Gato, a Spanish league in size, and, at least in 1848, he was pasturing fifty cattle there. Traces of this 180-year-old neighborhood trail exist today in the road that curves around Pintail Lakes. The farthest-east lake on the refuge today, holding water and providing a home to egrets, ibis, and cormorants, stretched into El Gato as part of a large, single resaca.

The Pintail Lakes are almost certainly this once unusually large resaca that Julio named Lake Pechuga. Immediately after the legal survey, he moved his extended family onto rising land, described as lying about six miles from the river near a resaca. This was the Resaca del Gato. A General Land Office map of Hidalgo County in 1880 depicts it as a long, stream-like formation several miles north of the Military Road. Although much of this resaca lies in the neighboring El Gato grant, Resaca del Gato was probably the reason for the location of the main Guzmán ranch enclave; when filled with seasonal rainwater, this long lake would have stretched over a half mile across the eastern league of Santa Ana. Near it, Julio built "some six or eight houses" and within a year had put up corrals, opened up fields, and enclosed the southern river frontage with fencing, establishing a river pasture. This pasture was extensive, estimated at five hundred acres. Very probably, it is the one refuge managers usually referred to as the "internal pasture" on Santa Ana. The field afforded Guzmán animals the chance to drink from the Rio Grande in months of extreme drought when Lake Pechuga and the other resacas had dried up. Although the pasture became severely overgrazed in the 1930s, once grazing leases ended and this acreage was left alone to be repeatedly flooded and replenished, the land recovered.[25]

Julio Guzmán had a sharp eye, and he would have noted the health and fertility of Santa Ana grassland. It is also likely that, just as Benigno Leal had in the 1830s, Julio and his sons saw the river forest as a source of food. As mentioned earlier, entrepreneurial Tejano ranchers were consummate hunters who supplemented their rancho corn and bean diet with wild birds, deer, and javelina. They were also vigilant hunters of stock predators such as coyote, jaguar, and mountain lion. Like the original north-bank settlers fifty years earlier, Julio had an intimate knowledge of the land and its resources. He and his grown sons, Amado and Julio Jr., came in with an eye for horseflesh and the kind of acreage needed to support these large grazers. As pointed out by Armando Alonzo as well, in just five years, Julio Guzmán's profile as a ranchero changed dramatically. In 1880 he had a net worth of under $1,500, the value of his horses and cattle only, as he owned no land and was "running horses and cattle" on acreage near Santa Ana and the river (his rented land on the Llano Grande grant). By 1885, Julio's net worth was over $8,000, and he now owned 10,860 acres of both the Santa Ana and El Gato grants. During the years that he raised horses near the river, Julio and his sons came to know the eastern league of Santa Ana and probably saw it as an ideal ranch, as it contained several large lakes.[26]

Census data indicate that at least two of Julio's sons had homes, small fields, and gardens on the eastern league of Santa Ana. While the main grazing acreage of La Pechuga Ranch lay to the north, Amado Guzmán, Julio's oldest son, almost certainly lived near the resaca known today on the refuge as Pintail Lakes, depicted on current refuge guides as five separate small bodies of water. Early-twentieth-century maps identify two ranches labeled "Santa Ana Ranch," one in the location of the old Rancho Adentro (the Leals) and one very close to Pintail Lakes. Both ranches lay inside what would become the refuge proper. As late as 1973, when manager Raymond Fleetwood drew his refuge map, Pintail Lakes still appeared as a single large lake, known then as East Lake. It takes imagination to envision the way this single wide and shallow resaca looked and functioned when Amado Guzmán and his family lived there. His wife, Teresa, and nine children would have planted gardens around its alluvial, flood-replenished margins. Five of Amado's children were born there, the last, Pablo, in 1896. Then, the lake was a rather amazing body of water in the wet season, covering perhaps two full acres. In places where cattle and goats were fenced out, the banks supported a thick fringe of cattails, rushes, and sedges. We know that cattails flourished around resacas, for the far western resaca on the refuge was named Cattail Lake by later managers.

Even today, the cattails that line the banks of one Pintail Lake are vibrantly tall. Cattails are a critically important aquatic plant, sustaining wetland life in many ways. One naturalist has put it simply: "Wherever there are cattails, there's food." Many birds feast on the tiny cattail seeds, as a single velvety-brown pod can release two hundred thousand of them. A cattail's roots and shoots also nourish many kinds of waterfowl and animals. Many observers know that red-winged blackbirds like to sit among the swaying stems of giant cattails, but grebes use them too. The marsh wren attaches a small nest to a cattail stalk and lines it with the soft seedy fluff. Geese and ducks, especially coots, dive for insects and vegetation in the safety of sturdy cattail stems. It is a good guess that when the Guzmáns lived near the large, single lake they knew as Pechuga, on some parts of it they saw cattails growing year-round. The children of Amado Guzmán are almost the only ones who can be verified through census records as being born and growing up on land

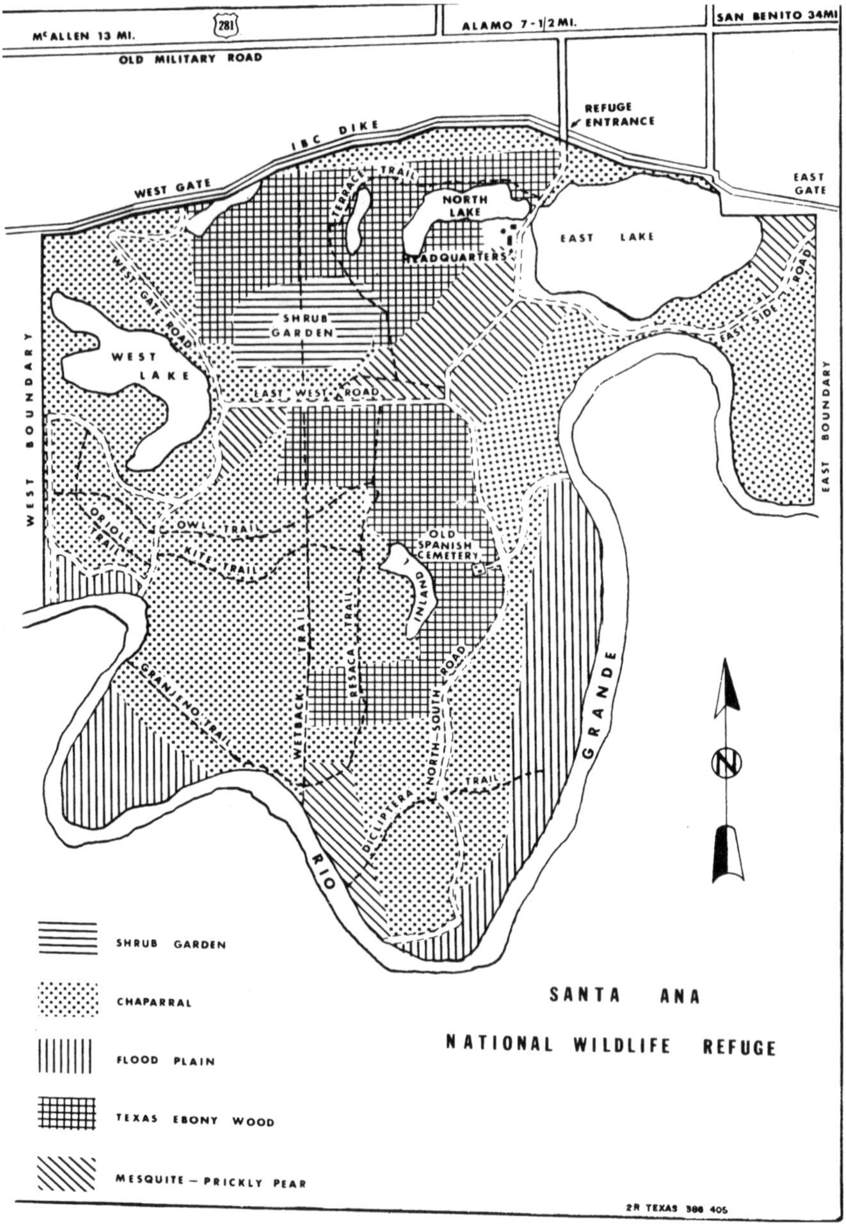

Portion of the 1973 map by refuge manager Raymond Fleetwood showing the large East Lake, East Side Road, and chaparral surrounding the old resaca. Map by Raymond J. Fleetwood, "Plants of Santa Ana National Wildlife Refuge."

that would become Santa Ana National Wildlife Refuge. Children everywhere, across centuries and continents, have played with cattails. Using a word derived from a Peruvian Indian language, the Guzmán children would likely have known them as *totora*.

While the basin of the lake created rich wetland habitat for waterfowl, some unusually fertile grazing acreage also stretched to the south, down toward the floodplain (in the 1970s, Raymond Fleetwood labeled this area "chaparral"). The Rio Grande ash, tepeguaje, and cedar elm on the banks of the river's bend, as today, were inviting perches for hunting falcons and hawks. Although the lake lay just south of the Military Road, in the last decades of the nineteenth century, the Rio Grande was powerful enough to keep this resaca full and its nearby forest well watered. The river loops high here at the eastern boundary of the refuge, evidence of the Rio Grande's twisting course.

On the refuge today, Pintail Lake Trail has the steepest elevation gain, rising sharply uphill to the north and the first levee, winding through terraces filled with the dry, bony rattle of dead tree limbs. Drought-killed trunks lie across trails, brought down by hot Gulf winds. The earth no longer grows the luxuriant mixtures of substory shrubs and vines found on the terraces nearer the river. Managed flooding in some of the Pintail Lakes produces the steamy, moist environment where buried tortoise eggs will hatch and wading birds will find juicy invertebrates like snails. It is still the Rio Grande waters sustaining this range of life, still the river pooling to shimmering, light-filled surfaces. Yet it is always approximate, never equaling those spring rises of wind-driven floodwater. Then, the Rio Grande rolled over parched acres as the rains came down. When the water

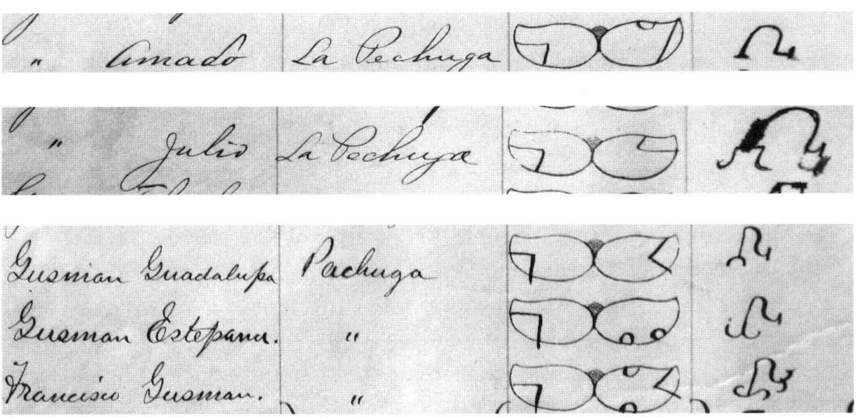

The Guzmán family ear marks and brands: Amado, Julio Jr., Guadalupe, Estéfana, and Francisco Guzmán, from 1877 and 1886. From the Hidalgo County Marks and Brands.

retreated, black, odorous, tacky mud had killed many plants, snails, and fish, but soon, the green surged back. Today, the vivid greening up of the earth around the lakes on Santa Ana connects visitors with the past in a distinct, visual way. The flooding of past centuries is rare now, happening only during hurricanes. The photograph in the gallery, taken at the end of May 2013, shows part of old Lake Pechuga.

Small ranchers like Amado Guzmán, who for most of his tenure on La Pechuga never grazed more than thirty-five horses and twenty-five cattle above and below the lake, maintained a sustainable ratio. Controlled numbers of animals will allow grasses to reach maturity and reproduce, the seed heads to form, and the birds to eat. Where grasses flourish, root systems hold fast the black, nutrient-filled soil, the tiny caches of precious moisture. Where there are deeply buried pockets of water, tree roots will go down to find them, holding the swaying canopy of riparian forests sturdy in the wind. And where the big trees thrive, so thrive birds. The management of stock in relatively low numbers on the acreage that became Santa Ana National Wildlife Refuge preserved it for many years.

Only after 1898 did Amado Guzmán work with sizable herds. When he inherited land from his mother, he had enough acreage to expand; in 1898, for example, he paid taxes on 25 horses, 150 cattle, 65 sheep, and 85 goats. He would certainly also have grazed these animals on the land north of the Military Road. At this time, Hidalgo County tax rolls indicate that his father, old Julio, had also begun to switch emphasis from horses to sheep and goats. During the late 1870s and 1880s, prices for sheep and goat products began to rise, especially the price of wool; in response, Tejano ranchers invested in sheep. The number of goats and sheep owned by small ranchers at this time doubled. As noted by Armando Alonzo, Hispanic owners preferred to raise both sheep and goats at the same time. Since the range and diet of these animals were similar, shepherds could care for both kinds of stock easily. Arnoldo De León, writing in *The Tejano Community*, furnishes a memorable description of these shepherds, called *pastores*. They were muscular, spirited, keenly observant of land and animals, and they employed "sounds and motions" to move large numbers of animals with ease. Vaqueros used horses, but pastores more often worked on foot.

We do not know whether the Guzmáns employed pastores; most likely, they tended their own goats. Mexican American families routinely ate goat kid, *cabrito*. The barbecuing of sweet, tender kid was a standard ranch dietary practice. Women slow-cooked an entire kid over deep-buried coals. They also prepared calf head in this way. "Perhaps the favorite of favorites was *cabrito en sangre*," writes Emilia Schunior Ramírez, author of *Ranch Life in Hidalgo County after 1850*. "But the head of a steer or calf baked all

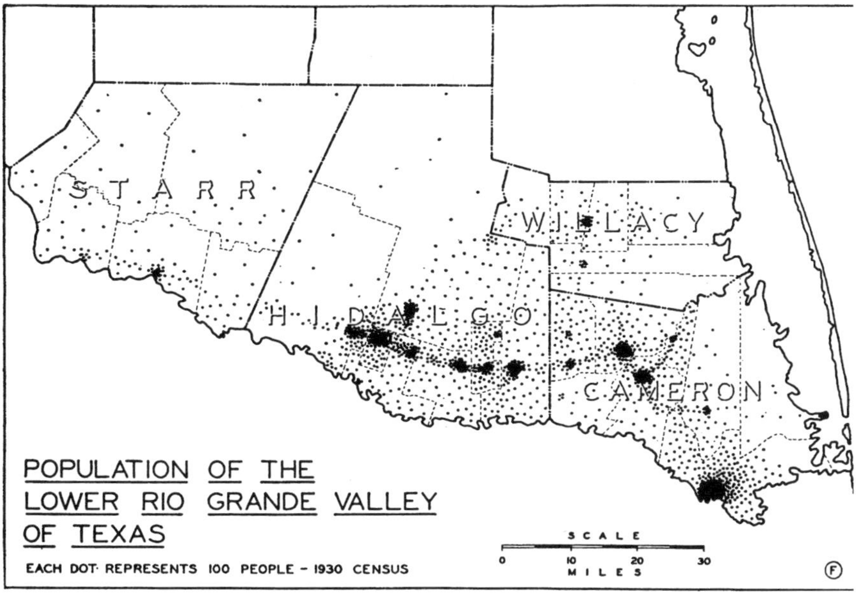

A 1930 census map showing the Mission Rise towns that formed along the "second lift" of land in Hidalgo County. Map by Edwin J. Foscue, "The Distribution of Population in the Lower Rio Grande Valley of Texas."

night, wrapped in a damp burlap sack, in a pre-heated pit and served for breakfast . . . seems to have run the *cabrito* a close second." Some limited memories of the ranch at La Pechuga connect the Guzmáns with goat raising. Rufino Garza of Alamo, Texas, is a great-grandson of Julio Guzmán. His father, Juan Garza, lived on La Pechuga well into the 1930s. Rufino mentions that old Julio eventually became known for raising and selling goats. Perhaps some of the eighty-five goats Amado and his sons managed in 1898 were part of Julio's goat herd.[27]

From 1882 to at least 1905, the Guzmáns ran cattle, horses, sheep, and goats north and south of the Military Road crossing their land, for *Hidalgo County Marks and Brands* records many family brands for them. The second son, Julio Jr., lived closer to the main ranch house of his parents near the Resaca del Gato, and he also became a modest stock raiser, with horse and cattle numbers about the same as his brother Amado's. A third son, Francisco, and two of Julio's daughters also registered brands. There is a consistent, recognizable shape in his children's brands, suggesting an original Guzmán family design: Julio's.

As is clear from how Julio Guzmán managed to buy his Santa Ana land, with profits derived from skillful horse breeding and wholesale stock sell-off, this man had a dream. There were two Pechuga ranches as well as a Lake Pechuga. Although there is limited information about how La Pechuga Ranch on Santa Ana was managed, there is noticeable record of what the Guzmáns *did not* do. For twenty years of multigenerational livelihood on the Santa Ana eastern league, despite an industrializing landscape of sugarcane and cotton farms, railroad shipping, and avid buyers, the Guzmáns neither overgrazed nor sold their league. It is easy to imagine land sharks approaching Julio and Estéfana throughout the 1890s, offering ready cash and plausible arguments for selling. After all, by 1890, the entire western league of Santa Ana had been sold. Most of the old El Gato grant was in the hands of American ranchers and farmers, as was Los Toritos. But the Guzmáns held on. Nor did they cut down much of their riverine forest. The giant trees that Irby Davis fought for in 1940—whose canopy shot to the sky, offering nests to bird species that had been coming there for millennia—these trees sat drinking up the Rio Grande in the 1890s. Except for those cleared along the river frontage for the southern pasture, they were spared.[28]

Because a Tejano family bought this land, returning it full circle to Hispanic ownership, the Santa Ana forests survived. This fact is unarguable. At least until 1903, forest preservation on these two leagues in South Texas was not a product merely of happenstance, fate, luck, or general neglect and lack of interest. Human beings living there were custodians of the land. We cannot know the relationship between Victoria Leal and Julio or Amado Guzmán, whose lifetimes overlapped. In the 1880s, Victoria was living at Rancho Adentro in the forested southern half of the western league of Santa Ana; Julio Guzmán had built his ranch house above the Military Road on the eastern league, and his son Amado lived near the East (Pintail) Lake, placing him quite close, within a mile, of the Leals. Julio and Victoria were neighbors diagonally, separated by the Military Road but sharing a common cultural heritage and landscape. We know that Julio Guzmán fenced some of his southern acreage, but likely the grazing land north of the Military Road was not fenced, as this would have required over ten miles of wood and barbed wire to be inspected and maintained. Side by side, the eastern and western leagues of Santa Ana stretched north toward what would become a strip of modern cities. A map constructed from the 1930 census shows how a string of necklace towns developed parallel to the Rio Grande, all founded on what is termed the Mission Rise. But before these towns began to grow, the Santa Ana grant had crossed that rise, gently ascending and rippling with grass.

Between 1882 and 1887, on this gradually rising pastureland, Victoria Leal's cattle and Julio Guzmán's cattle, sheep, and goats grazed and probably mingled. In the roundups for branding and selling, ranch vaqueros could greet each other, their horses weaving expertly around and through milling animals. In 1887, when Victoria was nearly ninety and Julio in his fifties, the southern forests on both of their leagues were yet thriving. This suggests that perhaps Victoria and Julio also shared what would come to be known much later as a land ethic. It does not really matter if that ethic was more about preserving Hispanic family title to land than about conservancy. Though we have not a single word that either of them ever personally spoke or wrote, other than Julio's signature, the tenacity of Julio Guzmán and Victoria Leal suggests a feeling for place: for river and earth, forest and resaca, horizon, sky, and stars. They stayed on their land until they died on their land. Sometimes in the past, thankfully, title and custodial outlook were one and the same.[29]

CHAPTER SEVEN

Land Redefined

The story of what happened to the Santa Ana land grant in the early twentieth century is still intimately connected to the life-giving waters of the Rio Grande. Between 1900 and the Great Depression, interest in South Texas lands focused intensely on the action of water. In these decades, pump irrigation, catastrophic flooding, and the proposed building of a dam system created the dominant themes of recorded history in Hidalgo County. Ironically, the first efforts to irrigate the alluvial bottomland of the river arose because of the drought of the 1890s. John Closner experimented with a pump on the banks of the Rio Grande between 1889 and 1895, using a mesquite-fired, twenty-five-horsepower centrifugal pump and a portable steam engine on his San Juan "plantation." This operation, successfully irrigating two hundred acres, eventually developed into a large sugarcane farm near Santa Ana on old Porción 72. The language of irrigation had arrived in the valley—canals, laterals, first and second rise, pumping stations, and eventually, pump houses. Ten years later, in 1905, the American Rio Grande Land and Irrigation Company began building canals and laterals. This company, like the many others that would follow it, bought up the old porciones and land grants fronting on the Rio Grande; they generally did so by buying parcels of land from Tejano heirs or the small farmers and developers those heirs had sold to.[1]

Land belonging to the Leals and Guzmáns disappeared in this way. In the late 1880s, Cristóbal Leal began selling off portions of what remained of Santa Ana. Significantly, the first sales began within a year of the death of his grandmother, Victoria, in May 1887. By 1890, he had sold both halves of the western league, and in 1890 he and his wife sold to Emilio Forto, a land developer, the "homestead interest" of what was entered as "the Benigno Leal grant." Victoria Leal, the matriarch of the old Mexican land grant family, had made a will naming Cristóbal as her "universal heir." Yet keeping the land in the family proved very difficult. At this time, there were no heirs listed for Cristóbal and Ascensión; they were childless. This meant no direct inheritance of Santa Ana. There were also considerable pressures on ranchers in the 1880s and 1890s, as the cattle industry had declined, marketing livestock had become much harder, and drought had devastated even the small riverfront farming economy. The expedient of selling acreage in order to pay land taxes on remaining acreage became all too common.

When Cristóbal Leal sold a portion of the "west half of the western league" of Santa Ana to Emilio A. Forto, he may have been approached by the first representatives for irrigated agriculture. Forto, described as a "Spanish-born politician in Cameron County," likely had his eye on the potential for irrigation, for at the same time, he was involved in the building of a seven-mile canal near Santa María. Less than ten years later, we find the Guzmán land, the eastern league of old Santa Ana, also being partitioned. In 1898, when Julio Guzmán's wife, Estéfana, died, La Pechuga Ranch was divided to award 705 1/2 varas of land to the widower Julio, still living, and 705 1/2 varas to his eight children, apportioned equally among them. Three years later Julio died, leaving his holdings on the "east side of Santa Ana" to his children. Each of his eight offspring now also inherited a portion of his land, and they sold these holdings almost immediately. By 1902, Peter Ebenezer Blalock, a land developer, owned the Guzmán land.[2]

The decisions to sell so quickly the hard-earned family and stock business acreage may today seem arbitrary and misguided. Yet one reason surely had to do with the rise of social unrest along the border in the last decades of the nineteenth century. Population and labor were changing rapidly as Americans arrived in the valley and became dominant. Electoral races and demographic changes of the 1880s, especially, had produced political and sometimes interracial riots in Laredo and Rio Grande City so severe that the governor had declared martial law and sent in Texas Rangers. There is no evidence for how the families of Rancho Adentro or La Pechuga were affected by rising racism, diminishing economic opportunities, and an atmosphere in which English-language newspapers excoriated Mexican laborers, painting them as dangerous and filled with "blood-lust." Yet it can be assumed that Julio Guzmán's children did sense these ominous changes. Newspapers such as the *San Antonio Express*, the *Beeville Bee*, and even the *New York Times* were printing stories of Mexicans "taking over" small Texas towns, rioting, raiding, stealing stock, and fleeing to Mexico. The Texas governor sent in Ranger units and placed the sheriffs of Hidalgo, Cameron, and Zapata Counties on alert. Arnoldo De León, the historian who has studied these decades most closely, points out that sadly, these tensions and riots, these struggles for power, were occurring at a time when Mexicans in South Texas still outnumbered Anglo-American residents ten to one.

For Hispanic families, it must have seemed a threatening and uncertain time in which to undertake a fresh ranching or farming venture. In addition, most of the Guzmán children were girls. Unless they brought their husbands into the ranch economy, clustering in a large extended family around the original ranch home, there did not seem much point in keeping Guzmán land in the Guzmán family. No heir owned enough land individually to graze stock successfully. This was also true of Julio Jr. and Amado, who had never owned land but only grazed their animals on their father's holdings. In the early 1900s, some of Julio's grandchildren were under the guardianship of the well-known and well-liked William Brewster, son of the physician William Brewster who had married into the Singleterry family after the Civil War. That the Guzmán grandchildren were under his care in the early 1900s suggests Guzmán family dispersal. Likely Julio's surviving children were offered ready money for their land. Except for Estéfana, born in Texas in the late 1860s, the five inheriting Guzmán girls—Dolores, Estéfana, Anastacia, Manuela, and Higinia—had grown up and married before Julio created La Pechuga Ranch in 1882. Census data and baptismal records from Nuestra Señora de Guadalupe Church in Reynosa, Tamaulipas, show that most of Julio's children were born between 1846 and 1869. At some point, likely in 1865 after the American Civil War was over, the family moved across the river into the state of Texas and became Tejanos.

Like all ranch children, Julio's daughters would have been skilled horsewomen as well as hard workers in the critical duties of food preparation and clothing production. In addition to carding, spinning, and weaving wool, they likely "crocheted, embroidered, did drawnwork and *canaba* [cross-stitch on hemp cloth, similar to needlepoint]." Some ranch women even made leather jackets and chaps, learning to tan hides themselves. But bright and visible change—modernity—was everywhere in the air of the new century. Railway lines were bringing in consumer goods more steadily, including dress materials such as linen, silk, and chambray, which were shipped to the southern cities of Brownsville and Matamoros. Even denim, known as "Kentucky jean," was now available. Transportation and commercial webs created more day laborer possibilities for men. Town sites were springing up to the west of La Pechuga: McAllen in 1903 and Mission in 1908. Irrigated citrus farms were the new venture as cattle and sheep ranching declined. Thus, in time, the Guzmán girls married into other ranch families or perhaps lived in early towns. Julio's sons may have been living on La Pechuga in other dwellings; the Federal Census of 1900 shows that in that year, only grandchildren and his youngest daughter, Estéfana, were living with him in his ranch house on La Pechuga. The earlier tight laws of inheritance (in Texas, based on Spanish law), and the social expectations of heirship and land continuity were dissolving. The previously sturdy understanding that had kept Texas land in Tejas families faced pressure from land and irrigation companies as well as growing racism. The old Hispanic ranchos were breaking up.[3]

The reconsolidation of farm and ranch land on the Mexican grants of Santa Ana, Los Toritos, and El Gato happened at an astonishing speed. In

1902, Emilio Forto also sold his holdings on the western league of Santa Ana to Peter Ebenezer Blalock. By 1905, the last documented land transaction involving the Santa Ana heir took place, when Cristóbal Leal, by warranty deed, sold to D. B. Chapin "all rights under the will of Victoria Balli, deceased." It is possible that this warranty deed was part of a transaction preserved in local anecdotal memory as the one in which Cristóbal received a violin and a suit of clothes. The deed record clearly shows that Cristóbal received $600 for selling a tract "fronting 1320 varas on the Rio Grande River." The deed language does include "for purposes and considerations," a phrase sometimes appearing in other deeds as "for the sum of . . . and other considerations." Possibly the "considerations" did involve a violin and clothing; there is no way to know. However, Cristóbal received cash in hand for the land as well, and this river acreage was actually in the Llano Grande Grant, Cristóbal's last holdings from his inheritance through his grandmother's Balli family line. Judge Chapin was a slick political operator, soon involved in the clandestine relocation of courthouse records from old Hidalgo to the site of a new county seat he wanted to name for himself—Chapin. In 1912, Judge Chapin was brought to trial in San Antonio for shooting a potential assassin in a saloon. As a result of this scandal, the name of his town was changed to Edinburg. Judge Chapin's legal training and knowledge of local people placed him opportunely to acquire land from struggling Tejano ranchers like Cristóbal Leal. A Harlingen newspaper article from 1970 stated that Cristóbal, "the weak-minded son traded the last of his lands for a fiddle and a suit of clothes." An earlier account in 1964 stated without any evidence that "the last of the heirs of the original grantees to Santa Ana was insane . . . he was so mad that he swapped his interest in Santa Ana for a fiddle and a new suit of clothes." Again, there is no credible source for these statements. The accounts build on each other, but Judge Chapin is never mentioned. After the 1905 land sale, it is difficult to find any trace of Cristóbal or Ascención Leal.[4]

Surveys, Sales, and Rails

During the first decade of the new century, entrepreneurs in the valley held competing visions of agricultural development. The same year that Cristóbal Leal sold the last parcels of his inheritance, a survey defined the boundaries of the Blalock Town and Improvement Company. Striking in its dependence on rail lines, the survey describes 3,182 acres out of the El Gato, Santa Ana, and Los Toritos grants. These acres would change name from the Blalock Town and Improvement Company to Camp Ebenezer to Alamo. The survey points include rail stations, railway lines, and railway rights-of-way. One survey measurement actually ends in the middle of a railway track, bringing to mind the precedent of dividing states and countries down through the middle of rivers. This newly arrived form of land definition replaced the old survey markers such as mesquite and ebony trees and the organic boundaries of rivers, salt lakes, arroyos, and resacas. With both irrigation and rail structures in place, companies swarmed in. The American Rio Grande Land and Irrigation Company sold land to farmers in small tracts of ten to forty acres; the new owners would then purchase pumped water at a set annual rate. These pre-1910 irrigation efforts placed "raw lands" on the market for forty to seventy-five dollars an acre. Small, and sometimes entrepreneurial, farmers from the upper Midwest arrived in the area anticipating bumper crops and prosperity.

The deed history of Hidalgo County before 1920 shows a frenzy of buying and selling. In 1917, for instance, an investor from Minnesota bought up eighty acres in the Santa Ana "subdivision," sight unseen, from the J. C. Engelman Land Company. Garfield Foster paid $17,000, or $212 per acre, drawn by the promise of a year-round growing season and unlimited river water. By 1924, when the town of Alamo was formally named, land companies and sales agents were described as "swarming" in the valley. A wide variety of sales terms existed—half down in cash, promissory notes, Liberty bonds, and the interesting method of accepting northern property in trade for a South Texas tract. One historian describes sales agents carrying leather-bound notebooks called "deal books." The Rio Grande sometimes flooded during excursion months, as in 1919, when brown river water rose to twenty feet deep near Mercedes. Some of the agents reportedly told land seekers that local farmers were "irrigating their rice."[5]

There was indeed irrigation, a mature infrastructure of canals, but for relocating farmers, it came at the cost of adapting to a climate and landscape they experienced as alien. Purchasing these smaller tracts of ten to forty acres, newlyweds from Michigan, Ohio, and Iowa came south to farm on the Alamo Tract. Here they endured perhaps two or three seasons of blazing heat, cactus, thorn trees, evaporating surface water, and biting insects, those "swarms . . . of sandflies at night and day" described by early travelers into lower Texas. A young couple from the broad-leaved, green, and hilly watershed of the Muskingum River in Ohio, arriving to teach in a newly established school at La Feria, encountered a wall of heat their first night. Years later, Laura Rich Cleary recounted to her children how she "roasted in her wool suit, the heat a dramatic change." She described thirteen miles of "mostly desolate countryside, dotted with mesquite, cactus, dense underbrush and the occasional live oak." The nights were hot and miserable, and she longed for the cool, seventy-degree weather of the Muskingum River

Valley. After finding a local man dangling from a tree in their schoolyard, lynched by outlaws, Laura and Ed Cleary left after only a year.[6]

For the hopeful, south-migrating farmers, the Lower Rio Grande Valley environment became a settlement filter. Thousands left, but people who stayed on found a match. Their adaptive personalities and general toughness of spirit allowed them to succeed in South Texas. The ebb and flow of young landowners in Hidalgo County was striking during this time. Many would sell out, often to another couple just like them. Their out-migration paralleled the minidiaspora of Tejano ranching people leaving their family lands. The decline in Tejano ranching and farming between 1895 and 1910 can be seen in a single, telling statistic: swings in the number of bushels of corn produced in the county. On small ranches such as La Pechuga and Rancho Adentro, owners using both family and paid, seasonal labor had produced considerable corn. This corn, like the frijol (usually the pinto bean), was an absolute staple of local diet. Corn was a dry-crop agriculture, watered by hand at times or grown in fields near the river. On the census of 1880, 226,899 bushels of corn were recorded in Hidalgo County; by 1900, only 51,490 bushels were produced. Yet by 1920, well over *one million* corn bushels flowed from this single Texas county, much shipped out on the new rail lines. In these figures can be seen the broad narrative: loss of ranch and farm acreage and thereby crop productivity; relocation of Tejano ranching families; and the staggering impact of irrigation on those same lands, now being watered, sold, and resold by land and irrigation companies.[7]

Between 1910 and 1925, these companies descended on Hidalgo County to root out the thorn scrub detritus of cattle ranching and the oases of original plant communities, including graceful Texas ebony trees that had often formed ring groves in the fertile alluvium of the river. Changes in the riverine land were profound and visible. In a talk given to the Lower Rio Grande Historical Society in 1952, Sarah Sanborne Weaver remembered, "[In] Hidalgo County in 1919, the fires were burning in wide circles all about our night driving; clearing, clearing, clearing, burning, burning, burning; destroying bird and beast . . . along with their homes and their food and the shade that the soil needed." To construct over 300 miles of feeder canals, most 8 to 10 feet deep, as well as trunk canals 110 to 130 feet across, companies first burned off the vegetation and then used mules and Mexican labor. That labor was plentiful, based on the flow of Mexican peoples across the Rio Grande during the Mexican Revolution years. The success of this animal and human team before the advent of mechanized dredgers, plows, chain saws, or stump removers can be measured in another set of revealing numbers. Described as "the rapid progress of farming," acres of cultivated land in Hidalgo County were documented in 1880 as 2,000; in

1910, as 8,940; by 1920 there were 74,128 farmed acres; and just four years later, in 1924, 127,220 acres. Yet, somewhat miraculously, the southernmost acreage of the three Mexican land grants that had become the Alamo Tract—including the massive Santa Ana forests—remained untouched. This is visible on all maps of Hidalgo County from the 1920s on. On an undated but likely pre-1950 map of Hidalgo County, in use in the County Appraisal Office in Edinburg, the startling dark, verdant outline of the forest stands out next to a series of cleared fields labeled "Klump Field" or "Toritos Field." Across the Rio Grande from Section 29 (Santa Ana) lies a field labeled "Mexicano Field." There is no corresponding forest left on the Mexican side.[8]

The economic effect on Hidalgo County was akin to land fever, to a land rush. Newspaper accounts fueled the heat of interest in acquiring land that was now seen as having miraculous or "magic" prospects. In 1903, the *Hidalgo Advance* reported that a Wisconsin purchaser who in 1902 had bought eight thousand acres for thirty-seven cents an acre was selling his land for twenty-five dollars an acre. The same issue celebrated the largest stalk of sugarcane ever raised in Hidalgo County. Standing nearly fifteen feet, with "44 joints," this mammoth cane had sprung from the irrigated soil of John Closner's San Juan plantation. The entire issue of the *Advance*, in fact, re-creates the celebratory, energetic feel of land change, agricultural progress, and economic boom times. At Montgomery Onion Patch, "75–100 men, women, and children" were working daily, setting the onions that would grow to admirable size. Those workers were Mexican and Tejano people, some perhaps digging into soils that had once been owned by their families. The paper also celebrated the shooting of wild turkeys "all along the line" of the St. Louis, Brownsville, and Mexico railroad. An advertisement placed by the lawyers Bell and Browne stated, "Land business is our specialty. We will bring suits to recover lands either for stated fees or portions of lands recovered." The *Advance* sang with the energy of a frontier zone.[9]

That feeling did not last long. Once irrigation was linked to an effective transportation system, the Rio Grande Valley was catapulted out of isolated, small-scale farming and into commercial agriculture. Windmills had reached the valley in 1903, but with rail lines, they could now be shipped in on flatcars. Although there was a period of overlap with traditional ranch watering methods, the days were soon to pass when water was drawn from a deep, hand-dug well by a man on horseback, slowly pulling a long rope attached to a leather bucket. Windmills and mechanized pumps spread rapidly. The possibility of shipping crops out by rail became a reality when, in 1904, the St. Louis, Brownsville, and Mexico railroad reached Hidalgo County. By 1907, 761 car lots of Lower Rio Grande Valley vegetables had been shipped out. Then, early in 1909, John Closner and W. F. Sprague financed the building of a spur from the railroad at San Juan to Edinburg. Eight miles long, Closner's spur was known as the San Antonio–Rio Grande Railroad. By 1912, with additional rail lines coming in, the citrus king John Shary had arrived in Mission to purchase the fifty-five thousand acres known as "Sharyland."[10]

Yet despite the laying of rail lines, the arrival of large-scale developers and irrigation companies, and the land boom, between 1909 and 1916, irrigation companies were reported in poor financial condition. Many were in receivership. The Rio Grande had not cooperated with dream-visions depending on the control of water. Beginning in 1909, the old river had flooded catastrophically. Up in Starr County in that year, the overflow had washed away twenty-one thousand cubic feet of earthworks and levees. The greater floods of 1914 and 1916 washed away the infrastructure of irrigation—canals, laterals, and the land itself. In addition, these floods left a gritty, odorous layer of sand over the whole area. In 1912, the Jackson Ranch Church near Santa Ana was reported to be "half full of water." Between 1914 and 1916, a channel change in the river was noted. Nevertheless, in 1914, Peter Ebenezer Blalock sold his holdings, the parcels and larger acreage he had been steadily amassing from a host of old families in Hidalgo County; this sale also included a five-acre pump site on the Rio Grande. The Alamo Land and Sugar Company arrived to claim and relabel the three old Mexican land grants of Los Toritos, Santa Ana, and El Gato. The new name was the Alamo Tract.[11]

This new "subdivision" attracted local and Midwest buyers almost overnight. Purchasing water from the Rio Grande Land and Irrigation Company, farmers who cleared their small holdings in the Alamo Tract received bursts of river water from steam-driven pumps. These pumps all ran on mesquite in the first decade, wood obtained by work crews who were "clearing adjacent lands." By the mid-1920s, no fewer than seven Hidalgo County irrigation companies were pumping from the Rio Grande. In 1920, the farmers themselves living on the Alamo Tract bought and began operating what was at first named Hidalgo County Water Improvement District #2. Of the sixty-eight thousand acres served by the district, fully sixty-two thousand were cultivated. In the six thousand uncultivated acres were counted the lower three miles of the old Santa Ana grant, a dense, often flooded forest that by the 1920s had still not been cleared. Because of levee construction, irrigation canals were not run into this acreage; farmers passed them by. By 1927, Water District #2 was pumping one hundred thousand acre-feet of water from the Rio Grande. A soil survey for the county in 1925 exulted that "the settlement and development of the county is continuing rapidly."[12]

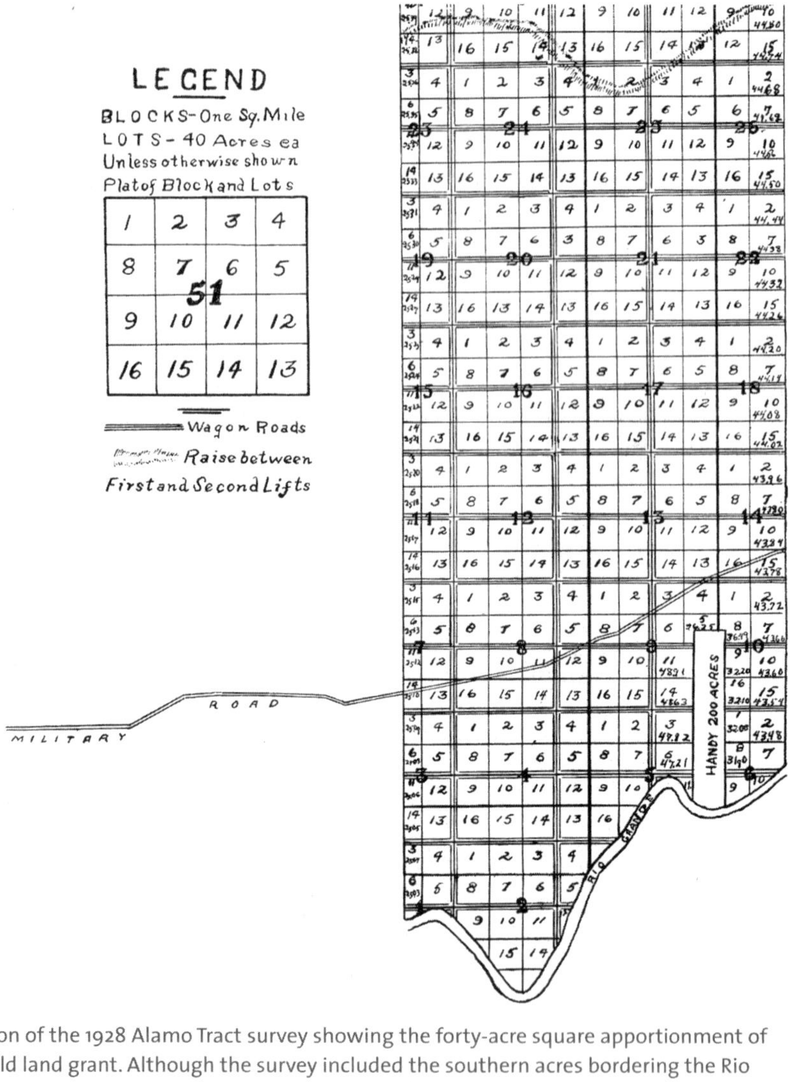

Portion of the 1928 Alamo Tract survey showing the forty-acre square apportionment of the old land grant. Although the survey included the southern acres bordering the Rio Grande, no one bought or cleared those densely forested mile-square farms sitting below the Military Road. From the Alamo Tract survey map, available at Hidalgo County Irrigation District #2, Edinburg, TX.

Two different stories are told by the records. One emphasizes population growth, double-cropping, extraordinary crop yield and size of vegetables, and the triumph of irrigated citrus farming. But the other story is about river flooding. During the dry summers, seven irrigation companies were releasing river water into dank, black-dirt canals; yet the river itself continued to leap its banks. Between 1900 and 1939, the Rio Grande "overflowed" twenty-three times. In 1915, as an initial flood control effort, construction began on the Hidalgo County levee along the second lift of land. A flood in 1919, followed by a stronger one in 1922, resulted in a genuine flood control movement. The same Soil Survey of 1925 that had reported rapid development of the county also noted that farm size was decreasing and lamented a general breakup of farms. A severe agricultural depression following World War I had caused many bank failures across the Midwest and the South, and the ripple effect on small-tract owners reached the Rio Grande Valley as well. In the southern part of the county, where the forest of Santa Ana often stood in brown, swirling floodwaters, most of the farms were operated by nonresidents, absentee owners who gleaned a profit by employing tenant farmers and sharecroppers. The Soil Survey reported that less than 5 percent of these laborers paid any cash rent.[13]

The transformation of Santa Ana had been strikingly fast. Inside a decade, the long, chaparral-dominated grazing leagues, filled in to the south with riverine forest and dotted with small cornfields, became the neatly surveyed Alamo Tract. The cartography of forty-acre farms was a relentless grid marching across floodplain terraces formed through eons of river deposition. A decade more, and many of those square tracts were unoccupied or had become impoverished, sharecropped farms.

Santa Ana in the Great Depression Years

As the Great Depression loomed, a final effort evolved to make the leagues of Santa Ana commercially productive. Although it failed, the enterprise generated a name that local people eventually used for the forest: Santa Ana Groves. In the late 1920s, an investment group including locals like William Brewster as well as two outside investors from Chicago—female physicians, in fact—attempted to enter the citrus market with an orchard called the Santa Ana Citrus Groves. Records show that by 1933, the company needed to borrow considerable sums to further its development. Despite the economic depression, the First National Bank of Chicago advanced four promissory notes to the ten investors in 1933. Perhaps the investors had been initially encouraged by the construction of yet another rail line across the old grant: in 1926, tracks were laid for the San Benito and Rio Grande Valley Railroad, known as the "Spiderweb." In the early 1920s, the Alamo Land and Sugar Company was bringing in "trainloads" of future buyers and lodging them in the infant town of Alamo, incorporated in 1924. Once rail lines fed the new town, it became a shipping point for irrigated agricultural products, many grown on old Santa Ana lands: cotton, cottonseed, broomcorn, and winter crops like cabbage and onions. The idea of growing both sugarcane and grapefruit on Santa Ana must have been a natural segue in the thinking of investors.

The Santa Ana Citrus Groves company was yet another form of the irrigated dream. A newspaper article from 1942 described how the two physicians fought to keep the company viable. "One remained in St. Louis practicing her profession while the other stayed on the property trying to meet expenses." Apparently, 147 acres of the lakes (resacas) on the old grant were "dammed and drained" so that crops and citrus saplings could be planted in the lake beds themselves. Because this company soon failed in the Great Depression and foreclosure occurred in 1940, it is not known exactly how many orange or grapefruit trees were originally set out on Santa Ana—if any were. This is one instance in which fate did intervene in the saving of Santa Ana: the Great Depression prevented forest clear-cutting. It was much cheaper to drain the resacas and use the spongy lake beds for planting than to burn off and root up the forest. But despite financial restraints, through the 1920s at least, the heated, ephemeral visions of great agricultural wealth continued.[14]

Yet the opposite forces of development and nascent environmental awareness were both at work on Santa Ana in these decades before refuge acquisition. The Chicago physicians who had invested in the failed citrus orchard, Dr. Mary A. Miller and Dr. Ann Rinehart, often stayed at the clubhouse just south of the Military Road; public information at Santa Ana today states that the Alamo Land and Sugar Company built the clubhouse to house potential buyers for its subdivision parcels. A study of the Alamo Tract development published in 1971 reveals that the two physicians had hoped to eventually create a retirement community, an "elite retirement settlement with grand homes on the winding road . . . all would face the beautiful lake on the tract." Yet drought years and probably the Great Depression itself prevented this vision from materializing. In 1939, Irby Davis mentioned that the International Boundary Commission (IBC) had given permission to Dr. Rinehart to continue living in the clubhouse, although plans for a levee were under way. The physician-owners of the failed citrus enterprise and retirement community were still in the area, and perhaps at this time, we can note a growing appreciation for welcome shade, for the tree, vine, shrub, and flower vigor, for the bird and butterfly life on Santa Ana. For the contrast was stark: as soon as visitors crossed the Military Road at the edge of the forest, they stood on a bald, treeless plain of searing sunlight. Pungent fields mired them; insects rose up in a loud, black swarm, drawn to the manuring of the cotton crop. The Santa Ana forested acres, however, retained a lushness. Early photographs of the clubhouse from the first years of the refuge show it sitting comfortably under Texas ebony and towering bald cypress trees; some cypress have been replanted and today still mark the edges of the northern resaca.[15]

Because a building created a meeting place for potential investors and, later, refuge visitors, the clubhouse figures prominently in the early accounts of Santa Ana Refuge. In 1943, the refuge manager detailed its architecture: "[It is] constructed along Spanish lines; stucco walls with high-beamed ceilings, a red tile roof over the central portion and a flat metal roof covering the Spanish Fortress type wings." The report also noted assertions from local people that during high flood stages of the Rio Grande, water reached up to two feet inside the clubhouse, borne out by visible watermarks and damage. From the clubhouse, a horse trail had once led down through the upland thorn forest to Rancho Adentro. The trail wound through the Texas ebony grove, past ironwood, purple sage, and sharp Spanish dagger. Perhaps this trail was wider on the upland than on the lower reaches, as the forest in the first mile up from the river was dominated by thorny species. In general, the earliest workers on the refuge described the paths they found as little more than overgrown wagon roads or thin stock trails, and personnel rode horses down into the forest. Consistently they noted edge habitats browsed, grazed, or eaten away. In 1990, a researcher speculated that "every hectare on the refuge . . . has been affected by grazing or farming before creation of the refuge in 1940."[16]

There is no way to ascertain whether this is true. Yet the living heart of Santa Ana, the source of its richness, is arboreal. The big trees outlasted wood use for brick kilns, as well as riverbank clearing for steamboats, ranch communities, and ferry crossings. The forest escaped exploitation by incoming American entrepreneurs when it was erroneously auctioned in 1850, and the trees—especially the grand, immense Texas ebony grove surrounding the Leal homestead—were recertified to Benigno and Victoria Leal. The forested southern acres survived despite erosional loss from floods, clear-cutting of mesquite and other small woody species for irrigation steam pumps, and consistent grazing and browsing by domestic animals. Precisely because of its towering density, the thorn forest of Santa Ana presented a formidable obstacle to the twentieth-century humans who wanted to strip the land, even when gasoline-powered engines were available. Most significant was the frequent inundation of the bottomland, where in 1933, after a Gulf hurricane swept up the river, the look of the place changed overnight. Suddenly, the familiar twin lobes of the refuge as it appears today protruded into the current. In 1942 the war correspondent Ernie Pyle visited the Lower Rio Grande Valley. His reaction on viewing the surviving forests was dramatic: "Suddenly you pop right into the heart of this luxuriant tropical greenery. It is like bursting through a wall into another room."[17]

Realizing that the only true building on the refuge was a draw for visitors, managers made repair of the clubhouse a priority, and by the fall of 1943, local clubs and visitors were meeting there. "Approximately 60 persons registered at the Clubhouse for a trip over the refuge," wrote Earl Craven in late 1943. This number is the first ever recorded for the refuge. It had been only a few months before, in September, that Santa Ana National Wildlife Refuge had been "officially acquired." Local interest was immediate. Many of the people who registered for that first outing came to Santa Ana with binoculars; they wanted to find, watch, and learn about birds. It was winter on the refuge, and also a time of great, engulfing world war. Yet the trees, hanging mosses, vines, thickets, river terraces, and edge habitats of the Santa Ana resacas were profound with birds, with life. In their observations, the managers conveyed an audible, visible scurrying and rustling, climbing, swooping, and sky-wheeling. In those days of seventy years past, bird numbers were yet dramatic compared with our present-day experience. As weeks passed into spring and flocks arrived to nest, a manager exclaimed of the "beautifully-colored" hooded orioles: "From scarcely any point on the refuge could one fail to observe a mating pair."[18]

Yet only twenty years before, preserving this amazing habitat had not been important. Through the 1920s and 1930s, highly depressed decades in the county, local hunters went into the thorn forest to take deer, javelina, ocelot, coyote, and white-winged doves. Oral accounts mention Tejano ranching families still living in the area, some in dirt-floored jacales, foraging in the woods for "berries, nuts and herbs." Deep inside the woods, the vandalized family graveyard of the Leals spewed bones out of a cracked tomb. This tomb, or *bóveda*, held the honored remains of Cristóbal Leal and his wife, Rafaela Treviño Leal, who died in 1908. During the years of violence and looting surrounding the Mexican Revolution of 1910, many cemeteries along the river were desecrated by thieves (often termed "bandits" in the newspapers) who crossed from northern Mexico. Once again, residents of the Rio Grande Valley sent "urgent requests for help" as random theft, stock killing, ambush, and murder escalated. By 1916, over 110,000 men occupied and patrolled the US side of the river. Some—the Texas Rangers—had been mobilized by the Texas governor, but the area also saw the arrival of federal troops and National Guard units. Despite this voluminous military traffic, most of which patrolled on horseback, and despite the attention given to river crossing points such as the one at Santa Ana, the forest environment on the old grant remained sturdy. Intricate and irreplaceable plant and animal species flourished in minihabitats that would later be labeled the upland thorn forest, the resacas, the riparian terraces, and the bottomland.[19]

Santa Ana had survived as a mosaic of land types, including several internal fields deep in the forest as well as the northern pastures the Guzmáns had used; and soon the Chicago bank holding the lien on the Citrus Grove company issued grazing leases. When absentee lease-holders ran stock on the internal fields, they allowed too many cattle. Assessment of animal load on the remaining overgrazed fields was not carried out until the refuge managers arrived in the 1940s. Through the Depression years, the use of Santa Ana was haphazard and indiscriminate. Early managers reported Mexican squatters with goat herds. Even after managers fenced parts of the refuge, goats were jumping the fences, long used to finding supplementary browse. Before the Rio Grande Valley Nature Club took an interest in the late 1930s, no one gathering plant resources, hunting, or running stock on the old grant had concern for its surviving precious habitat. The floods came to Santa Ana, but the forests profited from them. The droughts followed, and although plants and animals died, when the rains returned, the ecosystem rebounded. When farmers and investors redefined the land for double-cropped agriculture, coerced it through irrigation and mechanization, they recast this long-evolved drought-flood cycle as destructive. The priorities engendered by the agricultural boom were sharply new and powerful.[20]

In these years, forces gathering outside the Santa Ana forest were creating a future that surely would have finally destroyed it. Repeated calls for the construction of a series of flood control dams on the Rio Grande had resulted in discussions with Mexico. The perennial problem of the river boundary had intensified because of excessive irrigation upstream in the El Paso area, as well as channel changes on the lower river. One writer has estimated that before the construction of the Falcon Dam, 70 percent of the river's flow below El Paso came from Mexico. The agreements were not all about irrigation or floods, however. In 1936, the United States and Mexico signed a Migratory Bird Treaty. The groundwork for this treaty had been laid seven years earlier, by the Migratory Bird Conservation Act of 1929. The status of endangered migratory birds using the river had become a concern to both nations. Ornithologists chose the spotted owl as a case study to drive the legislation, but one report stated that a wide variety of birds arriving from Central and South America faced "many hunters."

By this time, the hunters included northern Mexican landless laborers and local Rio Grande hunter-ranchers as well as professional game bird marksmen. The Migratory Bird Treaty, signed in Mexico City, set out twenty-three species of birds no longer to be considered game birds, including cranes and rails. It also included a category called "Other," a fluid, evolving construct that would allow new birds to be added and protected. In 1972, for example, authorities added the crow family, protecting rare crow species, including the Tamaulipas crow, from hunters. This pivotal 1936 treaty changed forever the nature of the Santa Ana borderlands. No longer would the single, ominous shot of a casual hunter on either side of the Rio Grande echo daily through the riparian forest, although illegal hunting persisted for decades. A firm new ethic had arrived, and it was law. In the late nineteenth century, when market hunting swept across all of Texas, a hunting license issued at Galveston granted a perpetual right, described as "playful": "Without respect to feather, slay . . . every bird of every feather." The glorious, unlimited sky once perceived as a realm in itself, a fresh country of exotic targets, now had guardians. And although this would prevail, the protection of birds was not the only consideration in preserving the Santa Ana ecosystem.[21]

Epilogue: The Future of a River and Its Trees

A new future was made possible for Santa Ana when newspapers began publicizing proposed regulation of the Rio Grande. The protection of natural, living resources in the skies through international law laid the foundation for the protection of riverine habitat. It was in the 1930s that the birders of Hidalgo County began to be seriously alarmed. With the need for regulation of the river boundaries, for control of floodwaters, and for the sharing of vital irrigation water, members of the International Boundary Commission (IBC) began buying up land. "International storage" and "diversion dams" were phrases appearing in the newspapers of the day. Birders and naturalists of the valley read about these programs. Although between 1934 and 1938, the IBC proceeded with what it called "rectification" of the Rio Grande channel in the El Paso area, the commission also gained control of the river farther south by buying up the floodplain. In his late 1930s letters to J. Clark Salyer, Irby Davis noted that the IBC was purchasing old, often-flooded river acreage. Should this commission obtain Santa Ana, the forest would be at high risk. The IBC could—and did—remove trees. In the 1960s, for instance, IBC workers probably removed many Montezuma bald cypress from the lower Rio Grande banks during a period of channelization. This action occurred despite the clear trend of severe national depletion of bald cypress, which, after the American chestnut, has suffered the greatest reduction of any tree in the nation. The authority of the IBC also extended to the placement of hundreds of boundary markers along the river border, and the IBC checked and regulated the river channel to make legal determination of which country owned land that may have shifted. The commission often worked with the Army Corps of Engineers to ensure a free-flowing river. Two consistent strategies endangered original habitat: alteration of the riverbanks through vegetation removal, and channelization. By narrowing the river channel, agencies could control the historically seasonal, riotous flow of the Rio Grande.[22]

Modern studies of stream bank stability in areas as far west as Arizona have shown that these actions imperil riverine wildlife habitat. In one area, following vegetation removal, bank retreat rates doubled. When trees crash into the river, bringing topsoil with them, the secure cover many birds and mammals need in order to drink from the river disappears as well. In the 1940s, a manager at the refuge noted that chachalacas would approach the Rio Grande to drink only if they could dart out of a thickety ground cover. He added, "This type of watering place is scarce on the Santa Ana Refuge." By 1939, the local naturalists of Hidalgo County had visited the old tract often enough to observe worrisome changes. The Santa Ana forest was vulnerable. How vulnerable would become clear much later, when the IBC, now the IBWC (International Boundary and Water Commission), defined an aspect of its role as late as the 1990s. An IBWC memorandum details an "annual vegetation clearing program along the banks of the Rio Grande for a distance of 34.5 miles upstream [from Brownsville]." These activities would begin at the water's edge, move inland for a short distance, and involve mowing, removal of trees, and clearing and removal of underbrush by hand. The goal was to prevent debris accumulation that would in turn reduce the river's carrying capacity. As authorized to remove, carry, and take away, the IBWC worked in seeming counterpoint to land protection and restoration agendas. But at least by the mid-1980s, the IBWC was working *with* the Lower Rio Grande Valley Wildlife Refuge System, arriving at best practice for both river and thorn forest habitat.

Proposed actions for the midvalley riparian woodland, ninety tracts that included Santa Ana, were to "post and protect brush from further clearing and negotiate with IBWC to protect river banks." Inadvertently, in streamside clearing, a tree may be taken out—and it may be the last representative of a rare species. In addition, the old giants along the river can decline so quickly. After the upriver dams and reservoirs were constructed, researchers documented tree death at a markedly visible rate. Natural flooding was nearly eliminated: the Rio Grande has overflowed its banks only three times since 1970 and only a few times after 1997 (with the hurricane season of 2010 a major exception). The spring arrival of life-giving water had been a yearly event. Slowly but inexorably, water tables in the soil sank. Mature native trees died off, a mortality documented in the important 1997 study by environmental researcher Charles David Castillo. Mexican ash, cedar elm, and Texas persimmon were felled by winds. Their root systems had parched and were neither healthy nor strong enough to secure the trunks.

Castillo found his study site near the old resacas littered with decaying trees, with the fallen and broken trunks of native riparian giants. Continual dry-weather stress weakened the forest and resulted in a tree graveyard not far from the old Leal cemetery. Yet on wildlife refuges, trees come back. One small, evergreen citrus valiantly illustrates this.[23]

The dominant citrus crops of orange, lemon, and grapefruit have defined Texas fruit farms. Yet Texas has long been a land of other citrus trees, some extremely rare and precious today. The modest citrus tree *Esenbeckia runyonii*, or jopoy, once grew at the edges of old resacas along the lower Rio Grande. Found only in Texas, jopoy (also known as limoncillo) is an evergreen once considered extinct through the clearing of native vegetation during the South Texas agricultural boom. Jopoy grows very slowly in a habitat known for extremes of heat and for flooding during intense rainy seasons, when the dry-bed resacas burst with water and wash out over the surrounding plant communities. Like all successful species along the southern Rio Grande, jopoy has adapted to this drought-flood cycle. Its leaves are shiny, a bit curly, and fragrant, cherished by horticulturists as one of the most imperiled plants in all of Texas. In 1929, a botanist discovered a few surviving mature jopoy trees near Los Fresnos and obtained seeds. He was successful in starting more than one hundred jopoy seedlings in Brownsville, and a 1976 bulletin states that some of the hardier saplings were eventually transplanted to Santa Ana. Refuge personnel verified that in 2013, jopoy was still growing near the visitor's center. As botanist Raymond Fleetwood noted in his 1973 plant inventory, new species enter the refuge all the time, through floodwaters, animal and bird movement and droppings, and human passage. Border patrols, inspectors, refuge personnel, and thousands of visitors unwittingly transport seeds, some so tiny they seem like a speck of grit on an ankle sock. Yet extirpated species rarely surge back by accident. The return of jopoy to an area where it once naturally grew keenly highlights the importance of wildlife refuges.

Unfortunately, on refuges and in natural areas, plant arrival is inadvertent as well as intentional. The spread of plant species without natural controls has led to invasive species on Santa Ana, most especially salt cedar trees and buffelgrass. These plant seeds often wash in with flooding; according to Kimberly Wahl, plant ecologist on Santa Ana today, one species of salt cedar tree reaches sexual maturity just three months after germination and flowers year-round. Refuge workers must combat this highly virile tree, originally from Africa; for without any check on its constant reproduction, salt cedar trees gradually eliminate diversity. Buffelgrass is also so robust and vigorous that Wahl has seen "entire fields" completely covered with it. Today, preservation of original habitat means balance: no single species can be permitted to crowd out others. This was not a problem on the early-nineteenth-century porciones and grants, even in the presence of active flooding; for the land all around these grants was neither fragmented nor damaged. Commercial agriculture changed the earth, establishing uneasy relationships between cleared fields and original habitat. Land left fallow in rotation is an open invitation for the seeds of invasive species. And lying right next to the boundaries of Santa Ana today are such fields. "We want diversity," Wahl emphasizes. That diversity was inherent in the original ecosystem of the riparian forest. Diversity preserves an interlocking web of relationships—tiny wildflowers thriving wherever mesquite shades the soil, or reptiles digging holes for eggs in earth unchoked by buffelgrass.[24]

The management plans from the 1980s and 1990s for the Lower Rio Grande Valley National Wildlife Refuge System (Cameron, Hidalgo, Starr, and Willacy Counties) stress the urgent nature of preservation. In 1983, a report warned that the "conversion of native brush is continuing at a rapid pace." Discussions about the nature of the early Rio Grande Valley floodplain, whether or not it was "brush country," appear in reports from the 1990s. Cited in the 1983 report, a Texas Parks and Wildlife bulletin documented local memories: "Old-timers still live who remember that when they were young at least parts of the Rio Grande plain would not have qualified as what we now call, 'brush country.'" These reports with their mandates and actions indicate changing attitudes toward brush: that it is inherently valuable as a habitat in its own right, providing nesting, sheltered trails, shade, and food for birds in fall feeding flights. Reports gave priority status to floodplain habitat along the river, seeking to protect existing scattered brush tracts in the refuges. Brushland, with small trees and understory thickets, had been historically viewed as difficult for agriculture and an impediment to grazing, a place where snakes, predators, and poisonous insects lay in wait. It has taken modern understanding to realize that where luxuriant brush grows, it is being supported by the same rich river soils so touted for agriculture. Historically, few observers noted the degree of health and hardiness in brush communities. It all seemed the same. As late as 1938, just a few years before the creation of Santa Ana National Wildlife Refuge, a writer for *National Geographic* called the Rio Grande delta a "virtually worthless wilderness area." Even in 1975, a writer describing the land of South Texas before the arrival of railways called it "a desert of brush, cactus, and mesquite."[25]

In the same way that first settlers to the midwestern prairie states erroneously read prairie as treeless and therefore infertile, some observers of South Texas have also misread the land. Once viewed as "wasteland," brush country by the late 1990s had a new value: *ecologically complex and irreplaceable.* Santa Ana National Wildlife Refuge would preserve it—and the forest—"for use as an inviolate sanctuary." This inviolate sanctuary also ensured that upland thorn forests of the Tamaulipan biotic province—Santa Ana—would remain a wildland corridor for migrating raptors. In the 1980s, these raptors, Swainson's hawks and broad-winged hawks in particular, were described as funneling through in spectacular numbers. Today, their kettling circles high above the river may be merely a remnant of the numbers of birds present when the first Escandón settlers arrived at the Río Bravo del Norte in 1749. The process of recovery that began on Santa Ana with the opening of the refuge is ongoing. Yet it is heartening to realize how quickly land and water respond to skilled management. The protection of resident and migratory birds requires the protection of land: topsoil, subsoil, and grass. We cannot overemphasize the importance of healthy grass on Santa Ana. Only a year after acquisition, a manager wrote that "little openings in the brush and timber" were developing a fresh, vibrant growth of grasses, including *Setaria* (foxtails, or plains bristlegrasses) and *Chloris* (windmill grasses). Waterfowl, especially teals, mallards, and rails, eat the tiny seeds of the brushy foxtails, but so do upland game birds, from the wild turkey to the tiny bobwhite quail. All species of sparrows and songbirds, like the many overwintering warblers who come to Santa Ana, love both bristlegrass and windmill grass seeds. The resurgence of Santa Ana grass was a critical sign of recovery.[26]

By 1905, the families with the longest tenure at Santa Ana—the Leals and the Guzmáns—had dispersed across South Texas. Later, grandsons of old Julio Guzmán held civic offices in Edinburg. Newspapers in Hidalgo County ran feature articles on them, such as the 1931 piece on Santiago G. Guzmán, Hidalgo County treasurer at age twenty-seven. In the 1930s, Guzmán family members such as Santiago were political activists in the urban areas that had spread over their original ranch birthplaces. Santiago Guzmán, in fact, created an important civic organization, the Association of Latin American Citizens. He also founded and published a Spanish-language newspaper, *El Defensor*, in Edinburg. In the article about him, his father, Don Julio Guzmán, is described as a "pioneer stock raiser." But this was actually his grandfather, old Julio, who had leveraged a small inheritance, savings from his horse-breeding business, and carefully timed stock sales into an entire league-and-a-half ranch on Santa Ana and El Gato. These Guzmáns living on La Pechuga Ranch were not "pioneers" in the sense that we usually use this term; they had lived in South Texas long enough to be counted on at least five censuses. The name Guzmán is found as well among the earliest grantees of New Spain porciones. Like the Leals, they were in the original wave of Spanish and then Mexican settlers arriving to imprint Tejas between 1749 and the 1830s.[27]

As people who lived longest in the Lower Rio Grande Valley, their century of tenure had provided them with decades of observation of the natural world. And intimacy and observation create knowledge, culture, and feeling. It was the early Mexican settlers in the valley who identified the raucous call of the great-tailed grackle as "the cry of the widow." From Fray Domenech, a French missionary in South Texas, comes one of the only extant accounts of the feeling for land held by Mexican settlers and ranchers. An old Mexican servant, once a soldier, began talking to the priest one night in the late 1850s: "What silence in all nature!" he began. Then he added, as a noisy grackle chattered in the canopies, "Why does she not sleep beneath the broad shade of the ebony tree? Mystery of God . . . and those majestic palm-trees, whose graceful branches gently poise themselves against the clear sky, seeming as if at night-time they bear fruit of fire, suspended from every branch?" The old soldier went on to praise the wide Texas sky so filled with stars, saying their splendor "lights the plains like the timid, doubtful twilight." Travelers had described this territory over and over as a "veritable furnace," filled with harsh light. To passing observers, towns sat without shade, "roasted by the sun." Yet the land had nonetheless seduced and claimed its owners, those who had lived as witnesses to its drought and flood cycles. There was a feeling of enormity, of power, and of formidable and resilient beauty.[28]

And long before Julio and Estéfana Guzmán moved onto La Pechuga Ranch, before clusters of huts and jacales changed into Brownsville, Roma, or Hidalgo, Benigno Leal had crossed the Rio Grande on his horse from Reynosa and begun to create a central, protected homestead on the first rise of his western league. He discovered a thriving Texas ebony forest included in his grant, and he left it alone; eventually the family cut a few trees to hand-carve the heavy, somber palisade fence around the Leal ranch cemetery. The matriarch Victoria Balli Leal, who sought to make sure Santa Ana stayed in the Leal family by willing it to her grandson, left another legacy: a rather impressive family line. The Leal name is today prevalent in Hidalgo, Cameron, and Starr Counties. Even by 1920, there were thirty-four census listings for Leal in Hidalgo County alone, although only five were born in Texas. The historian Daniel Arreola has found that by 1930, it is clear that the population of South Texas was "culturally linked to a trans-Rio Grande homeland." The Mexican Americans of this region had come mainly from just across the river and had not migrated from central Mexico. The implication is that the Leal branch from northern Mexico had emigrated well before but also during the Mexican Revolution years. Today, Leal descendants tracing family history share anecdotal evidence that their forebears were born "at Santa Ana."[29]

It was neither the Leals nor the Guzmáns who overgrazed the grassland of Santa Ana. Neither did these people decimate the great thorn forest for firewood, building materials, field clearance, or commercial use such as fuel for a brick-making industry, wood for steamboats in the pre–Civil War years, or ties and palings for railway companies later. Only when they could no longer survive in an economy in which irrigated farming had replaced ranching—and where rising discrimination and racial prejudice also prevented their success—only then did they sell their land. Across the geographic sweep of South Texas, this story played out from Laredo to Brownsville. Homogenized agriculture cleared the exotic, teeming habitat of the Rio Grande corridor, floodplain terraces once stridently alive and flexed into the drought-flood cycle. Ecological recognition came slowly to the Rio Grande Valley, the critical understanding that "in order to survive, each species requires a unique combination of plants, animals, climate, soil, and water." Ironically, the Mexican and Tejano peoples who long lived on this land could probably have told the scientific community many of the things that today we wish we had understood so much earlier. Yet that knowledge *has* arrived; wildlife sanctuaries bespeak it. Thousands of species find their "unique combinations" in a thorn forest environment.

We hear those combinations in the voices of Santa Ana birds. "White-winged doves began to show up on April 15th," wrote manager Luther Goldman in 1949. "And in a few days, [they] were singing over much of the area. Their calls, mixed with white-fronted doves, red-billed pigeons, mourning doves and chachalacas make mighty good refuge music in the early morning." Today in South Texas, that music still resounds in the largest remaining tract of original landscape, just over two thousand acres: the forest that stands at Santa Ana National Wildlife Refuge. When Luther Goldman wrote of doves and pigeons singing in the morning, he was listening to birds on the original Santa Ana land grant. Since then, the refuge may have expanded slightly to the east, incorporating riverine forest on the old El Gato grant as well.

Santa Ana was among the last leagues granted to Mexican settlers in 1834. In that year, it is almost certain that Benigno Leal participated in a ritual claiming ceremony, the traditional act of possession performed when Spanish and Mexican grantees received their land. This ceremony is not preserved for Santa Ana, but it is recorded for the granting of Los Toritos to Máximo Domínguez, immediately after Benigno Leal received Santa Ana. Then, the alcalde of Reynosa stood with the grantee on a surveyed boundary; for Santa Ana, this would have been the eastern border shared with Agostadero del Gato. The alcalde recorded: "I took [the grantee] by the hand, manifesting that I was putting him in possession of the pasture land . . . and [he] performed his patriotic duty . . . to demonstrate his present ownership, he pulled grass, sprinkled water, and walked to and fro . . . and he remained in complete and peaceful possession of the said pastureland." That pastureland also included in its southern acreage a massive forest. There, one hundred years later, Irby Davis and the Rio Grande Valley Nature Club would note the richness of tropical bird species, each with a unique nesting history: in the trees along the river, the shaded thickets of intermittent chaparral, or the water-softened edges of flooded resacas on the terraces. The birders of South Texas began to petition to save this variegated land.

Irby and Anna May Davis conducted both Christmas Bird Counts and several breeding bird censuses for South Texas. Irby's 1940 census on Santa Ana verified nearly two hundred different species, including thirty-four species of nesting birds (observed nests with fledglings or eggs). The heart of that amazing count was the homestead forest that had spread over the site of the Leal ranch: fifteen acres filled with an arresting variety of nests. Still today, visitors may glimpse pendent oriole nests swinging out over water, or rarely, the thatchy, globular, foot-long nest of a rose-throated becard. The acreage also holds cuplike bearded flycatcher nests and the heavy stick nests of red-billed pigeons protecting but a single, pure-white egg. Nests hang thick in the trees, but the understory is important as well: down in the thorny brush, nests of resident olive sparrows tilt lightly, each woven basket of grasses, mosses, and bark sheltering three large eggs. And in the watery resacas, thick with reeds and cattails, the warm wind nudges the bobbing platform nests of pied-billed grebes. Minihabitats continue to receive and nourish migrating birds that fly directly there. With a green canopy floating above the earth of Santa Ana, the thorn forest signals familiar sanctuary to tired, arriving birds. The trees are now threaded with hiking and birding trails, but in size and complexity, this forest is the enduring last of its kind in the world.

To people who walk it, prowling through tunnels of entwined branches and mosses, it feels at times formidable. The impenetrable thickets and dark mats of vines suggest an obscure history, hinting of human struggle and contention. Yet the Santa Ana forest is truly only a remnant, no longer a jungle. Its predators are gone or highly endangered, and the once unbroken canopy often straggles out into piecemeal clearings. In these open patches, enormous gray tree skeletons lie bleaching. If we venture deep into the living trees, though, we can just glimpse the virile, verdant, towering swath of woodland that once enriched the Rio Grande on either side. And still, the birds come, bringing in turn their human admirers. The torch of preservation has been passed to refuge visitors. Through their passion, donations, and desire to learn, they are now the custodians of the forest.[30]

Notes

The Land of Santa Ana

1. See "Refuge Establishment Dates," National Conservation Training Center, US Fish and Wildlife Service, accessed November 29, 2014, http://training.fws.gov/history/ListsRefugeDates.html; for the best overview of the tangled legal history of Mexican grants, see the section "Once Upon a River" in Galen D. Greaser, *New Guide to Spanish and Mexican Land Grants in South Texas* (Austin: Texas General Land Office, 2009); *Titus E. Merriman et al. v. P. E. Blalock et al.*, June 28, 1909, Texas Civil Appeals Reports, vol. 56; for Irby Davis map, see Irby Davis to J. Clark Salyer, July 11, 1940, SANWR, General Correspondence, 1890–1956; information on endangered species appears on the Santa Ana National Wildlife Refuge Web site, http://www.fws.gov/refuge/santa_ana/.
2. For a thorough discussion of the birds of Santa Ana National Wildlife Refuge, see Timothy Brush, *Nesting Birds of a Tropical Frontier: The Lower Rio Grande Valley of Texas* (Kingsville: Texas A&M University Press, 2005); "Abstract of Title to Alamo Tract: The Alamo Land and Sugar Company Subdivision of Porcion Seventy-Two, Los Torritos, Santa Ana, and El Gato Grants in Hidalgo County, Texas" (Edinburg, TX, Hidalgo and Starr Counties Abstract Co., n.d.).
3. This study is particularly indebted to the Frank Cushman Pierce collection at the University of Texas–Pan American, Edinburg, and the Clotilde García collection at Texas A&M University, Corpus Christi. Several individual family histories have also been critically important, especially the Balli family genealogy by Joel Escobar y Sáenz.
4. The phrase "shared experience" is a useful one to define Borderlands approaches; it is also the title of an important book in this study, edited by Mario L. Sánchez, *A Shared Experience: The History, Architecture, and Historic Designations of the Lower Rio Grande Heritage Corridor* (Austin: Los Caminos del Río Heritage Project and the Texas Historical Commission, 1994); see, for instance, Félix D. Almaraz Jr., *The San Antonio Missions and Their System of Land Tenure* (Austin: University of Texas Press, 1989); Keith J. Volanto, *Texas, Cotton, and the New Deal* (College Station: Texas A&M University Press, 2005). See the helpful overview of Spanish regulations for ranchers in the first paragraphs of Armando C. Alonzo, "Hispanic Farmers and Ranchers in the Soil and Water Conservation Movement in South Texas, 1940s to Present," *Agricultural History* 78, no. 2 (Spring 2004): 204. For a study of water rights in the area of El Paso and Mesilla Valley, Mexico, see Douglas R. Littlefield, *Conflict on the Rio Grande: Water and the Law, 1879–1939* (Norman: University of Oklahoma Press, 2008). For northern New Mexico, see José A. Rivera, *Acequia Culture: Water, Land, and Community in the Southwest* (Albuquerque: University of New Mexico Press, 1998). For an especially good analysis of problems arising in a proposed shared borderlands park, see Emily Wakild, "Border Chasm: International Boundary Parks and Mexican Conservation, 1935–1945," *Environmental History* 14 (July 2009).

For land degradation in Mexico, see M. G. Manzano, J. Navar, M. M. Pando, and A. Martínez, "Overgrazing and Desertification in Northern Mexico: Highlights on Northeastern Region," *Annals of Arid Zones* (India) 39, no. 3 (2000). Important exceptions to this are foundational works that do examine the changes in land acquisition and use by Mexican and then Tejano ranchers as well as the social history connected to their changing status: see Armando C. Alonzo, *Tejano Legacy: Rancheros and Settlers in South Texas, 1734–1900* (Albuquerque: University of New Mexico Press, 1998); Arnoldo De León, *The Tejano Community, 1836–1900* (Albuquerque: University of New Mexico Press, 1982); and Kenneth L. Stewart and Arnoldo De León, *Not Room Enough: Mexicans, Anglos, and Socio-Economic Change in Texas, 1850–1900* (Albuquerque: University of New Mexico Press, 1993); see also Daniel D. Arreola, *Tejano South Texas: A Mexican American Cultural Province* (Austin: University of Texas Press, 2002), 9–42, especially "South Texas as an Environmental Region," 11–19.

5. Rosalinda González, "Work and Play on a Border Ranch," in *The Golden Log*, Texas Folklore Society Publication 31, ed. Mody Coggin Boatright (Dallas: Southern Methodist University Press, 1962), 144–45. See Andrés Tijerina and Martha Doty Freeman, *Pharr Reynosa International Bridge: Continued Archeological and Historical Research at El Capote Ranch Community, Hidalgo County, Texas* (Austin: Prewitt and Associates, 1994); Mary Amberson, James A. McAllen, and Margaret H. McAllen, *I Would Rather Sleep in Texas: A History of the Lower Rio Grande Valley and the People of the Santa Anita Land Grant* (Austin: Texas State Historical Association, 2010); Hermina Balli de Chavana, *The History of the Prestigious Balli Family: Story of the First Pioneer Settlers of the Rio Grande Valley* (Austin: Nortex Press, 1989); and Jane Clements Monday and Frances Brannen Vick, *Petra's Legacy: The South Texas Ranching Empire of Petra Vela and Mifflin Kenedy* (Kingsville: Texas A&M University Press, 2007), chap. 1. See, for instance, Sandra Carrizales and Ana Martínez, "Joe Cantú Jr. and Sylvia Cantú García," directed by Dr. Russell Skowronek, University of Texas–Pan American Oral History Project, spring 2010. This interview is part of the UTPA Community History Archaeology Project with Schools (CHAPS), available online at www.utpa.edu/chaps. The most important information to date concerning the Domínguez family is in the endnotes of *I Would Rather Sleep in Texas*, providing evidence that Máximo and Cecilia Domínguez, who were siblings, grew up on Santa Anita Ranch.
6. For an account of the founding of the Rio Grande Valley Nature Club and its goals, see the *Harlingen (TX) Valley Morning Star*, September 2, 1937. "An inviolate sanctuary" is the wording contained in 16 U.S.C. 715d, Migratory Bird Conservation Act of 1929.
7. SANWR, May–August 1944, 2. Of special importance among all accounts of the South Texas land is Jean Louis Berlandier, *Journey to Mexico during the Years 1826 to 1834*, vol. 2, trans. Sheila M. Ohlendorf, Josette M. Bigelow, and Mary M. Standifer (Austin: Texas State Historical Association and Center for Studies in Texas History, University of Texas at Austin, 1980); also important is the *Report of the United States and Mexico Boundary Survey*, vol. 2 (Washington, DC: Department of the Interior, 1859; copy in archives at Texas A&M University, Kingsville).
8. An excellent reproduction of these contrasting photographs can be found in

Brush, *Nesting Birds*; the frequently cited statistic of 95 percent original habitat loss comes from S. Jahrsdoerfer and D. M. Leslie Jr., *Tamaulipan Brushland of the Lower Rio Grande Valley of South Texas: Description, Human Impacts, Management Options*, Biological Report 88 (36), (Washington, DC: US Fish and Wildlife Service, 1988). For the statistic of 91 percent loss in Cameron County, see Thomas A. Tremblay, William A. White, and Jay A. Raney, "Native Woodland Loss during the Mid 1900s in Cameron County, Texas," *Southwestern Naturalist* 50, no. 4 (2005): 481.

9. On Los Toritos, the only pre-1870 ranch community that has come to light is the Sanforth Kidder ranch, occupied as early as 1842. The original grantee, Máximo Domínguez, established no ranch of his own on his land, selling it within the first year. See the Texas General Land Office File for Los Toritos.

Chapter One

1. SANWR, December 31, 1943, 2. Information on white-winged dove history and hunting is from Texas Parks and Wildlife, accessed January 20, 2013, http://www.tpwd.state.tx.us/. For early settler accounts of white-wings, see Dorothy Lee Pope, *Rainbow Era on the Rio Grande* (Brownsville, TX: Springman-King, 1971), especially 134, 172.
2. For early birding societies, see Mark V. Barrow Jr., *A Passion for Birds: American Ornithology after Audubon* (Princeton, NJ: Princeton University Press, 1998), 148; for *A Crisis of Conservation*, see p. 164. For Irby Davis on nest and egg collectors, see Karen Harden McCracken, *The Life History of a Texas Birdwatcher: Connie Hagar of Rockport* (College Station: Texas A&M University Press, 2001), 96. For rose-throated becards, see Brush, *Nesting Birds*, 133; and *Harlingen (TX) Valley Morning Star*, September 2, 1937.
3. Mark Schmitz and Price V. Fishback, "The Distribution of Income in the Great Depression: Preliminary State Estimates," *Journal of Economic History* 43, no. 1 (March 1983): 222. For an excellent overview history of the flow of Mexican farm workers across national borders, including South Texas, in the late 1930s and 1940s, see Kelly Lytle Hernández, "The Crimes and Consequences of Illegal Immigration: A Cross-Border Examination of Operation Wetback, 1943 to 1954," *Western Historical Quarterly* 37, no. 4 (Winter 2006); for Mexican cotton pickers and the Border Patrol, see p. 426. For migrant tent camps, in many parts of Texas, see Yolanda Romero, "Migrant Housing and Labor Camps in Northwest Texas, 1930s–1940s," in *Tejano Epic: Essays in Honor of Félix A. Almaraz, Jr.*, ed. Arnoldo De León (Austin: Texas State Historical Association, 2005); Keith J. Volanto, "Burying White Gold: The AAA Cotton Plow-Up Campaign in Texas," *Southwestern Historical Quarterly* 103, no. 3 (January 2000): 327; Volanto, *Texas, Cotton, and the New Deal*, 4 (see the staggering statistics on cotton sharecroppers, both nonwhite and white, between 1880 and 1959, on p. 7).
4. See L. Irby Davis to J. Clark Salyer, May 8, 1941, SANWR, 1939–44; K. Hernández, "Crimes and Consequences," 424. Although statistics for migrants into South Texas are not uniform, the city of San Antonio reported that in 1932, every train arriving from the east carried 50 to 100 homeless men, and on "big nights" the number could be as high as 250; see Donald W. Whisenhunt, *The Depression in Texas: The Hoover Years* (New York: Garland Publishing, 1983), 118–19. For

a vivid photographic essay of migrant camps in Hidalgo County, see "America from the Great Depression to World War II: Black-and-White Photographs from the FSA-OWI, 1935–1945," Library of Congress Farm Security Administration/ Office of War Information Black-and-White Negatives, accessed December 16, 2014, www.loc.gov/pictures/collection/fsa/; Volanto, "Burying White Gold," 336.

5. Volanto, "Burying White Gold," 348; David Roth, "Texas Hurricane Histories," National Weather Service, Camp Springs, Maryland, 2010, accessed November 29, 2014, http://www.hpc.ncep.noaa.gov/research/txhur.pdf, especially p. 42. See also "The Deadliest, Costliest, and Most Intense United States Tropical Cyclones from 1851 to 2010 (and Other Frequently Requested Hurricane Facts)," NOAA Technical Memorandum NWS NHC-6, accessed November 29, 2014, http://www.nhc.noaa.gov/pdf/nws-nhc-6.pdf.
6. For a thorough discussion of the joint Mexican-US Bracero Program, 1942–1964, see K. Hernández, "Crimes and Consequences." See manager's discussion of conditions on the refuge, SANWR, January–April 1944; Henry Wadsworth Longfellow, *Evangeline, a Tale of Acadie* (Boston: William D. Ticknor, 1847). Little information exists about the Rio Grande Valley Nature Club. Brief mentions in the *Harlingen (TX) Valley Morning Star* report trips, for instance, to the nearby sabal palm forest (see the issue of November 18, 1941); Irby Davis, the first president, was a trained ornithologist who eventually published *A Field Guide to the Birds of Mexico and Central America* (1972). His obituary mentions that he assisted Cornell University researchers in the recording of bird songs and served as a member of the Conservation Committee of the American Ornithologists' Union. See obituary of Louie Irby Davis in the *Lockhart (TX) Post Register*, January 28, 1988. In the late 1930s, the vice president and secretary-treasurer positions in the Rio Grande Valley Nature Club were held by women, Mrs. D. C. Ring and Mrs. F. W. Rompf, both of Alamo, Texas. We have only limited surviving club correspondence in the Santa Ana Record Group of the National Archives. Yet these letters indicate the sense of mission this group certainly had. In another source, Irby Davis is described as being "in the forefront of the movement to save the area." See McCracken, *Life History*, 95.
7. T. E. Fulbright and Fred A. Bryant, "The Wild Horse Desert: Climate and Ecology," in *Ranch Management: Integrating Cattle, Wildlife, and Range*, ed. C. A. Forgason, F. C. Bryant, and P. C. Genho (Kingsville, TX: King Ranch Institute, 2003), 9; NOAA Technical Memorandum NWS NHC-6, 17; L. Irby Davis to [J. Clark] Salyer, May 8, 1941, SANWR, 1939–44, Entry 162, General Correspondence, 1890–1956, Bureau of Biological Survey.
8. James C. Merrill, *Notes on the Ornithology of Southern Texas: Being a List of Birds Observed in the Vicinity of Fort Brown, Texas, from February, 1876 to June, 1878* (Washington, DC: Government Printing Office, 1878), 159; Wayne R. Marion and Raymond J. Fleetwood, "Nesting Ecology of the Plain Chachalaca in South Texas," *Wilson Bulletin* 90, no. 30 (1978): 390–93; SANWR, January–April 1943, 4; John Cassin, *Illustrations of the Birds of California, Texas, Oregon, British and Russian America* (Philadelphia: J. P. Lippincott, 1862); SANWR, May–August, 1950, 4; Austin Paul Smith, "Miscellaneous Bird Notes from the Lower Rio Grande," *Condor* 12 (May 1910): 94. For the chachalaca, see "Chachalacas," Texas Parks and Wildlife, accessed April 3, 2013, www .tpwd.state.tx.us/landwater/land/habitats/southtx_plain/upland_birds/

chachalaca.phtml; Lower Rio Grande Valley and Santa Ana National Wildlife Refuges Interim Comprehensive Management Plan, US Fish and Wildlife Service, Department of the Interior, September 1997, 16 (copy available in Special Collections, University of Texas–Pan American, Edinburg).

9. L. Irby Davis to J. Clark Salyer II, Bureau of Biological Survey, Washington, DC, September 27, 1939, SANWR, 1939–44. For the clearing of the Alamo Tract, see Pope, *Rainbow Era*, 69; J. Clark Salyer II, chief, Division of Wildlife Refuges, to L. Irby Davis, August 9, 1940, SANWR, 1939–44.

10. González, "Work and Play," in Boatright, *Golden Log*, 146; L. Irby Davis to [J. Clark] Salyer, July 11, 1940, SANWR, 1939–44; insect noise recorded in author's field notes, early June 2011, Santa Ana National Wildlife Refuge, Hidalgo County, TX; copy of Breeding Census Report as prepared for *Bird-Lore*'s annual census by L. Irby Davis, enclosed in letter from L. Irby Davis to [J. Clark] Salyer, July 11, 1940, SANWR, 1939–44.

11. For the Davis address on Polk Street in Harlingen, see the 1940 Federal Census. For Anna May Davis, see Harlingen High School yearbooks, 1941–1944. Sarah Sanborne Weaver, "Nature Conditioned Hidalgo," address to the Lower Rio Grande Valley Historical Society, April 24, 1952, later published in *Selections from the Collected Papers of the Lower Rio Grande Valley Historical Society, 1949–1979*, vol. 1 (Harlingen, TX: Lon A. Hill Memorial Library, 1979), 32–33; Eileen Matte, *At the Crossroads: Harlingen's First 100 Years, 1910–2010* (Rio Grande Valley Museum Association), 88–89; McCracken, *Life History*, 95; *Mission (TX) Times*, January 12, 1940. A concise overview of the creation of the 1930s refuges is Mari N. Jensen, "Coming of Age at 100: Renewing the National Wildlife Refuge System," *BioScience* 537, no. 4 (April 2003). Irving Brant, Harold K. Steen, and Alice E. Ingerson, "Adventures in Conservation: Putting It Up to FDR," *Journal of Forest History* 32, no. 1 (January 1981): 41. See "Refuge Establishment Dates," National Conservation Training Center, US Fish and Wildlife Service, accessed November 29, 2014, http://training.fws.gov/history/ListsRefugeDates.html. For the use of duck stamps as funding for refuges, see Jensen, "Coming of Age at 100."

12. "Santa Ana Tract on Rio Grande Is Now Wildlife Refuge Where Many Outstanding Species Located," *Harlingen (TX) Valley Morning Star*, May 26, 1942; Memo No. 46, Procedures, Santa Ana, Texas, J. Clark Salyer II, chief, Division of Wildlife Refuges, to Dr. [Ira N.] Gabrielson, August 21, 1941, SANWR, 1939–44. See Stanley D. Casto, "Economic Uses of Texas Birds," appendix in "The Market Hunting of Texas Birds," *Bulletin of the Texas Ornithological Society* 16, nos. 1 and 2 (1983): 9.

13. Merrill, *Notes on the Ornithology*, 169; Don Delnicki and Eric G. Bolen, "Natural Nest Site Availability for Black-Bellied Whistling Ducks in South Texas," *Southwestern Naturalist* 20, no. 1 (October 10, 1975): 371, 373, 377; SANWR, January–April 1949, 11; Minnie Gilbert, "The Valley's Wildlife Refuges," *La Feria (TX) Border Scope*, June 1949; SANWR, May–August 1949, 2. See "Historical Results by Count," Santa Ana National Wildlife Refuge, Hidalgo County, Texas, National Audubon Society Christmas Bird Count, accessed February 22, 2013, http://netapp.audubon.org/cbcobservation/; L. Irby Davis to [J. Clark] Salyer, May 10, 1941, SANWR, 1939–44; *Land Protection Plan for Lower Rio Grande Valley National Wildlife Refuge: Cameron, Hidalgo, Starr and Willacy Counties,*

Texas, US Fish and Wildlife Service, Region 2, Albuquerque, NM (Austin: Dolph Briscoe Center for American History, University of Texas at Austin, June 1983), 4. For manager's estimate of refuge acreage, see SANWR, January–April 1943, 6. First National Bank of Chicago to Rudolph Dieffenbach, chief of land acquisition, SANWR Correspondence, September 8, 1943.

14. Brush, *Nesting Birds*, 105; *Lower Rio Grande Valley and Santa Ana National Wildlife Refuges Interim Comprehensive Management Plan and Draft Environmental Assessment*, US Fish and Wildlife Service, US Department of the Interior (March 1997), 20 (copy available in Special Collections, University of Texas–Pan American, Edinburg); Gilbert, "Valley's Wildlife Refuges."
15. SANWR, October 5, 1948, 1; SANWR, September 2, 1943, 2; SANWR, September 1, 1948, 1. See Paul Horgan, *Great River: The Rio Grande in North American History* (Hanover, NH: University Press of New England, 1984); and Pat Kelley, *River of Lost Dreams: Navigation on the Rio Grande* (Lincoln: University of Nebraska Press, 1986).

Chapter Two

1. Tiffany Tanya Terneny, "A Re-Evaluation of Late Prehistoric and Archaic Chronology in the Rio Grande Delta of South Texas" (PhD diss., University of Texas at Austin, 2005), 10.
2. *Coahuiltecan* appears as early as 1915; see note 6 below. For the possible origin of the name "Coahuila" from Coahuiltecan Indians, I am indebted to Beatriz de la Garza. For a later overview, see Charles Shaw, *Indian Life in Texas* (Austin, TX: State House Press, 1987), 7–8; Juan Bautista Chapa, *Texas and Northeastern Mexico, 1630–1690*, ed. William A. Foster, trans. Ned F. Brierly (Austin: University of Texas Press, 1997), 99. For the classic overview of South Texas Indian tribes and bands, including their many names and identities, see Martin Salinas, *Indians of the Rio Grande Delta: Their Role in the History of Southern Texas and Northeastern Mexico* (Austin: University of Texas Press, 1990). For the Escandón reports of 1747 and 1757, see Salinas, 28, 38–39. For *Tampacuas*, see Salinas, 62–63. Early attempts to group these diverse Indian languages include John R. Swanton, "Linguistic Position of the Tribes of Southern Texas and Northeastern Mexico," *American Anthropologist* 17, no. 1 (January–March 1915): 17–40. For Indians in canoes, see Salinas, 131.
3. Chapa, *Texas and Northeastern Mexico*, 15; Salinas, *Indians of the Rio Grande*, 29, 128–129; John C. Ewers, "The Influence of Epidemics on the Indian Populations and Customs of Texas," *Plains Anthropologist* 18, no. 60 (May 1973): 107.
4. There are many studies of the founding of Nuevo Santander. For a detailed and thorough account, see Herbert Eugene Bolton, *Texas in the Middle Eighteenth Century* (New York: Russell and Russell, 1962), 292–300; Harriet Denise Joseph, "José de Escandón and the Settlement of South Texas in the Late Colonial Era, 1746–1821," in *Studies in Brownsville and Matamoros History*, ed. Milo Kearney, Anthony Knopp, and Antonio Zavaleta (Brownsville: University of Texas, 1995), 3. For a description of chaparral see Horgan, *Great River*, 711.
5. See the description of flooding at Reinosa Viejo in De Chavana, *History of the Prestigious Balli Family*, 60.

6. Frank W. Blair first identified the Tamaulipan Mezquital in an important 1950 article, "The Biotic Province of Texas," *Texas Journal of Science* 2, no. 1; see also "Southern North America: Southern United States into Northeastern Mexico," World Wildlife Fund, accessed November 28, 2014, http://www.worldwildlife.org/ecoregions/na1312. Sonny Hinojosa (manager of Hidalgo County Irrigation District #2), interview by author, June 28, 2010, Edinburg, TX.
7. James Rowe, "History of the King Ranch," in *King Ranch: 100 Years of Ranching, 1853–1953* (Corpus Christi, TX: Caller-Times, 1953); David A. Edwards, *The History of Texas, or The Emigrant's, Farmer's, and Politician's Guide to the Character, Climate, Soil, and Productivity of That Country, Arranged Geographically from Personal Observation and Experience* (1836, repr., Austin: Texas State Historical Association, 1990), 49, 68 (citations refer to the 1990 edition); V. W. Lehmann, *Forgotten Legions: Sheep in the Rio Grande Plain of Texas* (El Paso: Texas Western Press, 1969), 116.
8. Michael F. Small, Timothy H. Bonner, and John T. Baccus, "Hydrologic Alteration of the Lower Rio Grande Terminus: A Quantitative Assessment," *River Research Applications* 25, no. 3 (2009): 248; see also Jeff B. Breeden et al., "Vegetative Composition of Areas with and without Breeding Red-Billed Pigeons (*Patagioenas flavirostris*) in Texas," *Southwestern Naturalist* 54, no. 1 (March 2009). See reference to this lake as "Perchuga" in *Titus E. Merriman et al. v. P. E. Blalock et al.*, June 28, 1909, Texas Civil Appeals Reports, vol. 56, 601–2. Land agent map showing "Santa Ana Lake" in Pope, *Rainbow Era*, 11. Berlandier, *Journey to Mexico*, 439–40; George Miksch Sutton and Olin Sewall Pettingell Jr., "Birds of the Gómez Farías Region, Southwestern Tamaulipas," *The Auk* 59, no. 1 (January 1942): 12.
9. González, "Work and Play," in Boatright, *Golden Log*, 143. For an excellent overview of the Texas horned lizard, see Scott E. Henke and William Scott Fair, "Management of Texas Horned Lizards," *Wildlife Management Bulletin*, no. 2, Caesar Kleberg Wildlife Research Institute (Kingsville: Texas A&M University, 1998). Conrad Richter first used the phrase "sea of grass" in his 1934 novel of the settling of the American Southwest, *The Sea of Grass* (Cleveland: World Publishing, 1946). For presettlement grasses of South Texas, see overview in "Grasslands," Handbook of Texas Online, Texas State Historical Association, http://www.tshaonline.org/handbook/online/articles/gqg01. See also Frank W. Gould, *The Grasses of Texas* (College Station: Texas A&M University Press, 1975), 316, 353. Raymond J. Fleetwood, "Plants of Santa Ana National Wildlife Refuge," unpublished inventory, Santa Ana National Wildlife Refuge, Bureau of Sport Fisheries and Wildlife, Alamo, Texas, 1973 (copy available in Special Collections, University of Texas–Pan American, Edinburg; for windmill grass species, see p. 17).
10. For evaporation and soil types common near Santa Ana, see F. W. Gould, *Texas Plants: A Checklist and Ecological Summary* (College Station: Texas A&M University, Texas Agricultural Experimental Station), 1969, 12. See Christina Mild, "From Threatened to 'Threatening,'" *The Sabal* 27, no. 5 (May 2010); Fleetwood, "Plants of Santa Ana," 50, and especially map detailing Dicliptera Trail, 14; Wayne R. Marion, "Plain Chachalaca Food Habits in South Texas," *The Auk* 93, no. 2 (April 1976): 377; Alfred Richardson and Ken King, *Plants of Deep South Texas: A Field Guide to the Woody and Flowering Species* (Kingsville: Texas A&M University Press, 2011), 49. As endangered species, see *The Sabal* 3, no. 4

(May 1986); author's field notes on dicliptera along the Arroyo Colorado from January 2011; photographs of dicliptera in photo gallery by Christina Mild.

11. See González, "Work and Play," in Boatright, *Golden Log*, 151; Arthur Brennan, "Some Superstitions of the Mexican Indians," *Folklore* 28, no. 3 (September 1917): 327–28. For boom-and-bust population dynamics, see Fidel Hernández, Fred S. Guthery, and William P. Kuvlesky Jr., "The Legacy of Bobwhite Research in South Texas," *Journal of Wildlife Management* 66, no. 1 (January 2002). Linda Campbell-Kissock, Lytle H. Blankenship, and J. W. Stewart, "Plant and Animal Foods of Bobwhite and Scaled Quail in Southwest Texas," *Southwestern Naturalist* 30, no. 4 (November 1985): 543–53, especially 552. For a good overview of paloverde, see the Lady Bird Johnson Wildflower Center at www.wildflower.org.
12. Margaret Harrison Smith, "The Lower Rio Grande Region in Tamaulipas, Mexico," (PhD diss., University of Texas, 1961), 208. For the drought of 1963, see International Boundary and Water Commission Water Bulletin, no. 23, 1953. For broader discussion of climate, drought, and rainfall patterns, see M. Smith, "Lower Rio Grande Region," 208–225; SANWR, September 2, 1943, 1; SANWR, September 12, 1944, 1. See "General Soil Map, Hidalgo County, Texas," in *Soil Survey of Hidalgo County, Texas* (US Department of Agriculture, Soil Conservation Service), 1925, publ. 1929; see also discussion of Harlingen soil type, 28.
13. Brush, *Nesting Birds*, 26; Kenneth D. Pruitt et al., "Importance of Native Seeds in White-Winged Dove Diets Dominated by Agricultural Grains," *Journal of Wildlife Management* 72, no. 2 (February 2008): 434. See also discussion of white-winged doves' original food sources and their adaptability in Blair O. Wolf and Carlos Martínez del Río, "Use of Saguaro Fruit by White-Winged Doves: Isotopic Evidence of a Tight Ecological Association," *Oecologia* 124 (2000): 536–43; SANWR, May 7, 1944, 2.
14. José Fernando Villaseñor-Gómez, "Habitat Use of Wintering Bird Communities in Sonora, Mexico: The Importance of Riparian Habitats," in *Birds of the US-Mexico Borderlands: Distribution, Ecology, and Conservation*, Studies in Avian Biology, no. 37, ed. Janet M. Ruth, Tim Brush, and David Krueper (Cooper Ornithological Association, September 2008). Villaseñor-Gómez notes that riparian forests "influence the ecological dynamics of adjacent upland habitats" (53). The Jean Louis Berlandier sketch is included in Spencer Baird, "Mammals of the Boundary," in *United States and Mexican Boundary Survey*, vol. 2 (Washington, DC: Department of the Interior, 1859); for Armstrong letter, see Vernon Bailey, "Biological Survey of Texas," *North American Fauna* 25 (October 1905); Scott Nicol, "Broken Promises and Border Walls Push Jaguarundi to the Brink," accessed November 29, 2014, http://notexasborderwall.blogspot.com/2013/01/broken-promises-and-border-walls-push_13.html; Raymond J. Hock, "Southwestern Exotic Felids," *American Midland Naturalist* 15, no. 2 (April 1955): 327.
15. SANWR, January–April 1948, 6. For jaguarundi habitat and Mexican studies, see Cat Specialist Group, "Jaguarundi (*Herpailurus yagouaroundi*)," http://www.catsg.org/index.php?id=93, accessed November 29, 2014. For excellent information on the importance of brush to jaguarundi, see "Jaguarundi," Texas Parks and Wildlife, accessed February 17, 2013, http://www.tpwd.state.tx.us/publications/pwdpubs/media/pwd_bk_w7000_0013_jaguarundi.pdf

16. See *testimonio* proceedings of 1777 surveys of Llano Grande and La Feria grants, discussed in Herbert Davenport and Joseph K. Wells, "The First Europeans in Texas, 1528–1536," *Southwestern Historical Quarterly* 22, no. 3 (January 1919): 218, 221; SANWR, May 6, 1943, 4; Minnie C. Gilbert, "Valley Wildlife: Part II, Children of the Chaparral," in *Gift of the Rio: Story of Texas Tropical Borderland* (Mission, TX: Border Kingdom Press, 1975), 243.
17. See Freerk Molleman et al., "Is Male Puddling Behavior of Tropical Butterflies Targeted at Sodium for Nuptial Gifts or Activity?" *Biological Journal of the Linnean Society* 86, no. 3 (November 2005): 345–61. For butterfly and bird species correlation, see Robert K. Robbins and Paul A. Opler, "Butterfly Diversity and a Preliminary Comparison with Bird and Mammal Diversity," in *Biodiversity II: Understanding and Protecting Our Biological Resources*, ed. Marjorie L. Reaka-Kudla, Don E. Wilson, and Edward O. Wilson (Washington, DC: Joseph Henry Press, 1997).

Chapter Three

1. The narrative of Escandón's successful *entrada* to northern New Spain and his settlement-building years appears in many works. See especially Joseph, "José de Escandón," 3–11; Sánchez, *Shared Experience*, 24–33; Edwin J. Foscue, "Agricultural History of the Lower Rio Grande Valley Region," *Agricultural History* 8, no. 3 (July 1934): 124–37. See Escandón's report in Saldívar, *Ramo de Provincias Internas*, in M. Smith, "Lower Rio Grande Region," 95.
2. See discussion of irrigation technology in Juan Fidel Zorrilla, *Tamaulipas: Fértil planicie entre sierra y laguna. Monografía estatal*, 2nd ed. (Secretaria de Educación Publica, Impreso en México, 1994), 65; Alonzo, *Tejano Legacy*, 36.
3. Sánchez, *Shared Experience*, 27; Salinas, *Indians of the Rio Grande*, 153.
4. Salinas, *Indians of the Rio Grande*, 154. For a detailed overview of the settlement of Reynosa, see Greaser, *New Guide*, 67–79.
5. Foscue, "Agricultural History," 125; Davenport and Wells, "First Europeans in Texas," 210; Berlandier, *Journey to Mexico*, 149–50.
6. Berlandier, *Journey to Mexico*, 351; A. Starker Leopold, *Wildlife of Mexico: The Game Birds and Mammals* (Berkeley: University of California Press, 1959), 342; M. L. Brown, *Firearms in Colonial America: The Impact on History and Technology, 1492–1792* (Washington, DC: Smithsonian Institution Press, 1980), 172–73; Census of Reynosa, July 21, 1750, extracted and compiled from Inspección y Revista de la Reynosa, AGN (Mexico) Provincias Internas, vol. 180, Expediente 2, in Dr. Clotilde P. García Collection, Texas A&M University Archives, Corpus Christi. See map of gun distribution in the New World, including Spanish guns on the northern frontier, in Carl P. Russell, *Guns on the Early Frontiers* (Lincoln: University of Nebraska Press, 1957), 41, 176.
7. John K. Strecker, "The Trade in Deer Skins in Early Texas," *Journal of Mammalogy* 8, no. 2 (May 1927): 108; Elinor G. K. Melville and Bradley Skopyk, "Disease, Ecology, and the Environment," in *The Oxford History of Mexico*, ed. William H. Beezley and Michael C. Meyer (New York: Oxford University Press, 2010), 222.
8. Melville and Skopyk, "Disease, Ecology," 224–27. For ojos de agua as springs, see "Ojo de Agua Cemetery aka San Jose or Abram Cemetery," Hidalgo County His-

torical Commission, accessed December 6, 2014, http://www.cemeteries-of-tx.com/Etx/Hidalgo/Cemetery/Ojo%20de%20Agua.htm

9. Census of Reynosa, July 21, 1750; agricultural census data for Reynosa found in Lehmann, *Forgotten Legions*, 13–14; see Escandón's accounts in M. Smith, "Lower Rio Grande Region," 96; "Provincial Inspection of Nuevo Santander in 1795" by Félix Calleja, in David M. Vigness, "Nuevo Santander in 1795: A Provincial Inspection by Félix Calleja," *Southwestern Historical Quarterly* 75, no. 4 (April 1972): 475.
10. Lehmann, *Forgotten Legions*, 41.
11. C. Wayne Hanselka and Joe C. Paschal, "Brush Utilization on the Rio Grande Plains," *Rangelands* 14, no. 3 (June 1992): 169–70; L. E. Warren et al., "Spanish Goat Diets on Mixed-Brush Rangeland in the South Texas Plains," *Journal of Range Management* 37, no. 4 (July 1984): 340–42.
12. Arnoldo De León, *Mexican Americans in Texas: A Brief History*, 2nd ed. (Wheeling, IL: Harlan Davidson, 1999), 21–22. For trade laws, see Andre F. Sjoberg, "The Bidai Indians of Southeastern Texas," *Southwest Journal of Anthropology* 7, no. 4 (Winter 1951): 394.
13. For accurate wording on jurisdictions and villas, I am indebted to Beatriz de la Garza; Leonardo Andrade, "Upper Valley's Main Mexican Neighborhood Dates to Colonial Days," *McAllen (TX) Evening Monitor*, November 21, 1996; Sánchez, *Shared Experience*, 32.
14. For discussion of the growth of early ranch communities, see John J. Leffler, *Refuge on the Rio Grande: A Regional History of Bentsen-Rio Grande Valley State Park* (Texas Parks and Wildlife Department, 2013). For information on early Peñitas, see text of Texas Historical Marker, accessed November 30, 2014, http://atlas.thc.state.tx.us/shell-kword.htm.
15. "Provincial Inspection of Nuevo Santander in 1795" by Félix Calleja, in Vigness, "Nuevo Santander in 1795," 472; for Reynosa and the salt trade, see John Suval, "Region's Rich History Still Visible Today," *McAllen (TX) Evening Monitor*, August 23, 1998; Zorrilla, *Tamaulipas*, 68.
16. Stanley D. Casto, "Perceptions of Vultures by the Indians and Early Texans," *Bulletin of the Texas Ornithological Society* 21, nos. 1 and 2 (1988): 3.
17. For a photograph of vultures, see SANWR, September 1, 1948; SANWR, October 4, 1950, 6; SANWR, October 5, 1948, 7.
18. For the best discussion of the kinds of grants awarded in Hidalgo County, see Alonzo, *Tejano Legacy*, 55–58; Alonzo, *Tejano Legacy*, 39; Leffler, *Refuge on the Rio Grande*, 9–12; see discussion of the Petition of 1763 in "Reynosa Is 216 Years Old," *McAllen (TX) Valley Town Crier*, August 22, 1979. Information for this article taken from John R. Peavey, *Echoes from the Rio Grande* (McAllen, TX: privately printed, 1963).
19. Minnie C. Gilbert, "Valley Wildlife: Part I, Chaparral County," in *Gift of the Rio: Story of Texas Tropical Borderland*, photo opposite p. 229; goats are seasonally adaptive and move to autumn mast easily. See Hanselka and Paschal, "Brush Utilization," 169–70; SANWR, January–April 1944, 4; for high preference for ebony in fencing, see Eduardo C. Estrada et al., "Diversity and Distributional Patterns of Legumes in Southern Nuevo León, Mexico," *Southwestern Naturalist* 51, no. 1 (March 2006). See also Tejano mesquite and "large log" fencing on

ranches in Andrés Sáenz, *Early Tejano Ranching: Daily Life at Ranchos San José and El Fresnillo* (College Station: Texas A&M University Press, 2001), 8.

20. Mesquite has been described as a "dramatic increaser." See Gould, *Grasses of Texas*, 4; also Gould, *Texas Plants*, 12.
21. Timothy E. Fulbright and Fred A. Bryant, *The Last Great Habitat*, Special Publication No. 1 of the Caesar Kleburg Wildlife Research Institute (Kingsville: Texas A&M University Press, 2002; repr., 2004), 5; see the list of birds and mammals relishing granjeno in Richard B. Taylor, Jimmy Rutledge, and Joe G. Herrera, *A Field Guide to Common South Texas Shrubs* (Austin: University of Texas at Austin, Texas Parks and Wildlife Press, 1997), 41; V. Havard, "Report on the Flora of Western and Southern Texas," *Proceedings of the United States National Museum* 8, no. 29 (September 23, 1885): 507; Chris Hathcock (acting director, Santa Ana National Wildlife Refuge), personal communication, July 28, 2010.
22. John Phillip Santos, *Places Left Unfinished at the Time of Creation* (New York: Penguin Books, 1999), 113; for aerial photograph, see SANWR, February–April 1947.

Chapter Four

1. Florence Johnson Scott, *Historical Heritage of the Lower Rio Grande* (1937; repr., Rio Grande City, TX: La Retama Press, 1965), 83, 79; for the burning of Nuevo León forests, see Conan T. Wood, "Cerralvo as the Mother City of the Lower Rio Grande Valley," talk presented to the Lower Rio Grande Valley Historical Society, October 28, 1964, published in *Selections from the Collected Papers of the Lower Rio Grande Valley Historical Society, 1949–1979*, vol. 1 (Harlingen, TX: Lon A. Hill Memorial Library, 1979), 13.
2. Eugene George, *Lost Architecture of the Rio Grande Borderlands* (College Station: Texas A&M University Press, 2008), 32; see also Andrés Tijerina, *Tejano Empire: Life on the South Texas Ranchos* (College Station: Texas A&M University Press), 1998, 32; George, *Lost Architecture*, 26; see also Tijerina, *Tejano Empire*, 32: "Tejanos systematically transplanted construction grasses."
3. Tijerina, *Tejano Empire*, 33, 34; Laurence A. Walker, "Wood from Five Forests of Texas," *Texas Natural History*, Summer 1985, 15; Beth A. Middleton, "Effects of Hurricane Katrina on Tree Regeneration in *Taxodium distichum* of the Gulf Coast," *Wetlands* 29, no. 1 (March 2009): 135, 140; Paul W. Cox and Patty Leslie, *Texas Trees: A Friendly Guide* (San Antonio: Corona, 1993), 4–5; Matt Warnock Turner, *Remarkable Plants of Texas: Uncommon Accounts of Our Common Natives* (Austin: University of Texas Press, 2009), 104.
4. Tijerina, *Tejano Empire*, 69; Havard, "Report on the Flora," 475.
5. George, *Lost Architecture*, 31.
6. Ibid., 23; Tijerina, *Tejano Empire*, 36, 26. Desert willow, *flor de mimbres*, withstands high heat and aridity. The fragrant blooms appear on new wood growth, so that frequent pruning produces more blossoms. See "Desert Willow, Flowering Willow, Willowleaf Catalpa, Desert Catalpa, Flor de Mimbre, Mimbre, Bow Willow," Aggie Horticulture, Texas A&M University, accessed November 30, 2014, https://aggie-horticulture.tamu.edu/ornamentals/natives/chilopsislinearis.htm

7. See the excellent discussion of outside spaces in Tijerina, *Tejano Empire*, 28. The term "primitive" appears in many descriptions of early settler homes and, regrettably, resurfaces in late-twentieth-century histories as well; Berlandier, *Journey to Mexico*, 428.
8. Bernard Doyon, *The Cavalry of Christ on the Rio Grande* (Milwaukee, WI: Bruce Press, 1956), 129; see also Maurine Duncan, "The Oblate Trail," in *Gift of the Rio: Story of Texas Tropical Borderland* (Mission, TX: Border Kingdom Press, 1975); José M. Peña, *Inherit the Dust from the Four Winds of Revilla: A 250-Year Historical Perspective with Emphasis on Ancient Guerrero, Its People and Its Land Grants* (Bloomington, IN: Xlibris, 2006), 85; for "muskit grass," see Edwards, *History of Texas*, 67; for beauty of mesquite, see Rogelia O. García, *Dolores, Revilla, and Laredo (Three Sister Settlements)* (Waco, TX: privately printed, 1970), 44.
9. See Ann Reed Washington, "Ranches in the Rio Grande Valley of Texas," *La Porcione* 1, no. 2 (December 1986).
10. "Reynosa Census of 1855," *La Porcione* 2, no. 1 (Spring 1987): 59; see discussion of Indians in families in Patricia Galindo, "*Con un Pie en Cado Lado*: Ethnicities and the Archaeology of Spanish Colonial Ranching Communities along the Lower Rio Grande Valley" (PhD diss., University of Texas at Austin, 2003), 55–56 (*con un pie en cado lado* translates to "with a foot on each side of the river"); for Borrego Indians, see Galindo, 54; Guillermo Garmendía Leal, *Origen de los Fundadores de Cadereyta (1635–1763)* (Monterrey, Nuevo León: Derechos Reservados, 1993), 76; Doyon, *Cavalry of Christ*, 133; for Leal children, see folder, "Bautismos de Reynosa," Libro No. 1 A-R, 1800–1912, Frank Cushman Pierce Genealogical Collection, Special Collections, University of Texas–Pan American, Edinburg; for Mexican colonization laws, see the excellent overview in Leroy P. Graf, "Colonization Projects in Texas South of the Nueces, 1820–1845," *Southwestern Historical Quarterly* 50, no. 4 (April 1947), especially p. 437 and note 11.
11. For original grants, see "Abstract of Title to Alamo Tract"; for history of the Balli family, see "Balli Ranch Cemetery," Hidalgo County, Cemeteries of Texas, Hidalgo County Historical Society, accessed September 1, 2012, http://www.cemeteries-of-tx.com/Etx/Hidalgo/Cemetery/balliranch.htm; *Titus E. Merriman et al. v. P. E. Blalock et al.*, June 28, 1909, Texas Civil Appeals Reports, vol. 56, 554; see also Joel René Escobar y Sáenz, *Balli Family History (La Barreta and Padre Island Branches)* (McAllen,TX: privately printed, 2008) (copy available at Corpus Christi Public Library, Corpus Christi, TX); Clotilde P. García, "Rosa María Hinojosa De Balli (1752–1803)" and "Cavazos Family Tree," Dr. Clotilde P. García Genealogical Collection, Camargo (27), Texas A&M University, Corpus Christi; for demographic data on Laredo, see Gilberto Miguel Hinojosa, *A Borderlands Town in Transition: Laredo, 1755–1870* (College Station: Texas A&M University Press,1983), 34–35; for Captain José María Balli, see Escobar y Saenz; for sale of El Gato land to Francisco Balli, see *Titus E. Merriman et al. v. P. E. Blalock et al.*; for Concepción and Tomás, see Federal Census of 1880, Hidalgo County, Enumeration District 80; for Domínguez family, see "Bautismos de Reynosa," Frank Cushman Pierce Genealogical Collection; see also Amberson, McAllen, and McAllen, *I Would Rather Sleep in Texas*, 563n81;

for Gómez grant, see "Santa Anita Cemetery," Hidalgo County, Cemeteries of Texas, Hidalgo County Historical Commission, accessed October 10, 2013, www.cemeteries-of-tx.com/Etx/Hidalgo/Cemetery/santaanita.htm; Federal Census of 1870, Precinct 1, Hidalgo County, Texas.

12. For location of Leal ranch house, see William L. MacWhorter and Frances W. Isbell, application for a Texas Historical Marker, Hidalgo County Historical Commission (McAllen, Texas, n.d.) (copy available at Weslaco Public Library, Weslaco, Texas), 1 ; this map reproduced in MacWhorter and Isbell, 10; 1911 International Boundary Survey map, Special Collections, University of Texas–Pan American, Edinburg; see the connection between the family cemetery and the main house in Tijerina, *Tejano Empire*, 22; for ranch locations, see Leroy P. Graf, "The Economic History of the Lower Rio Grande Valley, 1820–1875" (PhD diss., Harvard University, 1942), 436; see also Willard B. Robinson, "Colonial Ranch Architecture in the Spanish-Mexican Tradition," *Southwestern Historical Quarterly* 83, no. 2 (October 1979): 129; see map in Fleetwood, "Plants of Santa Ana," 14.
13. Texas Forest Service, *Famous Trees of Texas*, 1st ed. (College Station: Texas A&M University, 1970); Pete Smith (Big Tree Registry coordinator, Texas Forest Service), e-mail message to author, September 21, 2011; see also "History of Old Cemetery at Bird Sanctuary Sought," *Harlingen (TX) Valley Morning Star*, October 28, 1970; see also Bryan Robinson, "Chachalaca Trail Reveals Valley Nature at Its Very Best," *Harlingen (TX) Valley Morning Star*, October 25, 1975; SANWR, January–April 1949, 8; for photograph of the Big Ebony, see SANWR, January–April 1950.
14. Estrada et al., "Diversity and Distributional Patterns," 1; see "Texas Ebony," Arizona State University, accessed June 2011, http://www.public.asu.edu/~camartin/plants/Plant%20html%20files/ebenopsisebano.html; see excellent, detailed discussion of Texas ebony in Mary Irish, *Trees and Shrubs for the Southwest: Woody Plants for Arid Gardens* (Portland, OR: Timber Press, 2006); Cox and Leslie, *Texas Trees*, 258–59.
15. Cox and Leslie, *Texas Trees*, 259; for ebony and lightning, see John G. Bourke, "Medicine, Customs, and Superstitions of the Rio Grande," *Journal of American Folklore* 7, no. 25 (April–June 1894): 130; Nick Reid, Jorge Marroquín, and Peter Beyer-Munzel, "Utilization of Shrubs and Trees for Browse, Fuelwood and Timber in the Tamaulipan Thornscrub, Northeastern Mexico," *Forest Ecology and Management* 36 (1991): 74.
16. For accounts of the Balli family's flight to Reynosa to escape Indians, see "Balli Ranch Cemetery History," Hidalgo County, Cemeteries of Texas, Hidalgo County Historical Society, accessed July 2011, www.cemeteries-of-tx.com/Etx/Hidalgo/Cemetery/balliranch.htm; for Hispanic names for plants, see Fleetwood, "Plants of Santa Ana," for tepeguaje and canopy, see Chris Best, Santa Ana Wildlife Refuge ecologist, cited in Russell D. Butcher, *America's National Wildlife Refuges: A Complete Guide* (Lanham, MD: Rowman and Littlefield, 2008), 258; Máximo Martínez, *Las plantas medicinales de México*, 5th ed. (Mexico City: Edicíon Botas, 1969); see also "Guayacan," Texas Beyond History, accessed June 2011, http://www.texasbeyondhistory.net/ethnobot/images/guayacan.html

17. SANWR, May–August 1949, 4; SANWR, January–April 1949, 3; for Nicolás Garza, see Scott, *Historical Heritage*, 31.
18. For a comprehensive examination of natural foods of the Rio Grande Valley, see John G. Bourke, "The Folk Foods of the Rio Grande Valley and of Northern Mexico," *Journal of American Folklore* 8, no. 28 (January–March 1895); for Spanish dagger, see p. 48; Santos, *Places Left Unfinished*, 60; for cenizo leaves, see Pope, *Rainbow Era*, 136.
19. See discussion of anacua's importance on ranches in Tijerina, *Tejano Empire*, 35; Havard, "Report on the Flora," 510.
20. Robinson, "Colonial Ranch Architecture," 139; for fur exports, see Graf, "Economic History," table 6: "Exports from Matamoros, 1825–1828"; Graf, "Economic History," table 11: "Value of Exports from Camargo to the United States, 1874, 1877–1878"; for hunting on the Esperanza Ranch in the late nineteenth century, see González, "Work and Play," in Boatright, *Golden Log*, 144; see A. Starker Leopold, *Wildlife of Mexico*, 69; Tijerina, *Tejano Empire*, 60.
21. Federal Census of 1850, Cameron, Starr, and Webb Counties; Tijerina and Freeman, "History of El Capote," 26.
22. For Estéfana Garza Guzmán identified as being from El Capote Ranch, see "Pechuga Ranch Cemetery," Hidalgo County, Cemeteries of Texas, Hidalgo County Historical Society, accessed February 17, 2013, http://www.cemeteries-of-tx.com/Etx/Hidalgo/Cemetery/pechuga.htm. The possibility that Estéfana Guzmán (daughter of Santiago Guzmán) did live as a child on El Capote is noteworthy, however, since the eastern edge of El Capote, on Porción 70, lay only four miles west of La Pechuga Ranch, where Estéfana spent the last fifteen years of her life. Marcos Guzmán, Estéfana's brother, had transferred 112 acres from old Porción 70 to Estéfana's husband, Julio, by 1882. Hidalgo County Tax Rolls record Julio Guzmán's increased holdings in 1882; see "The Brickmaking Industry in the Lower Rio Grande Valley," *Heritage* 13, no. 1 (Winter 1995), accessed June 2011, http://texashistory.unt.edu/ark:/67531/metapth45408/m1/23/?q=brickmaking industry; Scott Cook, *Mexican Brick Culture in the Building of Texas, 1800s–1980s* (College Station: Texas A&M University, 1998), 33; see this reference from Chatfield, 1893, in Cook, *Mexican Brick Culture*, 69; Cook, *Mexican Brick Culture*, 37; see also Tijerina and Freeman, "History of El Capote," 114.
23. For mesquite and numbers of bricks, see Tijerina and Freeman, "History of El Capote," 117. See especially the photograph of mesquite being unloaded at a 1995 kiln in Cook, *Mexican Brick Culture*, 49.
24. Cook, *Mexican Brick Culture*, 20; see also his excellent discussion of the appeal of handmade bricks, 248; MacWhorter and Isbell, application for a Texas Historical Marker, Santa Ana.
25. Washington, "Ranches in the Rio Grande," 191; see the excellent discussion of these implements and food preparation in Emilia Schunior Ramírez, *Ranch Life in Hidalgo County after 1850* (Edinburg, TX: New Santander Press, 1971), 6–9; I am grateful to Beatriz de la Garza for the mention of *molcajete* use in grinding herbs and spices; Robinson, "Colonial Ranch Architecture," 13; Joe S. Graham, *El Rancho in South Texas: Continuity and Change from 1750* (Kingsville: Texas A&M University, University of North Texas Press, 1994), 26.

26. Ramírez, *Ranch Life in Hidalgo County*, 9; for female curanderas, see "Tia Joséfa, the *Curandera*," in A. Sáenz, *Early Tejano Ranching*; "The Power of Don Pedrito," *San Antonio Express Magazine*, February 26, 1993; for *gordo lobo*, see Elsie Clews Parsons, "Curanderos in Oaxaca, Mexico," *Scientific Monthly* 32, no. 1 (January 1931): 64; for heart of huisache, see Sarah Sanborne Weaver, "Nature Conditioned Hidalgo," address to Lower Rio Grande Valley Historical Society, Harlingen, TX, April 24, 1952; see this paper in *Selections from the Collected Papers of the Lower Rio Grande Valley Historical Society, 1949–1979*, vol. 1 (Harlingen: Lon A. Hill Memorial Library, 1979), 32–33; see also Eliseo Torres, *The Folk Healer: The Mexican-American Tradition of Curanderismo* and *Green Medicine* (Zurich, Switzerland: Nieves Press, 1984); "Curanderos Help Bridge Gap in Modern Medicine," *Harlingen (TX) Valley Evening Monitor*, September 27, 1992; for parteras, see "Curanderismo—An Optional Health Care System," script for slide presentation, University of Texas–Pan American Press, n.d. (copy at McAllen Public Library), 39, 48; for an authoritative and comprehensive study of Hispanic women along the southern Rio Grande, see Teresa Palomo Acosta and Ruthe Winegarten, *Las Tejanas: 300 Years of History*, Jack and Doris Smothers Series in Texas History, Life, and Culture (Austin: University of Texas Press, 2003); for women as early curanderas and midwives, see p. 26.
27. Wallace Hawkins, *El Sal del Rey* (Austin: Texas State Historical Association, 1947), 1794 surveyor map of San Salvador del Tule; for a vivid overview of the historical presence of dangerous animals and snakes, see Gilbert, "Valley Wildlife, Part II."
28. Graf, "Economic History," 455, 457; for Indian raids and the moon, see J. W. Wilbarger, *Indian Depredations in Texas* (Austin, TX: Hutchins Printing House, 1889), 661.
29. Lena Clara Koch, "The Federal Indian Policy in Texas, 1845–1860," *Southwestern Historical Quarterly* 28, no. 3 (January 1925): 224, 232; see this report in Anna Muckleroy, "The Indian Policy of the Republic of Texas, 1," *Southwestern Historical Quarterly* 25, no. 4, (April 1922): 235.
30. "Balli Ranch Cemetery," Hidalgo County, Cemeteries of Texas, Hidalgo County Historical Society; accessed July 2011, www.cemeteries-of-tx.com/Etx/Hidalgo/Cemetery/balliranch.htm; *Recuerdos: Escrito para las familias de los Cavazos/Cárdenas* (n.p., n.d., copy in Corpus Christi Public Library, Corpus Christi, TX), 7; Graf, "Economic History," 436; David M. Vigness, "Indian Raids on the Lower Rio Grande, 1836–1837," *Southwestern Historical Quarterly* 59, no. 1 (July 1955): 16–18.
31. Vigness, "Indian Raids," 19; for an excellent overview of early Spanish-language newspapers in Texas, see "Spanish-Language Newspapers," Texas State Historical Association, accessed June 26, 2013, www.tshaonline.org/handbook/online/articles/ees18
32. Wilbarger, *Indian Depredations*, 224; the story of Benigno Leal's death by Indian ambush is reported in MacWhorter and Isbell, application for a Texas Historical Marker; for the *defunción* of Benigno Leal, June 5, 1861, in Archivo General del Registro del Estado de Tamaulipas [Tamaulipas Civil Registry State Archives], see images of "México, Tamaulipas, Civil Registration, 1800–2002," FamilySearch, Church of Jesus Christ of Latter-Day Saints, accessed Novem-

ber 30, 2014, https://familysearch.org/search/collection/1916237; Wilbarger, *Indian Depredations,* 650–51. An alternative explanation for Benigno Leal's death at the hands of Indians is possible. In 1859, during the Cortina War, eleven warriors of the Tampacuas (a tribe living near Reynosa) joined Cortina, and their chieftain was killed at the Battle of La Bolsa in 1860. Rancho La Bolsa (south of the Hidalgo and Cameron County line) remained a gathering point in Mexico for a small group of Cortina followers (Cortinistas) who raided into Hidalgo County, killing cattle and "depredating in various ways" in the year of the grantee's death, 1861. The use of the phrase "killed by an Indian" in reference to Benigno remains undocumented and is entirely an oral tradition. For Cortinistas, see Jerry Thompson, *Cortina: Defending the Mexican Name in Texas* (College Station: Texas A&M University Press, 2007), 55, 83, 102.

33. Wilbarger, *Indian Depredations*, 556; Hidalgo County Tax Rolls, 1852–1905, available in archives at University of Texas–Pan American, Edinburg.
34. Cameron County Tax Rolls, 1848 and 1849, available at University of Texas–Pan American, Edinburg; SANWR, January–April, 1948, 2; see George B. Sennett and Elliott Coues, *Further Notes on the Ornithology of the Lower Rio Grande of Texas: Further Observations Made during the Spring of 1878* (Washington, DC: Department of the Interior, US Geological and Geographical Survey of the Territories, 1878); hooded orioles in photo gallery painted by John Cassin, *Illustrations of the Birds of California*, plate 8.

Chapter Five

1. Stephen A. Carney, *Guns along the Rio Grande: Palo Alto and Resaca de la Palma* (Washington, DC: US Center for Military History, 2006), 18 (copy available at Palo Alto National Battlefield Site and online at http://www.history.army.mil/catalog/pubs/73/73-2.html); Horgan, *Great River*, 711; see journal entry for December 12, 1846, in Graham A. Barringer, "The Mexican War Journal of Henry S. Lane," *Indiana Magazine of History* 53, no. 4 (December 1957).
2. Horgan, *Great River*, 711. Hugh Davenport gives the name of General Taylor's steamboat as the *Corvette* in "Notes on Steamboating on the Rio Grande," *Southwestern Historical Quarterly* 49, no. 2 (October 1945); Horgan, *Great River*, 712; R*eport of the United States and Mexico Boundary Survey*, 1859, vol. 2, pp. 7, 22, 24.
3. Jerome E. Petsche, T*he Steamboat Bertrand: History, Excavation, and Architecture* (Washington, DC: US Department of the Interior, National Park Service, 1974), 86; Horgan, *Great River*, 713.
4. "Jackson Ranch Church Founded in 1857," *Mid-Valley News Tourist Edition*, n.d., 18; SANWR, May–August 1948, 1; Jennifer Owen-White (manager of Santa Ana National Wildlife Refuge), interview by author, January 11, 2011, Santa Ana National Wildlife Refuge, Alamo, TX.
5. SANWR, September–December 1950, 1; Charles David Castillo, "Effects of Artificial Flooding on the Vegetation and Avifauna of Riparian Woodlands at Santa Ana National Wildlife Refuge, Hidalgo County, Texas" (master's thesis, University of Texas–Pan American, 1997), 26–28.
6. Castillo, "Effects of Artificial Flooding," 30, 41.

7. For the flooding on Santa Ana, see SANWR Narrative Report, September–December 1944, 1; Caleb Coker, ed., *The News from Brownsville: Helen Chapman's Letters from the Texas Military Frontier, 1848–1852* (Austin: Barker Texas History Center, Texas State Historical Association, 1992), 143–44; see, for instance, "Zacatal Ranch Cemetery," Hidalgo County, Cemeteries of Texas, Hidalgo County Historical Commission, http://cemeteries-of-tx.com/Etx/Hidalgo/Cemetery/Zacatal.htm; Hugh Davenport, "Notes on Steamboating," 289; for the incident involving the Comanches, see "Important News from the Rio Grande," *New York Times*, June 10, 1852; Ann Perry, "Studying Streambanks Reveals Their Weaknesses and Strengths," *Agricultural Research*, February 2011, 21.
8. Dixie L. Jones, "Old Military Road," Handbook of Texas Online, Texas State Historical Association, accessed December 7, 2014, http://www.tshaonline.org/handbook/online/articles/exo02
9. Berlandier, *Journey to Mexico*, 309; Walter Prescott Webb, *The Texas Rangers: A Century of Frontier Defense* (Austin: University of Texas, 1965), 98, 95; Horgan, *Great River*, 795–96; Michael L. Collins, *Texas Devils: Rangers and Regulars on the Lower Rio Grande, 1846–1861* (Norman: University of Oklahoma Press, 2008), 70, 73.
10. Graf, "Economic History," 452–54; Dan Flores, "Bringing Home All the Pretty Horses: The Horse Trade and the Early American West: 1775–1825," *Montana: The Magazine of Western History* 58, no. 2 (Summer 2008): 13–14.
11. Juan N. Almonte, "Statistical Report on Texas (1835)," trans. C. E. Castañeda, *Southwestern Historical Quarterly* 28, no. 3 (January 1925): 191; see Brian Robertson, *Wild Horse Desert: The Heritage of South Texas* (Edinburg, TX: New Santander Press, 1985); Flores, "Bringing Home," 18, 13.
12. Ernest Thompson Seton, *Lives of Game Animals*, vol. 1 (Boston: Charles T. Branford, 1953), 23; Berlandier, *Journey to Mexico*, 451; see this statement about destruction of horses and asses by Don Félix D'Azara in many sources; for instance, it is mentioned in R. S. Huidekoper, *The Cat: a Guide to the Classification and Varieties of Cats and a Short Treatise upon Their Care, Diseases, and Treatment* (New York: D. Appleton, 1895); Baird, "Mammals of the Boundary," 6; for jaguar bites, see Hugh Craig, *The Animal Kingdom, Based upon the Writings of Audubon, Wallace, Brehm, Wood, and Others*, vol. 1 (New York: Johnson and Bailey, 1897), 199.
13. Dale Weniger, *The Explorers' Texas: The Animals They Found*, vol. 2 (Austin, TX: Eakin Press, 1997), 81; see Rafael Hoogesteijn, *Manual on the Problem of Depredation Caused by Jaguars and Pumas on Cattle Ranches* (Tikal, Guatemala: Apure Ranches, Prohesa, Jaguar Advisory Council, Wildlife Conservation Society, and Cat Specialist Group, 2001), especially p. 16; Baird, "Mammals of the Boundary," 7.
14. Seton, *Lives of Game Animals*, 17, 24; Graf, "Economic History," table 6: "Exports from Matamoros, 1825–1828."
15. Sánchez, *Shared Experience*, 41, 196; for an excellent discussion of the value of horses to Comanches, see the section "Some Loved Their Horses More Than Their Wives" in James F. Brooks, *Captives and Cousins: Slavery, Kinship, and Community in the Southwest Borderlands* (Chapel Hill: University of North Carolina Press, 2002), 174–80; Berlandier, *Journey to Mexico*, 451.

16. Collins, *Texas Devils*, 191; Elizabeth Davis (DVM, PhD, DACVIM, associate professor and section head, Equine Medicine and Surgery, Kansas State University, Manhattan, Kansas), personal communication, February 19, 2013; for grazing needs, young horses, see L. J. Krysl et al., "Horses and Cattle Grazing in the Wyoming Red Desert: Food Habits and Dietary Overlap," *Journal of Range Management* 37, no. 1 (January 1984): especially 74–75; for grazing competition, see Patricia Evans and Scott McKendrick, "Equine Nutrition: Forages," Agricultural Extension, Utah State University, *Equine*, May 2006; Krysl et al., 74–75.
17. For a clear, effective overview of these wars, see Jerry A. Thompson, "Historical Survey, Part II," in Sánchez, *Shared Experience; Shared Experience* puts the number of men under General Santa Ana at six thousand (34). An official breakdown of the Mexican Army suggests a lesser number. See "Army of the Republic of Mexico Present in Bexar, March 6, 1836," Heart of San Antonio, accessed March 17, 2013, http://hotx.com/alamo/mexarmy.html; *Shared Experience*, 35; Hidalgo County Tax Rolls, 1852–1905.
18. Hidalgo County Tax Rolls, 1852–1905; census taker handwriting is problematic for the entry for horses. See Agricultural Census of 1860 (Schedule 4), Hidalgo County, Texas; Agricultural Census of 1870 (Schedule 2), Hidalgo County, Texas; for "muskit grass," see chapter 4 of this volume; Louis L'Amour, *The Man from Broken Hills* (New York: Bantam Books, 1975), 1; for equine digestion of mesquite seeds, see C. E. Fisher et al., "Control of Mesquite on Grazing Lands," Bulletin 935 (College Station: Texas Agricultural Experiment Station, 1959); D. N. Cole, "Experiments in Trampling of Vegetation. II. Predictions of Resistance and Resilience." *Journal of Agricultural Economics* 32 (1995): 215–24; D. Dale and T. Weaver, "Trampling Effects of Vegetation of the Trail Corridors of North Rocky Mountain Forests," *Journal of Applied Ecology* 11, no. 2 (August 1974); Erik Beaver, "Management Implications of the Ecology of Free-Roaming Horses in Semi-Arid Ecosystems of the Western United States," *Wildlife Society Bulletin* 31, no. 3 (Autumn 2003); Berlandier, *Journey to Mexico*, 432.
19. Amberson, McAllen, and McAllen, *I Would Rather Sleep in Texas*, 38; see this coat of arms in Karen Gerhardt and Rod Santa Ana III, *Images of America: Hidalgo County, Texas* (Chicago: Arcadia, 2000), 13; Report of Commissioners, as cited in Galen D. Greaser and Jesús F. de la Teja, "Quieting Title to Spanish and Mexican Land Grants in the Trans-Nueces: The Bourland and Miller Commission, 1850–1852," *Southwestern Historical Quarterly* 95, no. 4 (April 1992): 449. See also the detailed discussion of Bourland and Miller in Alonzo, *Tejano Legacy*, 152–59; for the best overview of the complex Bourland and Miller investigation, see Greaser and de la Teja, "Quieting Title."
20. Greaser and de la Teja, "Quieting Title," 450; Horgan, *Great River*, 789; Federal Census of 1850; Doyon, Cavalry of Christ, 124; Greaser, *New Guide to Spanish and Mexican Land Grants in South Texas* (Austin: Texas General Land Office, 2009), #190, Leal, Benigno. "Santa Ana," 9,883.16 acres, Hidalgo County; Abstract H-18.
21. As Galen Greaser noted in *New Guide to Spanish and Mexican Land Grants in South Texas*, there is no title for Santa Ana in the Texas GLO file; the Santa Ana and El Gato tax receipts are in the file, however; for Adolphus Glavecke, see Jerry Thompson, *Cortina: Defending the Mexican Name in Texas* (College Station: Texas A&M University Press, 2007), 27; for Domínguez records, see "Bau-

tismos de Reynosa, Libro No. 1 A-R, 1800–1912," Frank Cushman Pierce Genealogical Collection, University of Texas–Pan American, Edinburg; Federal Census of 1850; Doyon, *Cavalry of Christ*, 124; Greaser, *New Guide to Spanish and Mexican Land Grants*; for lawsuit mentioning Los Toritos, see *Strong v. Delhi-Taylor Oil Corporation*, 405 SW 2d 351 (Texas Court of Civil Appeals, 13th District, 1966); for sale of Los Toritos, see the seal and bill of sale for 1838 and 1839 in the Texas GLO file for Los Toritos; for Kidder livestock, see Hidalgo and Cameron County Tax Rolls; 1852 Boundary Survey map in *Report of the United States and Mexico Boundary Survey*, vol. 2; for Cecilia Domínguez's connection to Máximo Domínguez, see Amberson, McAllen, and McAllen, *I Would Rather Sleep in Texas*, 563n81; for Cecilia's connection to Matamoros, see p. 67; for Cecilia Domínguez's marriage record, see *Matamoros Church Marriage Records*, 1801–1848 (Corpus Christi: Spanish-American Genealogical Association, 1995) (copy in Special Collections, University of Texas–Pan American, Edinburg); for payment of taxes on El Gato, see tax receipt of September 13, 1850, in Texas GLO file for Santa Ana. Lack of documentary evidence for this period is partly due to a fire that conveniently destroyed the deeds acquired by Basse and Hord in 1852. For notes about Cameron County deeds, stating that volumes "containing recorded deeds from 14 August 1850 to 6 February 1851 were destroyed by fire in 1854," see "Cameron County Records," Texas State Library and Archives Commission, accessed November 30, 2014, https://www.tsl.texas.gov/arc/local/cameron.html

22. For Merriman as tax collector at Hidalgo/Edinburg, see GLO file, Santa Ana, tax receipt for 1852; Robertson, *Wild Horse Desert*, 87; Amberson, McAllen, and McAllen, *I Would Rather Sleep in Texas*, 67; Robertson, *Wild Horse Desert*, 89.
23. Greaser and de la Teja, "Quieting Title," 438, 458; see Record 82 of *Report of James R. Miller and W. H. Bourland Commissioners to Investigate Land Titles West of the Nueces*, 1852 (copy available in archives at University of Texas–Pan American, Edinburg). Thanks to Special Collections archivist George Gause for his very helpful assistance; Hildalgo County Tax Rolls, 1852–1905; for El Gato land transfers, see the Texas General Land Office file for Agostadero del Gato/Juan José Treviño; "Jackson Ranch Cemetery" Hidalgo County, Cemeteries of Texas, accessed June 19, 2013, http://www.cemeteries-of-tx.com/Etx/Hidalgo/Cemetery/jackson.htm; for La Blanca land sales and owners, see the Texas General Land Office file for Lino Cavazos/La Blanca; Ida May Segrest Decker, "Eli T. Merriman: A Biography Thesis" (Kingsville: Texas College of Arts and Industries, 1940); similar information is available at "Santa Ana National Wildlife Refuge," US Fish and Wildlife Service, http://www.fws.gov/refuge/santa_ana/; *Hidalgo County Marks and Brands* (copy available in archives at University of Texas–Pan American). For IBC Map of 1852, see Sánchez, *Shared Experience*; "Abstract of Title to Alamo Tract"; Decker, "Eli T. Merriman."
24. See "Jackson Ranch Church Founded in 1857," *Mid-Valley News Tourist Edition*, n.d., 18; Robertson, *Wild Horse Desert*, 87.
25. Robertson, *Wild Horse Desert*, 87; for Cortina War and ranch depopulation, see Amberson, McAllen, and McAllen, *I Would Rather Sleep In Texas*, 174; Report of Major Samuel P. Heintzelman, cited in Sánchez, *Shared Experience*, 52; see original, handwritten copy of Leal will, registered in Texas in 1862, at Hidalgo County Courthouse, Edinburg, TX; for livestock rustling during the Cortina War, see Thompson, *Cortina*, 70.

26. Agricultural Census of 1860 (Schedule 4), Hidalgo County, Texas.
27. For Cristóbal Peña, see Escobar y Sáenz, *Balli Family History*, 45; see Hidalgo County Clerk deed records, "Agreement July 21, 1859, between Benigno Leal and his wife Victoria Balli," Books A and B, p. 54; for Balli progeny, see "*Balli Ranch Cemetery*," Hidalgo County, Cemeteries of Texas, Hidalgo County Historical Society, accessed January 31, 2013, http://www.cemeteries-of-tx.com/Etx/Hidalgo/Cemetery/balliranch.htm; "Zacatal Ranch Cemetery," Hidalgo County, Cemeteries of Texas, Hidalgo County Historical Commission, accessed January 31, 2013, http://cemeteries-of-tx.com/Etx/Hidalgo/Cemetery/Zacatal.htm; "Handy Cemetery," Hidalgo County, Cemeteries of Texas, Hidalgo County Historical Commission, accessed January 31, 2013, http://www.cemeteries-of-tx.com/Etx/Hidalgo/Cemetery/handy.htm; Agricultural Census of 1870 and 1880 (Schedule 2), Hidalgo County, Texas; Federal Census of 1870, Precinct 1, Hidalgo County, Texas; for baptism of grandson Cristóbal Leal, see "Bautismos de Reynosa, Libro No. 1 A-R, 1800–1912," Frank Cushman Pierce Genealogical Collection, Special Collections, University of Texas–Pan American, Edinburg.
28. Federal Census of 1880, Hidalgo County, Texas (Enumeration District 80).
29. "Compiled Service Records of Confederate Soldiers Who Served in Organizations from the State of Texas, 1861–1865," Record Group 109, National Archives Publication No. M323; see "Military Units" in Roll 0221, contained in above record, National Archives; Thompson, *Cortina*; for Thomas's Rangers, see 41, 71; for the defense of Edinburg/Hidalgo, 102.
30. "Compiled Service Records of Confederate Soldiers"; see will of Benigno and Victoria Leal on file at Hidalgo County Courthouse, Edinburg, TX; Frances W. Isbell, ed., *Hidalgo County Ranch Histories* (Edinburg, TX: Hidalgo County Historical Society and Hidalgo County Historical Commission, 1994), 102.
31. Historians have examined the increasing dominance of Anglo-American land ownership, labor control, and market growth in South Texas after the Civil War; see especially Kenneth L. Stewart and Arnoldo De León, "Laborers and Regional Economic Disparities," chap. 2 in *Not Room Enough: Mexicans, Anglos, and Socioeconomic Change in Texas, 1850–1900* (Albuquerque: University of New Mexico Press, 1982); W. H. Goetzmann, "The United States-Mexican Boundary Survey, 1848–1853," *Southwestern Historical Quarterly* 62, no. 2 (October 1958): 189; Isbell, Hidalgo County Ranch Histories, 102; "Jackson Ranch Cemetery," *Hidalgo County, Cemeteries of Texas*, accessed June 19, 2013, http://www.cemeteries-of-tx.com/Etx/Hidalgo/Cemetery/jackson.htm; see also "Jackson Ranch Church Founded in 1857," *Mid-Valley News Tourist Edition*, n.d., 18; for the best history of the Oblates in South Texas, see Doyon, *Cavalry of Christ*; for the Oblate Trail map, see inside cover of *Gift of the Rio: Story of Texas Tropical Borderland* (Mission, TX: Border Kingdom Press, 1975); for priests on the trail, see especially Duncan, "Oblate Trail," in *Gift of the Rio*, 155; for the Chapel at Edinburg, see also Robert Wright, "Sacred Sites: Building Churches and Communities in 19th Century South Texas," *Heritage* 17, no. 1 (Spring 1999); for marriage record of Cristóbal Leal and Ascensión Ozuna in 1879, see "Marriage Records, 1852–1888," Hidalgo County records on microfilm (reel 1017253), University of Texas–Pan American archives, p. 247. Also see p. 143 of that source for a marriage witnessed by Cristóbal and Rafaela Leal in 1875; for cultural traditions of weddings on ranches, see, for instance, Beatriz de la Garza, *From the Republic of*

the Rio Grande: A Personal History of the Place and the People (Austin: University of Texas Press, 2013), 61–62.

32. Hidalgo County Tax Rolls, 1852–1905; see also Cameron County Tax Rolls, 1846–1852; 1870 Agricultural Census (Schedule 2), Hidalgo County, Texas; for Leal brands, see *Hidalgo County Marks and Brands*; for signature of Benigno Leal, see sale document, Cecilia Domínguez to John Webber, 1853, in Texas GLO File, El Gato.

Chapter Six

1. For flood of 1889 in Edinburg, see Wright, "Sacred Sites"; Patricia W. Freeman and Hugh H. Genoways, "Recent Northern Records of the Nine-Banded Armadillo (Dasypodidae) in Nebraska," *Southwestern Naturalist* 43, no. 4 (December 1998): 491; F. Wallace Taber, "Expansion of the Range of the Armadillo," *Journal of Mammalogy* 20, no. 4 (November 1939): 489–90; Vernon Bailey, "Biological Survey of Texas," in Schmidly, *Texas Natural History*, 53.
2. John K. Strecker, "The Extension of Range of the Nine-Banded Armadillo," *Journal of Mammalogy* 72, no. 3 (August 1926), 207–8; for Class 4 herds, see Alonzo, *Tejano Legacy*, 229.
3. Frank A. Pierce, *A Brief History of the Lower Rio Grande Valley* (Menasha, WI: George Banta, 1917), 142; for Olmstead quote, see C. W. Hanselka, "The Historical Use of Fire on South Texas Rangelands," in *Prescribed Range Burning in the Coastal Prairie and Eastern Rio Grande Plains of Texas*, ed. C. W. Hanselka, Texas Agricultural Extension Service Bulletin (College Station: Texas A&M University, 1980), 2–18; for barbed wire, see Earl W. Hayter, "Barbed Wire Fencing: A Prairie Invention; Its Rise and Influence in the Western States," *Agricultural History* 13, no. 4 (October 1939); K. A. Hibbard, D. S. Schimel, S. Archer, D. S. Ojima, and W. Parton, "Grassland to Woodland Transitions: Integrating Changes in Landscape Structure and Biogeochemistry," *Ecological Applications* 13, no. 4 (2003): 917; Hanselka, "Historical Use of Fire," 7; Horgan, *Great River*, 886.
4. Hanselka, "Historical Use of Fire," 7; Omer C. Stewart, *Forgotten Fires: Native Americans and the Transient Wilderness* (Norman: University of Oklahoma Press, 2002), 140; Hanselka, "Historical Use of Fire," 9; see information on burning trees and mesquite hardiness in C. E. Fisher, "The Mesquite Problem in the Southwest," *Journal of Range Management* 3, no. 1 (January 1950): 60–70.
5. Agricultural Census of 1880 (Schedule 2), Hidalgo County, Texas.
6. SANWR, February–April 1944, 4; SANWR, August 1943, 3; for grass poaching, see SANWR, February–April 1947, 3.
7. Gould, *Texas Plants*, 2.
8. "Laguna Seca Ranch," accessed December 7, 2014, http://lagunasecaranch.com/our-history.html; Graf, "Economic History," 484; Horgan, *Great River*, 883; Graf, "Economic History," 148.
9. See Alonzo, *Tejano Legacy*, 97, table 4.1: "Population of Counties in South Texas, by Decade, 1860–1900"; see Alonzo, *Tejano Legacy*, 216–17, tables 7.5 and 7.6; some sources give the number of "14,000" cattle for the 1870 census, not the 1880. There is conflicting information; Alonzo, *Tejano Legacy*, 217, table 7.7;

Clotilde P. García, "Rosa María Hinojosa de Balli," 1985, unpublished manuscript in Clotilde P. García Genealogical Collection, Texas A&M University, Corpus Christi.

10. See a good discussion of ongoing environmental change in Texas in Schmidly, *Texas Natural History*; Mary O. Parker, "Birds, Brush, and Fire," *Texas Parks and Wildlife*, May 2009, 34–37; Brush, *Nesting Birds*, 23.
11. SANWR, May–August 1945, 3.
12. Information on burning at Santa Ana is from Jennifer Owen-White (manager of Santa Ana National Wildlife Refuge), e-mail message to author, June 14, 2011; SANWR, January 5, 1945, 4; for disappearance of Leal home, see MacWhorter and Isbell, application for a Texas Historical Marker.
13. Federal Census of 1880, Hidalgo County, Texas (Enumeration District 80).
14. Federal Census of 1880, Texas. For specific ranch, see "Santa Ana Ranch in County of Hidalgo, 16th of June, 1880."
15. For 1870s violence, see letter of Lina Helen Box, May 13, 1875, in "Texas Frontier Troubles," House of Representatives, 44th Cong., 1st Sess., Report No. 343, p. 111; the ages of these boys ranged from fifteen to eighteen; see Federal Census of 1880, as above; Agricultural Census of 1880 (Schedule 2), Hidalgo County, Texas, Santa Ana Rancho; Pierce, *Brief History*, 108; Federal Census of 1880, Hidalgo County, Texas (Enumeration District 80).
16. See "Capote Rancho" on the Federal Census of 1880; see the Agricultural Census of 1880 Agricultural (Schedule 2), Hidalgo County, Texas, for Santa Ana Rancho.
17. Jane Manaster, *Javelinas: Collared Peccaries of the Southwest* (Lubbock: Texas Tech University Press, 2006), 59; Agricultural Census of 1880 (Schedule 2), Hidalgo County, Texas, Santa Ana Rancho.
18. For ranch life before 1900, see González, "Work and Play," in Boatright, *Golden Log*, 143–44; see also Ramírez, *Ranch Life in Hidalgo County;* Federal Census of 1880, Texas, "Santa Ana Ranch in County of Hidalgo, 16th of June, 1880"; Federal Census of 1880, Hidalgo County, Texas (Enumeration District 80); for Kidder family on Los Toritos, see the Texas GLO file for Los Toritos. The Federal Census of 1880 lists the family of Rosalía Cortez on Santa Ana. This is important, as her three sons are also identified as living with her. One of the boys was eight-year-old Gregorio. Although Rosalía's family left the county in the early 1880s, it is worth noting that Gregorio became famous in 1901 when he was accused of rustling. During an extensive manhunt, his shrewdness and endurance were widely admired. This is arguably the only verifiable connection between Santa Ana people and a historic event in South Texas that became legendary. For this connection, see Richard J. Mertz, "No One Can Arrest Me: The Story of Gregorio Cortez," *Journal of South Texas 1* (1974).
19. Federal Census of 1880, Texas, "Santa Ana Ranch in County of Hidalgo, 16th of June, 1880"; Federal Census of 1880, Hidalgo County, Texas (Enumeration District 80); see this story at "Santa Ana National Wildlife Refuge, Texas," US Fish and Wildlife Service, accessed July 8, 2010, http://www.fws.gov/refuge/santa_ana/
20. For images of Tejana women from the 1870s and 1880s, see especially the photographs following p. 62 in Hinojosa, *Borderlands Town; Hidalgo County Marks and Brands*, Book A (copy at University of Texas–Pan American, Edinburg);

Hidalgo County Probate Records, File 33, minutes, Book B, 523–27. Will of Victoria Balli; see will and contestations also in Alonzo, *Tejano Legacy*, 116; Escobar y Sáenz, *Balli Family History*, 45; see the section on "Tejano Children and the Adoption of Children" in Alonzo, *Tejano Legacy*, 115; for burial request, see will of Victoria Balli, above, and probate file no. 33, Estate of Victoria Balli, Hidalgo County Courthouse, Edinburg, TX.

21. "Abstract of Title to Alamo Tract"; Mary A. Sutherland, *The Story of Corpus Christi*, ed. Frank A. Harrison (Corpus Christi, TX: Corpus Christi Chapter, Daughters of the Confederacy, 1916), also online at "Old Bayview Cemetery: E. T. Merriman," Corpus Christi Public Libraries, accessed January 2013, http://www.cclibraries.com/localhistory/oldbayview/index.php/component/content/article/61/513-e-t-merriman; for sales of Merriman land, see Decker, "Eli T. Merriman"; for land transfers in Merriman family, see "Abstract of Title to Alamo Tract"; Hidalgo County Tax Rolls, 1852–1905.
22. Agricultural Census of 1880; Graf, "Economic History," 235; "Abstract of Title to Alamo Tract."
23. See "Pechuga, Hidalgo County," Agricultural Census of 1880, Schedule Two; this information included in "Pechuga Ranch Cemetery," Hidalgo County, Cemeteries of Texas, Hidalgo County Historical Society, accessed August 2012, http://www.cemeteries-of-tx.com/Etx/Hidalgo/Cemetery/pechuga.htm; for Tejano land valuation, see Alonzo, *Tejano Legacy*, 123; for poignant studies of racial discrimination, segregation, and the marginalization of Tejanos in the late nineteenth century, see especially Arnoldo De León, *They Called Them Greasers: Anglo Attitudes Toward Mexicans in Texas, 1821–1900* (Austin: University of Texas Press, 1983); see also the discussion and table on rural labor force competition, 1860–1900, in De León, *Tejano Community*, 1836–1900, chap. 3.
24. Alonzo, *Tejano Legacy*, 123; see also "Abstract of Title to Alamo Tract"; *Titus E. Merriman et al. v. P. E. Blalock et al.*, June 28, 1909, Texas Civil Appeals Reports, vol. 56, 601–2.
25. For evolution of "an indolent people," see De León, *They Called Them Greasers*, chap. 3; Hidalgo County Tax Rolls, 1852–1905; for survey of Guzmán land, see *Titus E. Merriman et al.*, 277–78; for Francisco Balli ranch, see Cameron County Tax Rolls, 1848 and 1849; for Resaca del Gato, see Hidalgo County General Land Office Map, 1880, photographed by author at Hidalgo County Courthouse, Edinburg, TX, June 2013.
26. See analysis of Julio Guzmán's net worth in Alonzo, *Tejano Legacy*, 169.
27. Federal Census of 1900; for "Santa Ana Ranches," see IBC Map, 1911 (copy available at Special Collections, University of Texas–Pan American, Edinburg); Carol Lee, "For Wildlife, Cattails Serve Many Functions," *Lubbock Avalanche-Journal*, October 7, 2007, accessed June 25, 2013, http://lubbockonline.com/stories/100707/gue_100707050.shtml; for shift to sheep and goats, see Alonzo, *Tejano Legacy*, 221; for pastores, see Arnoldo De León, *Tejano Community*, 57–60; for cabrito, see Ramírez, *Ranch Life in Hidalgo County*, 15; for Rufina Garza, see "Pechuga Ranch Cemetery," Hidalgo County, Cemeteries of Texas, Hidalgo County Historical Society, accessed June 2013, http://www.cemeteries-of-tx.com/Etx/Hidalgo/Cemetery/pechuga.htm; Fleetwood, "Plants of Santa Ana"; Hidalgo County Tax Rolls, 1852–1905.

28. *Hidalgo County Marks and Brands*, 1852–1905.
29. The concept known as the land ethic first appeared in the work of Aldo Leopold, *A Sand County Almanac*, 1948; see date of death for Victoria Leal in her probate file, Hidalgo County Courthouse, Edinburg, TX.

Chapter Seven

1. Alonzo, *Tejano Legacy*, 256; J. Lee Stambaugh and Lillian J. Stambaugh, *The Lower Rio Grande Valley of Texas: Its Colonization and Industrialization, 1518–1953* (Austin: San Felipe Press, 1974, reprint from 1954), 256; J. Lee Stambaugh and Lillian J. Stambaugh, *Historical Heritage of the Rio Grande Valley of Texas* (Austin: Jenkins Publishing, 1974), 190; for the historic pump house in Hidalgo County, see "Old Hidalgo Pumphouse Museum and World Birding Center," City of Hidalgo, Texas, accessed November 30, 2014, http://www.cityofhidalgo.net/pumphouse.html; as the Web site indicates, today this pump house and museum are part of the World Birding Center along the lower Rio Grande.
2. "Abstract of Title to Alamo Tract"; Alonzo, *Tejano Legacy*, 256; the eight Guzmán children who inherited were Amado, Julio, Dolores, Estéfana, Anastacia, Manuela, Higinia, and Francisco. I am grateful to Beatriz de la Garza for the point about Spanish law influencing Texas laws of inheritance. See "Abstract of Title to Alamo Tract," 62–63.
3. For analyses of profound changes in Tejano land ownership, labor, and political power, see the important works by Arnoldo De León, notably, *They Called Them Greasers*, especially chap. 8, "Frontier 'Democracy' and Tejanos—the Postbellum Period"; for Laredo and Rio Grande City riots, see 92–96; for Guzmán family history, see Federal Censuses of 1870, 1880, 1900, and 1910; information on Reynosa baptisms provided in an e-mail post on ancestry.com, June 19, 2007, relative to a query about the Guzmán family in Reynosa; for women's work on ranches, see Ramírez, *Ranch Life in Hidalgo County*, 9; for a history of McAllen, see Amberson, McAllen, and McAllen, *I Would Rather Sleep in Texas;* for Mission, see Richard D. Heller Jr., *History of Mission* (Mission, TX: privately printed, 2002); Federal Census of 1900.
4. "Abstract of Title to Alamo Tract"; warranty deed, Cristóbal Leal to D. B. Chapin, February 21, 1905, Hidalgo County Courthouse, Edinburg, TX; Gerhardt and Santa Ana, *Images of America*, 38; see the *San Antonio Light*, December 7, 1911, for coverage of the Chapin shooting; for Cristóbal Leal's insanity, see "History of Old Cemetery at Bird Sanctuary Sought," *Harlingen (TX) Valley Morning Star*, October 28, 1970, and "Valley Wildlife Refuge Visited by 12,806 Bird Lovers Last Year," *McAllen (TX) Valley Evening Monitor*, October 28, 1964.
5. "Abstract of Title to Alamo Tract," 81; Stambaugh and Stambaugh, *Lower Rio Grande Valley*, 190; warranty deed, 59, J. C. Engelman Land Company to Garfield Foster, State of Texas, County of Hidalgo, May 31, 1917; for a detailed overview of land sale excursions on the Alamo Tract, see Pope, *Rainbow Era*, especially chap. 1, "Landmen, Excursions, and Homeseekers." For methods of purchasing land, and flooding, see 28–30.
6. Edwards, *History of Texas*, 97; Mary Helen Straker, *The Hills of Home: Five*

Generations of a Pioneer Ohio Family (Nashport, OH: New Concord Press, 2008), 361–63.

7. For the concepts of environmental filtering, adaptation, and preadaptation, see Terry Jordan, "Preadaptation and European Colonization in Rural North America," *Annals of the Association of American Geographers* 79, no. 4 (1989): 489–500; these comparative agricultural census data for corn are found in Stambaugh and Stambaugh, *Lower Rio Grande Valley*, 233.
8. Sarah Sanborne Weaver, "Nature Conditioned Hidalgo," talk presented to the Lower Rio Grande Valley Historical Society, April 14, 1952, later published in *Selections from the Collected Papers of the Lower Rio Grande Valley Historical Society, 1949–1979*, vol. 1 (Harlingen, TX: Lon A. Hill Memorial Library, 1979). See p. 8 for quote. *The American Rio Grande Land and Irrigation Company Sales Office Brochure* (Dallas: Southland Life Building, ca. 1920) (copy at the Dolph Briscoe Center for American History, University of Texas at Austin); Wayne A. Showers, "The Vegetable Industry in the Lower Rio Grande Valley, Past, Present, and Future," *Journal of the Rio Grande Valley Horticultural Society* 25 (1971): 80; see this map in the County Appraisal Office in Edinburg, TX.
9. *Hidalgo Advance*, January 15, 1903.
10. For horses and wells, see Washington, "Ranches in the Rio Grande," 192; MacWhorter and Isbell, application for a Texas Historical Marker, 3; Stambaugh and Stambaugh, *Lower Rio Grande Valley*, 234; W. Clyde Norris, *History of Hidalgo County Texas* (Kingsville: Texas A&M University, 1942), 33, 40.
11. Norris, *History of Hidalgo County*, 91; Stambaugh and Stambaugh, *Lower Rio Grande Valley*, 193; for flooding, see "Jackson Ranch Church Founded in 1857," *Mid-Valley News Tourist Edition*, n.d; Norris, *History of Hidalgo County*, 48; "Abstract of Title to Alamo Tract."
12. Norris, *History of Hidalgo County*, 88–89; *Soil Survey of Hidalgo County, Texas* (US Department of Agriculture, 1925; publ. 1929), introduction.
13. *Lower Rio Grande Valley and Santa Ana National Wildlife Refuges Interim Comprehensive Management Plan and Draft Environmental Assessment*, US Fish and Wildlife Service, US Department of the Interior, 1997, 21; Norris, *History of Hidalgo County*, 95; see David C. Wheelock, "Regulation and Bank Failures: New Evidence for the Agricultural Depression of the 1920s," *Journal of Economic History* 52, no. 4 (December 1992); *Soil Survey of Hidalgo County, Texas*, 1925, 43.
14. See Notice of Lis Pendens, No. A-4573, *The First National Bank of Chicago v. Santa Ana Citrus Groves, Inc., et al.*, Record No. 33880, Hidalgo County Courthouse Records, Edinburg, TX; survey of the Alamo Tract in "Abstract of Title to Alamo Tract"; see Frances W. Isbell, "Spiderweb Railroad," application for a Texas Historical Marker, Hidalgo County Historical Commission, McAllen, Texas, 1981 (copy dated May 11, 1982, available in Hidalgo County Historical Marker Applications Collection, 1963–present, Museum of South Texas History); MacWhorter and Isbell, application for a Texas Historical Marker, 4; *Harlingen (TX) Valley Morning Star*, May 26, 1942.
15. For proposed retirement community, see Pope, *Rainbow Era*, 170; L. Irby Davis, president, Lower Rio Grande Valley Nature Club, to [J. Clark] Salyer, September 27, 1939; SANWR, 1939–44; Entry 162, General Correspondence, 1890–1956.

16. SANWR, January–April 1943, 5; Robin S. Vora, "Plant Communities of the Santa Ana National Wildlife Refuge, Texas," *Texas Journal of Science* 42 (1990): 118.
17. See Ernie Pyle writing in the *Mission (TX) Times*, January 12, 1942.
18. SANWR, September–December 1943, 2.
19. Chris Hathcock (acting manager, Santa Ana National Wildlife Refuge), personal communication, June 28, 2010; for foragers, see Leffler, *Refuge on the Rio Grande*, 60; for 1908 death of Rafaela Leal, see "Affidavit of Manuel Balli and his wife proving family history and children of Juan José Treviño, original grantee, El Gato Grant," deed record for Agostadero del Gato, Hidalgo County Courthouse, Edinburg, TX. See "Santa Ana National Wildlife Refuge," Guide to Texas Outside, accessed July 31, 2011, www.texasoutside.com/easttexas/SantaAnaNWR.htm; Leffler, *Refuge on the Rio Grande*, 55.
20. SANWR, May–August 1943, 3.
21. Norris, *History of Hidalgo County, 96; Department of the Interior Land Protection Plan: Lower Rio Grande Valley National Wildlife Refuge: Cameron, Hidalgo, Starr, and Willacy Counties, Texas* (Albuquerque, NM: US Fish and Wildlife Service, Region 2, June 1983), 4; see "US-Mexico Bird Migration Treaty (MIGRATE)," accessed August 22, 2011, http://www1.american.edu/TED/MIGRATE.HTM; Casto, "Market Hunting of Texas Birds," 3.
22. This action has also been credited to the Army Corps of Engineers; there is no clear history. See discussion of the milling of bald cypress, especially for shingles, water tanks, and rail lines, in Turner, *Remarkable Plants of Texas*, 106.
23. N. Pollen-Bankhead, A. Simon, K. Jaeger, and E. Wohl, "Destabilization of Streambanks by Removal of Invasive Species in Canyon de Chelly National Monument, Arizona," *Geomorphology* 10, no. 3 (2009): 363–74; see also comparable studies of the Mississippi in "Studying Streambanks Reveals Their Weaknesses and Strengths," *Agricultural Research*, February 2011, accessed February 2013, http://www.ars.usda.gov/is/AR/archive/feb11/streambanks0211.htm; SANWR, January–April 1948, 3; IBWC, US Section, *Revised Biological Assessment on the Lower Rio Grande Flood Control Project Vegetation Clearing Activities in Hidalgo, Cameron, and Willacy Counties, Texas, February 1993* (Austin: Dolph Briscoe Center for American History, University of Texas at Austin); *US Department of the Interior Land Protection Plan for Lower Rio Grande Valley National Wildlife Refuge in Cameron, Hidalgo, Starr, and Willacy Counties, Texas* (Albuquerque, NM: US Fish and Wildlife Service, Southwest Region, 1984–1985) (copy in archives of University of Texas–Pan American); for floods in Texas, see also Luna et al., "Levees in Texas: A Historical Perspective," http://www.halff.com/downloads/info_bank/levees_in_texas-historical.pdf; Castillo, "Effects of Artificial Flooding," 41, 42.
24. J. H. Everett, "Native Plant Thought Extinct Grows as an Ornamental," *Journal of the Rio Grande Valley Horticultural Society* 30 (1976): 113–14; Chris Hathcock (acting manager, Santa Ana National Wildlife Refuge), personal communication, August 29, 2011; Fleetwood, "Plants of Santa Ana," 1; Kimberly Wahl (plant ecologist, Santa Ana National Wildlife Refuge), interview with author, May 31, 2013.
25. *US Department of the Interior Land Protection Plan*, 1984–1985, 2; see J. M. Inglis, "A History of Vegetation on the Rio Grande Plain," *Texas Parks and*

Wildlife Bulletin, no. 45 (1964); *US Department of the Interior Land Protection Plan*, 1984–1985, 50; Kerby McFall, "The Texas Delta of an American Nile," *National Geographic Magazine* 74 (July–December 1938); Marjorie Johnson, "Outdoors in the Valley," in *Gift of the Rio: The Story of Texas Tropical Borderland* (Mission, TX: Border Kingdom Press, 1975), 146.

26. This wording contained in 16 U.S.A. 715d, Migratory Bird Conservation Act of 1929; SANWR, September–December 1944, 3; see Marc C. Woodin et al., "Grassland Birds Wintering at U.S. Navy Facilities in Southern Texas," project no. 07-189, US Department of the Interior, US Geological Survey, Open File Report 2010–1115, prepared in cooperation with Texas A&M University, Corpus Christi, July 2010, accessed January 2013, http://pubs.usgs.gov/of/2010/1115/
27. "Latin Americans Plan Elaborate Festival on Saturday and Sunday," *Brownsville (TX) Herald*, July 10, 1931; for cultural legacies, see Wilbur Zelinsky's "Doctrine of First Effective Settlement," described by Terry Jordan, "Preadaptation and European Colonization," 490–91.
28. Horgan, *Great River*, 798; see Fray Emmanuel Domenech, *Missionary Adventures in Texas and Mexico: A Personal Narrative of Six Years' Sojourn in Those Regions* (London: Longsman, Brown, Green, Longsman, and Roberts, 1858); see also Horgan, *Great River*, 789–90; for an imaginative and poignant exploration of Spanish settlers' love of land and trees in the area northwest of Santa Ana, see also Elena Zamora O'Shea, *El Mesquite: A Story of the Early Spanish Settlements between the Nueces and the Rio Grande* (College Station: Texas A&M University Press, 2000).
29. Federal Census of 1920, Texas, Precinct 2; for analysis of the 1930 census, see Daniel D. Arreola, "Mexico Origins of South Texas Mexican-Americans, 1930," *Journal of Historical Geography* 19, no. 1 (January 1993); for information about a child of Pedro Leal who was "born on the Santa Ana ranch in 1862," see information posted by Gustavo Hinojosa, January 10, 2010, at http://genforum.genealogy.com/leal/messages/428.html, accessed December 8, 2014.
30. John M. "Frosty" Anderson, *Places to Hide and Seek: Wildlife Sanctuaries and the Audubon Society* (Austin: University of Texas Press, 2000), xv; SANWR, January–April 1949, 3; for Spanish claiming ceremonies, see the Texas General Land Office 1877 Survey of Los Toritos; L. Irby Davis, breeding census, 1940, included in correspondence to J. Clark Salyer, July 11, 1940, SANWR, 1939–1940, Entry 162, General Correspondence, 1890–1956; see also Davis, "Rio Grande Region," in nesting data published in *Bird-Lore* magazine, 1940, 221–22. Readers may have questions about the controversial Border Wall/Fence erected along parts of the Rio Grande northwest of Brownsville. A succinct overview of how this wall has impacted Santa Ana National Wildlife Refuge states: "Thanks to uproar from the park staff and local environmentalist groups that had worked to restore and preserve this nearly lost habitat, the infamous border wall—a twelve-foot-high metal fence—stops at the Santa Ana's perimeter and starts up again on the other side. Next to the river, a sign reads: "This corridor will allow animals to safely pass along and across the Rio Grande." See Lauren Markham, "First the Fence, Then the System," *Virginia Quarterly Review* 89, no. 3 (Summer 2013), accessed June 25, 2014, http://www.vqronline.org/articles/first-fence-then-system.

Bibliography

Primary Sources

NATIONAL ARCHIVES RECORDS

"Compiled Service Records of Confederate Soldiers Who Served in Organizations from the State of Texas, 1861–1865." Record Group 109, National Archives Publication No. M323.

SANWR (Santa Ana National Wildlife Refuge) Narrative Reports, Entry 247, Narrative Reports; Records of the Division of Wildlife Refuges; Records of the Bureau of Sport Fisheries and Wildlife; US Fish and Wildlife Service, Record Group 22; National Archives at College Park, MD.

FEDERAL GOVERNMENT PUBLICATIONS

Agricultural Census of 1860 (Schedule 4), Hidalgo County, Texas.

Agricultural Census of 1870 (Schedule 2), Hidalgo County, Texas.

Agricultural Census of 1880 (Schedule 2), Hidalgo County, Texas.

"America from the Great Depression to World War II: Black-and-White Photographs from the FSA-OWI, 1935–1945." Library of Congress Farm Security Administration/Office of War Information Black-and-White Negatives. www.loc.gov/pictures/collection/fsa/

Baird, Spencer F. "Mammals of the Boundary." *Report of the United States and Mexican Boundary Survey*, vol. 2. Washington, DC: Department of the Interior, 1859.

Department of the Interior Land Protection Plan: Lower Rio Grande Valley National Wildlife Refuge: Cameron, Hidalgo, Starr and Willacy Counties, Texas. Albuquerque, NM: US Fish and Wildlife Service, Region 2, June 1983.

Federal Census of 1850, Cameron, Starr, and Webb Counties.

Federal Census of 1860, Hidalgo County, Texas.

Federal Census of 1870, Precinct 1, Hidalgo County, Texas.

Federal Census of 1880, Hidalgo County, Texas, Enumeration District 80.

Federal Census of 1900, Texas, Precinct 2.

Federal Census of 1910, Texas, Precinct 2.

Federal Census of 1920, Texas, Precinct 2.

Federal Census of 1940, Texas, Precinct 2.

Fleetwood, Raymond J. "Plants of Santa Ana National Wildlife Refuge." Unpublished inventory, Santa Ana National Wildlife Refuge, Bureau of Sport Fisheries and Wildlife, Alamo, Texas, 1973. Special Collections, University of Texas–Pan American, Edinburg.

IBWC, US Section. *Revised Biological Assessment on the Lower Rio Grande Flood Control Project Vegetation Clearing Activities in Hidalgo, Cameron, and Willacy Counties, Texas, February, 1993*. Austin: Dolph Briscoe Center for American History, University of Texas at Austin.

International Boundary and Water Commission Water Bulletin, no. 23. Austin: Dolph Briscoe Center for American History, University of Texas at Austin, 1953.

Leslie, D. M., Jr. *Tamaulipan Brushland of the Lower Rio Grande Valley of South Texas: Description, Human Impacts, Management Options*. Biological Report 88 (36). Washington, DC: US Fish and Wildlife Service, 1988.

Lower Rio Grande Valley and Santa Ana National Wildlife Refuges Interim Comprehensive Management Plan. US Fish and Wildlife Service, US Department of the Interior, September 1997. Special Collections, University of Texas–Pan American, Edinburg.

Lower Rio Grande Valley and Santa Ana National Wildlife Refuges Interim Comprehensive Management Plan and Draft Environmental Assessment. US Fish and Wildlife Service, US Department of the Interior, March 1997. Special Collections, University of Texas–Pan American, Edinburg.

Migratory Bird Conservation Act of 1929, 16 U.S.A. 715d., http://www.epw.senate.gov/mbca.pdf

National Audubon Society. "Historical Results by Count." Santa Ana National Wildlife Refuge, Hidalgo County, TX, National Audubon Archives, University of Texas Society Christmas Bird Count. http://netapp.audubon.org/cbcobservation/

National Register of Historic Places. Registration form, McAllen Ranch. National Park Service, US Department of the Interior, October 1990.

Report of James R. Miller and W. H. Bourland Commissioners to Investigate Land Titles West of the Nueces, 1852. Archives, University of Texas–Pan American, Edinburg.

Report of the United States and Mexico Boundary Survey, vol. 2. Washington, DC: Department of the Interior, 1859. Archives, Texas A&M University, Kingsville.

"Santa Ana National Wildlife Refuge." US Fish and Wildlife Service. http://www.fws.gov/refuge/santa_ana/

Sennett, George B., and Elliott Coues. *Further Notes on the Ornithology of the Lower Rio Grande of Texas: Further Observations Made during the Spring of 1878*. Washington, DC: Department of the Interior, US Geological and Geographical Survey of the Territories, 1878.

US Department of the Interior Land Protection Plan for Lower Rio Grande Valley National Wildlife Refuge in Cameron, Hidalgo, Starr, and Willacy Counties, Texas. Albuquerque, NM: US Fish and Wildlife Service, Southwest Region, 1984–1985. Archives, University of Texas–Pan American, Edinburg.

"US-Mexico Bird Migration Treaty (MIGRATE)." http://www1.american.edu/TED/MIGRATE.HTM

Woodin, Marc C., Mary Kay Skoruppa, Bryan D. Pearce, Amanda J. Ruddy, and Graham C. Hickman. "Grassland Birds Wintering at U.S. Navy Facilities in Southern Texas." Project no. 07-189, US Department of the Interior, US Geological Survey, Open File Report 2010–1115. Prepared in cooperation with Texas A&M University, Corpus Christi, July 2010. http://www.denix.osd.mil/nr/upload/07–189-Grassland-Birds-report.pdf

TEXAS SOURCES AND RECORDS

Almonte, Juan N. "Statistical Report on Texas (1835)." Translated by C. E. Castañeda. *Southwestern Historical Quarterly* 28, no. 3 (January 1925).

Bailey, Vernon. "Biological Survey of Texas, 1905." In David J. Schmidly, *Texas Natural History: A Century of Change*. Lubbock: Texas Tech University Press, 2002. Originally published in *North American Fauna* 25 (October 1905).

Blake (Robert Bruce) Papers. Dolph Briscoe Center for American History, University of Texas at Austin.

Box, Lina Helen. Letter to Texas House of Representatives, May 13, 1875. In "Texas Frontier Troubles." House of Representatives, 44th Cong., 1st Sess., Report No. 343.

Cameron County Tax Rolls, 1848–1852. University of Texas–Pan American, Edinburg. Microfilm.

Coker, Caleb, ed. *The News from Brownsville: Helen Chapman's Letters from the Texas Military Frontier, 1848–1852*. Austin: Barker Texas History Center, Texas State Historical Association, 1992.

"Desert Willow, Flowering Willow, Willowleaf Catalpa, Desert Catalpa, Flor de Mimbre, Mimbre, Bow Willow," Aggie Horticulture, Texas A&M University, https://aggie-horticulture.tamu.edu/ornamentals/natives/chilopsislinearis.htm

García, Dr. Clotilde P. Genealogical Collection. Texas A&M University, Corpus Christi.

Gould, F. W. *Texas Plants: A Checklist and Ecological Summary*. College Station: Texas A&M University, Texas Agricultural Experimental Station, 1969.

Greaser, Galen. *New Guide to Spanish and Mexican Land Grants in South Texas*. Austin: Texas General Land Office, 2009.

"Guayacán." Texas Beyond History. Texas Archeological Research Laboratory, University of Texas at Austin. http://www.texasbeyondhistory.net/ethnobot/images/guayacan.html

Guide to Spanish and Mexican Land Grants in South Texas. Austin: Texas General Land Office, 1999.

Harlingen High School Yearbooks, 1940–1941. Harlingen, TX.

Isbell, Frances W. "Spiderweb Railroad." Application for a Texas Historical Marker, Hidalgo County Historical Commission, McAllen, Texas, 1971. *Museum of South Texas History*.

MacWhorter, William L., and Frances W. Isbell. Application for a Texas Historical Marker, Hidalgo County Historical Commission, McAllen, Texas, n.d. Weslaco Public Library, Weslaco, Texas.

Matamoros Church Marriage Records, 1801–1848. Corpus Christi: Spanish-American Genealogical Association, 1995. Special Collections, University of Texas–Pan American, Edinburg.

Pierce, Frank Cushman. Genealogical Collection. Special Collections, University of Texas–Pan American, Edinburg.

"Santa Ana National Wildlife Refuge." Guide to Texas Outside. www.texasoutside.com/easttexas/SantaAnaNWR.htm

"Texas Ebony." Arizona State University. http://www.public.asu.edu/camartin/plants/Plant%20html%20files/ebenopsisebano.html

Texas General Land Office Records, http://www.glo.texas.gov/cf/land-grant-search/index.cfm

Texas History Online Sources

CEMETERY HISTORIES

"Cemeteries of Hidalgo County Texas." Cemeteries of Texas Project. http://www.cemeteries-of-tx.com/Etx/Hidalgo/ListHidalgo.html

HISTORICAL MARKERS

"Military Highway of the Lower Rio Grande Valley—Mercedes,Hidalgo County, Texas." Texas Historical Marker. http://www.9key.com/markers/marker_detail.asp?atlas_number=5215012064

"Peñitas." Texas Historical Marker. http://atlas.thc.state.tx.us/shell-kword.htm

"Santa Ana Land Grant—Alamo, Hidalgo County, Texas." Texas Historical Marker. http://www.9key.com/markers/marker_detail.asp?atlas_number=5215004570

RANCH HISTORIES

"Laguna Seca Ranch." http://lagunasecaranch.com/our-history.html

Hidalgo County, Texas, Sources and Records:

"Abstract of Title to Alamo Tract: The Alamo Land and Sugar Company Subdivision of Porcion Seventy-Two, Los Torritos, Santa Ana, and El Gato Grants in Hidalgo County, Texas." Edinburg, TX: Hidalgo and Starr Counties Abstract Co., n.d. Museum of South Texas and Hidalgo County Historical Society, Edinburg.

"Affidavit of Manuel Balli and his wife proving family history and children of Juan José Treviño, original grantee, El Gato Grant." Deed record for Agostadero del Gato, Hidalgo County Courthouse, Edinburg, TX.

Hidalgo County Clerk deed records. "Agreement July 21, 1859, between Benigno Leal and his wife Victoria Balli." Books A and B.

Hildago County clerk deed records. First National Bank of Chicago and USA, September 1, 1943. Deed number 32680.

Hidalgo County Map, 1880. Austin, TX: General Land Office. Hidalgo County Courthouse, Edinburg.

Hidalgo County Map, undated but pre-1950. County Appraisal Office, Edinburg, TX.

Hidalgo County Marks and Brands, 1852–1905, Books A and B. Archives, University of Texas–Pan American, Edinburg.

Hidalgo County Probate Records. File 33, minutes, Book B, 523–27. Estate of Victoria Balli. Hidalgo County Courthouse, Edinburg, TX.

Hidalgo County Tax Rolls, 1852–1905. Archives, University of Texas–Pan American, Edinburg. Microfilm.

"Marriage Records, 1852–1888." Reel 1017253. Archives, University of Texas–Pan American, Edinburg.

Soil Survey of Hidalgo County, Texas. US Department of Agriculture, 1925 (publ. 1929).

Survey of the Alamo Tract, 1928. Hidalgo County Irrigation District #2, Edinburg, TX.

USDA Farm Service Agency Map, 2008. Santa Ana National Wildlife Refuge, Hidalgo County, TX. Hidalgo County Irrigation District #2 Office, Edinburg, TX.

Warranty deed, Cristóbal Leal to D. B. Chapin, February 21, 1905. Hidalgo County Courthouse, Edinburg, TX.

Warranty deed 59, J. G. Engelman Land Company to Garfield Foster. The State of Texas, County of Hidalgo, May 31, 1917. Hidalgo County Courthouse, Edinburg, TX.

Newspaper Sources

Border Scope, La Feria, Texas
Brownsville Herald, Brownsville, Texas
Hidalgo Advance, Edinburg, Texas
Lockhart Post Register, Lockhart, Texas
Lubbock Avalanche-Journal, Lubbock, Texas
Mid-Valley News Tourist Edition, n.d. (copy at Museum of South Texas History)
Mission Times, Mission, Texas
San Antonio Express Magazine, San Antonio, Texas
San Antonio Light, San Antonio, Texas
Valley Evening Monitor, McAllen, Texas
Valley Morning Star, Harlingen, Texas
Valley Town Crier, McAllen, Texas

Additional Primary Sources

The American Rio Grande Land and Irrigation Company Sales Office Brochure. Dallas: Southland Life Building, ca. 1920. Dolph Briscoe Center for American History, University of Texas at Austin.

Audubon's Birds of America. Popular edition. New York: MacMillan, 1950.

Bailey, Vernon. "Biological Survey of Texas." *North American Fauna* 25 (October 1905).

Berlandier, Jean Louis. *Journey to Mexico during the Years 1826 to 1834*. Vol. 2. Translated by Sheila M. Ohlendorf, Josette M. Bigelow, and Mary M. Standifer. Austin: Texas State Historical Association and Center for Studies in Texas History, University of Texas at Austin, 1980.

Chapa, Juan Bautista. *Texas and Northeastern Mexico*, 1630–1690. Edited by William A. Foster. Translated by Ned F. Brierly. Austin: University of Texas Press, 1997.

Domenech, Fray Emmanuel. *Missionary Adventures in Texas and Mexico: A Personal Narrative of Six Years' Sojourn in Those Regions*. London: Longsman, Brown, Green, Longsman, and Roberts, 1858.

Escobar y Sáenz, Joel René. *Balli Family History (La Barreta and Padre Island Branches)*. McAllen, TX: privately printed, 2008. Corpus Christi Public Library, Corpus Christi, TX.

Havard, V. "Report on the Flora of Western and Southern Texas." Proceedings of the United States National Museum 8, no. 29 (September 23, 1885).

Martínez, Máximo. *Las plantas medicinales de México*. 5th ed. Mexico City: Edicíon Botas, 1969.
Merrill, James C. *Notes on the Ornithology of Southern Texas, Being a List of Birds Observed in the Vicinity of Fort Brown, Texas,* from February, 1876 to June, 1878. Washington, DC: Government Printing Office, 1878.
"México, Tamaulipas, Registro Civil, 1800–2002." Archivo General del Registro del Estado de Tamaulipas [Tamaulipas Civil Registry State Archives]. https://familysearch.org/search/collection/1916237
Recuerdos: Escrito para las familias de los Cavazos/Cárdenas, n.p., n.d. Corpus Christi Public Library, Corpus Christi, TX.
"Reynosa Census of 1855." *La Porcione* 2, no. 1 (Spring 1987).

Secondary Sources

Acosta, Teresa Palomo, and Ruthe Winegarten. *Las Tejanas: 300 Years of History*. Jack and Doris Smothers Series in Texas History, Life, and Culture. Austin: University of Texas Press, 2003.
Almaraz, Félix D., Jr. *The San Antonio Missions and Their System of Land Tenure*. Austin: University of Texas Press, 1989.
Alonzo, Armando C. "Hispanic Farmers and Ranchers in the Soil and Water Conservation Movement in South Texas, 1940s to Present." *Agricultural History* 78, no. 2 (Spring 2004).
———. *Tejano Legacy: Rancheros and Settlers in South Texas, 1734–1900*. Albuquerque: University of New Mexico Press, 1998.
Amberson, Mary, James A. McAllen, and Margaret H. McAllen. *I Would Rather Sleep in Texas: A History of the Lower Rio Grande Valley and the People of the Santa Anita Land Grant*. Austin: Texas State Historical Association, 2010.
Anderson, John M. "Frosty." *Places to Hide and Seek: Wildlife Sanctuaries and the Audubon Society*. Austin: University of Texas Press, 2000.
Arreola, Daniel D. "Mexico Origins of South Texas Mexican-Americans, 1930." *Journal of Historical Geography* 19, no. 1 (January 1993).
———. *Tejano South Texas: A Mexican American Cultural Province*. Austin: University of Texas Press, 2002.
Barringer, Graham A. "The Mexican War Journal of Henry S. Lane." *Indiana Magazine of History* 53, no. 4 (December 1957).
Barrow, Mark V., Jr. *A Passion for Birds: American Ornithology after Audubon*. Princeton, NJ: Princeton University Press, 1998.
Beaver, Erik. "Management Implications of the Ecology of Free-Roaming Horses in Semi-Arid Ecosystems of the Western United States." *Wildlife Society Bulletin* 31, no. 3 (Autumn 2003).
Blair, Frank W. "The Biotic Province of Texas." *Texas Journal of Science* 2, no. 1 (1950).
Boatright, Mody Coggin, ed. *The Golden Log*. Texas Folklore Society Publication 31. Dallas: Southern Methodist University Press, 1962.
Bolton, Herbert Eugene. *Texas in the Middle Eighteenth Century*. New York: Russell and Russell, 1962.

Bourke, John G. "The Folk Foods of the Rio Grande Valley and of Northern Mexico." *Journal of American Folklore* 8, no. 28 (January–March 1895).

———. "Medicine, Customs, and Superstitions of the Rio Grande." *Journal of American Folklore* 7, no. 25 (April–June 1894).

Brant, Irving, Harold K. Steen, and Alice E. Ingerson. "Adventures in Conservation: Putting It Up to FDR." *Journal of Forest History* 32, no. 1 (January 1981).

Breeden, Jeff B., Michael F. Small, John T. Baccus, and Jack C. Eitnear. "Vegetative Composition of Areas with and without Breeding Red-Billed Pigeons (*Patagioenas flavirostris*) in Texas." *Southwestern Naturalist* 54, no. 1 (March 2009).

Brennan, Arthur. "Some Superstitions of the Mexican Indians." *Folklore* 28, no. 3 (September 1917).

"Brickmaking Industry in the Lower Rio Grande Valley." *Heritage* 13, no. 1 (Winter 1995). http://texashistory.unt.edu/ark:/67531/metapth45408/m1/23/?q=brickmaking industry

Brooks, James F. *Captives and Cousins: Slavery, Kinship, and Community in the Southwest Borderlands*. Chapel Hill: University of North Carolina Press, 2002.

Brown, M. L. *Firearms in Colonial America: The Impact on History and Technology, 1492–1792*. Washington, DC: Smithsonian Institution Press, 1980.

Brush, Timothy. *Nesting Birds of a Tropical Frontier: The Lower Rio Grande Valley of Texas*. Kingsville: Texas A&M University Press, 2005.

Butcher, Russell D. *America's National Wildlife Refuges: A Complete Guide*. Lanham, MD: Rowman and Littlefield, 2008.

Campbell-Kissock, Linda, Lytle H. Blankenship, and J. W. Stewart. "Plant and Animal Foods of Bobwhite and Scaled Quail in Southwest Texas." *Southwestern Naturalist* 30, no. 4 (November 1985).

Carney, Stephen A. *Guns along the Rio Grande: Palo Alto and Resaca de la Palma*. Washington, DC: US Center for Military History, 2006.

Cassin, John. *Illustrations of the Birds of California, Texas, Oregon, British and Russian America*. Philadelphia: J. P. Lippincott, 1862.

Castillo, Charles David. "Effects of Artificial Flooding on the Vegetation and Avifauna of Riparian Woodlands at Santa Ana National Wildlife Refuge, Hidalgo County, Texas." Master's thesis, University of Texas–Pan American, 1997.

Casto, Stanley D. "The Market Hunting of Texas Birds." *Bulletin of the Texas Ornithological Society* 16, nos. 1 and 2 (1983).

———. "Perceptions of Vultures by the Indians and Early Texans." *Bulletin of the Texas Ornithological Society* 21, nos. 1 and 2 (1988).

Cat Specialist Group. "Jaguarundi (*Herpailurus yagouaroundi*)." March 18, 2001. http://www.catsg.org/index.php?id=93

Cole, D. N. "Experiments in Trampling of Vegetation. II. Predictions of Resistance and Resilience." *Journal of Agricultural Economics* 32 (1995).

Collins, Michael L. *Texas Devils: Rangers and Regulars on the Lower Rio Grande, 1846–1861*. Norman: University of Oklahoma Press, 2008.

Cook, Scott. *Mexican Brick Culture in the Building of Texas, 1800s–1980s*. College Station: Texas A&M University, 1998.

Cox, Paul W., and Patty Leslie. *Texas Trees: A Friendly Guide*. San Antonio: Corona, 1993.

Craig, Hugh. *The Animal Kingdom, Based upon the Writings of Audubon, Wallace, Brehm, Wood, and Others*. Vol. 1. New York: Johnson and Bailey, 1897.

"Curanderismo—An Optional Health Care System." Script for slide presentation. University of Texas–Pan American Press, n.d. McAllen Public Library, McAllen, TX.

Dale, D., and T. Weaver. "Trampling Effects of Vegetation of the Trail Corridors of North Rocky Mountain Forests." *Journal of Applied Ecology* 11, no. 2 (August 1974).

Davenport, Herbert, and Joseph K. Wells. "The First Europeans in Texas, 1528–1536." *Southwestern Historical Quarterly* 22, no. 3 (January 1919).

Davenport, Hugh. "Notes on Steamboating on the Rio Grande." *Southwestern Historical Quarterly* 49, no. 2 (October 1945).

Davis, L. Irby. "The Rio Grande Region." *Bird-Lore: The Season*. National Association of Audubon Societies (March–April 1940).

De Chavana, Hermina Balli. *The History of the Prestigious Balli Family: Story of the First Pioneer Settlers of the Rio Grande Valley* (Austin: Nortex Press, 1989).

Decker, Ida May Segrest. "Eli T. Merriman: A Biography Thesis." Kingsville: Texas College of Arts and Industries, 1940.

De la Garza, Beatriz. *From the Republic of the Rio Grande: A Personal History of the Place and the People*. Austin: University of Texas Press, 2013.

De León, Arnoldo. *Mexican Americans in Texas: A Brief History*. 2nd ed. Wheeling, IL: Harlan Davidson, 1999.

———. *The Tejano Community*, 1836–1900. Albuquerque: University of New Mexico Press, 1982.

———, ed. *Tejano Epic: Essays in Honor of Félix A. Almaraz, Jr*. Austin: Texas State Historical Association, 2005.

———. *They Called Them Greasers: Anglo Attitudes Toward Mexicans in Texas, 1821–1900*. Austin: University of Texas Press, 1983.

Delnicki, Don, and Eric G. Bolen. "Natural Nest Site Availability for Black-Bellied Whistling Ducks in South Texas." *Southwestern Naturalist* 20, no. 1 (October 10, 1975).

Doyon, Bernard. *The Cavalry of Christ on the Rio Grande*. Milwaukee, WI: Bruce Press, 1956.

Duncan, Maurine. "The Oblate Trail." In *Gift of the Rio: Story of Texas Tropical Borderland*. Mission, TX: Border Kingdom Press, 1975.

Edwards, David A. *The History of Texas, or the Emigrant's, Farmer's, and Politician's Guide to the Character, Climate, Soil, and Productivity of That Country, Arranged Geographically from Personal Observation and Experience*. 1836. Reprint, Austin: Texas State Historical Association, 1990.

Estrada, Eduardo C., José A. Villarreal Q., Delgado S. Alfonso, Pando M. Marisela, Scott M. Laura, Enrique Jurado, and Yen M. Carmen. "Diversity and Distributional Patterns of Legumes in Southern Nuevo León, Mexico." *Southwestern Naturalist* 51, no. 1 (March 2006).

Evans, Patricia, and Scott McKendrick. "Equine Nutrition: Forages." Agricultural Extension, Utah State University, *Equine*, May 2006.

Everett, J. H. "Native Plant Thought Extinct Grows as an Ornamental." *Journal of the Rio Grande Valley Horticultural Society* 30 (1976).

Ewers, John C. "The Influence of Epidemics on the Indian Populations and Customs of Texas." *Plains Anthropologist* 18, no. 60 (May 1973).

Fisher, C. E. "The Mesquite Problem in the Southwest." *Journal of Range Management* 3, no. 1 (January 1950).

Fisher, C. E., C. H. Meadors, R. Behrens, E. D. Robison, P. T. Marion, and H. L. Morton. "Control of Mesquite on Grazing Lands." *Bulletin* 935. College Station: Texas Agricultural Experiment Station, 1959.

Flores, Dan. "Bringing Home All the Pretty Horses: The Horse Trade and the Early American West: 1775–1825." *Montana: The Magazine of Western History* 58, no. 2 (Summer 2008).

Forgason, Caroline Alexander, and Timothy E. Fulbright. "Cattle, Wildlife, and Range Management on King Ranch Over the Years." Kingsville: Caesar Kleberg Wildlife Research Institute, Texas A&M University, 2003. krirm.tamuk.edu/text/Resources/Forgason_and_Fulbright.pdf

Foscue, Edwin J. "Agricultural History of the Lower Rio Grande Valley Region." *Agricultural History* 8, no. 3 (July 1934).

———. "The Distribution of Population in the Lower Rio Grande Valley of Texas." *Field and Laboratory* 2, no. 2 (1934).

Freeman, Patricia W., and Hugh H. Genoways. "Recent Northern Records of the Nine-Banded Armadillo (Dasypodidae) in Nebraska." *Southwestern Naturalist* 43, no. 4 (December 1998).

Fulbright, Timothy E., and Fred A. Bryant. *The Last Great Habitat*. Special Publication No. 1 of the Caesar Kleberg Wildlife Research Institute. Kingsville: Texas A&M University Press, 2002. Reprint, 2004.

Galindo, Patricia. "*Con un Pie en Cado Lado*: Ethnicities and the Archaeology of Spanish Colonial Ranching Communities along the Lower Rio Grande Valley." PhD diss., University of Texas at Austin, 2003.

García, Rogelia O. *Dolores, Revilla, and Laredo (Three Sister Settlements)*. Waco, TX: privately printed, 1970.

George, Eugene. *Lost Architecture of the Rio Grande Borderlands*. College Station: Texas A&M University Press, 2008.

Gerhardt, Karen, and Rod Santa Ana III. *Images of America: Hidalgo County, Texas*. Chicago: Arcadia, 2000.

Gift of the Rio: Story of Texas Tropical Borderland. Mission, TX: Border Kingdom Press, 1975.

Gilbert, Minnie C. "Valley Wildlife: Part I, Chaparral Country." In *Gift of the Rio: Story of Texas Tropical Borderland*. Mission, TX: Border Kingdom Press, 1975.

———. "Valley Wildlife: Part II, Children of the Chaparral." In *Gift of the Rio: Story of Texas Tropical Borderland*. Mission, TX: Border Kingdom Press, 1975.

Goetzmann, W. H. "The United States-Mexican Boundary Survey, 1848–1853," *Southwestern Historical Quarterly* 62, no. 2 (October 1958).

González, Rosalinda. "Work and Play on a Border Ranch." In *The Golden Log*, Texas Folklore Society Publication 31, edited by Mody Coggin Boatright, 144–45. Dallas: Southern Methodist University Press, 1962.

Gould, Frank W. *The Grasses of Texas*. College Station: Texas A&M University Press, 1975.

Graf, Leroy P. "Colonization Projects in Texas South of the Nueces, 1820–1848." *Southwestern Historical Quarterly* 50, no. 4 (April 1947).

———. "The Economic History of the Lower Rio Grande Valley, 1820–1875." PhD diss., Harvard University, 1942.

Graham, Joe S. *El Rancho in South Texas: Continuity and Change from 1750*. Kingsville: Texas A&M University, University of North Texas Press, 1994.

Greaser, Galen D., and Jesús F. de la Teja. "Quieting Title to Spanish and Mexican Land Grants in the Trans-Nueces: The Bourland and Miller Commission, 1850–1852." *Southwestern Historical Quarterly* 95, no. 4 (April 1992).

Hanselka, C. W. "The Historical Use of Fire on South Texas Rangelands." In *Prescribed Range Burning in the Coastal Prairie and Eastern Rio Grande Plains of Texas*, edited by C. W. Hanselka, 2–18. Texas Agricultural Extension Service Bulletin. College Station: Texas A&M University, 1980.

Hanselka, C. Wayne, and Joe C. Paschal. "Brush Utilization on the Rio Grande Plains." *Rangelands* 14, no. 3 (June 1992).

Hathcock, Christopher R., and Timothy Brush. "Breeding Abundance and Nest-Site Distribution of the Altamira Oriole at Santa Ana National Wildlife Refuge, Texas." *Southwestern Naturalist* 49, no. 1 (March 2004).

Hawkins, Wallace. *El Sal del Rey*. Austin: Texas State Historical Association, 1947.

Hayter, Earl W. "Barbed Wire Fencing: A Prairie Invention; Its Rise and Influence in the Western States." *Agricultural History* 13, no. 4 (October 1939).

Heller, Richard D., Jr. *History of Mission*. Mission, TX: privately printed, 2002.

Henke, Scott E., and William Scott Fair. "Management of Texas Horned Lizards." *Wildlife Management Bulletin*, no. 2, Caesar Kleberg Wildlife Research Institute. Kingsville: Texas A&M University, 1998.

Hernández, Fidel, Fred S. Guthery, and William P. Kuvlesky Jr. "The Legacy of Bobwhite Research in South Texas." *Journal of Wildlife Management* 66, no. 1 (January 2002).

Hernández, Kelly Lytle. "The Crimes and Consequences of Illegal Immigration: A Cross-Border Examination of Operation Wetback, 1943 to 1954." *Western Historical Quarterly* 37, no. 4 (Winter 2006).

Hibbard, K. A., D. S. Schimel, S. Archer, D. S. Ojima, and W. Parton. "Grassland to Woodland Transitions: Integrating Changes in Landscape Structure and Biogeochemistry." *Ecological Applications* 13, no. 4 (2003).

Hinojosa, Gilberto Miguel. *A Borderlands Town in Transition: Laredo, 1755–1870*. College Station: Texas A&M University Press, 1983.

Hock, Raymond J. "Southwestern Exotic Felids." *American Midland Naturalist* 15, no. 2 (April 1955).

Hoogesteijn, Rafael. *Manual on the Problem of Depredation Caused by Jaguars and Pumas on Cattle Ranches*. Tikal, Guatemala: Apure Ranches, Prohesa, Jaguar Advisory Council, Wildlife Conservation Society, and Cat Specialist Group, 2001.

Horgan, Paul. *Great River: The Rio Grande in North American History*. Hanover, NH: University Press of New England, 1984.

Inglis, J. M. "A History of Vegetation on the Rio Grande Plain." *Texas Parks and Wildlife Bulletin*, no. 45 (1964).

Irish, Mary. *Trees and Shrubs for the Southwest: Woody Plants for Arid Gardens*. Portland, OR: Timber Press, 2006.

Isbell, Frances W., ed. *Hidalgo County Ranch Histories*. Edinburg, TX: Hidalgo County Historical Society and Hidalgo County Historical Commission, 1994.

Jahrsdoerfer, S., and D. M. Leslie, Jr. *Tamaulipan Brushland of the Lower Rio Grande Valley of South Texas: Description, Human Impacts, Management Options*. Biological Report 88 (36). Washington, DC: US Fish and Wildlife Service, 1988.

Jensen, Mari N. "Coming of Age at 100: Renewing the National Wildlife Refuge System." *BioScience* 53, no. 4 (April 2003).

Johnson, Marjorie. “Outdoors in the Valley.” In *Gift of the Rio: The Story of Texas Tropical Borderland*. Mission, TX: Border Kingdom Press, 1975.

Jones, Dixie L. “Old Military Road.” *Handbook of Texas Online*. Texas State Historical Association. http://www.tshaonline.org/handbook/online/articles/exo02

Jordan, Terry. “Preadaptation and European Colonization in Rural North America.” *Annals of the Association of American Geographers* 79, no. 4 (1989).

Joseph, Harriet Denise. “José de Escandón and the Settlement of South Texas in the Late Colonial Era, 1746–1821.” In *Studies in Brownsville and Matamoros History*, edited by Milo Kearney, Anthony Knopp, and Antonio Zavaleta. Brownsville: University of Texas, 1995.

Kelley, Pat. *River of Lost Dreams: Navigation on the Rio Grande*. Lincoln: University of Nebraska Press, 1986.

Koch, Lena Clara. “The Federal Indian Policy in Texas, 1845–1860.” *Southwestern Historical Quarterly* 28, no. 3 (January 1925).

Krysl, L. J., M. E. Hubbert, B. F. Sowell, G. E. Plumb, T. K. Jewett, M. A. Smith, and J. W. Waggoner. “Horses and Cattle Grazing in the Wyoming Red Desert: Food Habits and Dietary Overlap.” *Journal of Range Management* 37, no. 1 (January 1984).

L’Amour, Louis. *The Man from Broken Hills*. New York: Bantam Books, 1975.

Leal, Guillermo Garmendía. *Origen de los Fundadores de Cadereyta* (1635–1763). Monterrey, Nuevo León, 1993.

Leffler, John J. *Refuge on the Rio Grande: A Regional History of Bentsen-Rio Grande Valley State Park*. Texas Parks and Wildlife Department, 2013.

Lehmann, V. W. *Forgotten Legions: Sheep in the Rio Grande Plain of Texas*. El Paso: Texas Western Press, 1969.

Leopold, Aldo. *A Sand County Almanac*. Oxford: Oxford University Press, 1949.

Leopold, A. Starker. *Wildlife of Mexico: The Game Birds and Mammals*. Berkeley: University of California Press, 1959.

Littlefield, Douglas R. *Conflict on the Rio Grande: Water and the Law, 1879–1939*. Norman: University of Oklahoma Press, 2008.

Luna, Melinda, T. Lynn Lovell, Joe T. Barrow, John Ivey, and Jack Furlong. “Levees in Texas: A Historical Perspective.” http://www.halff.com/downloads/info_bank/levees_in_texas-historical.pdf

Manaster, Jane. *Javelinas: Collared Peccaries of the Southwest*. Lubbock: Texas Tech University Press, 2006.

Manzano, M. G., J. Navar, M. M. Pando, and A. Martínez. “Overgrazing and Desertification in Northern Mexico: Highlights on Northeastern Region.” *Annals of Arid Zones* (India) 39, no. 3 (2000).

Marion, Wayne R. “Plain Chachalaca Food Habits in South Texas.” *The Auk* 93, no. 2 (April 1976).

Markham, Lauren. “First the Fence, Then the System.” *Virginia Quarterly Review* 89, no. 3 (Summer 2013). http://www.vqronline.org/articles/first-fence-then-system

Matte, Eileen. *At the Crossroads: Harlingen’s First 100 Years, 1910–2010*. Rio Grande Valley Museum Association, 2009.

McCracken, Karen Harden. *The Life History of a Texas Birdwatcher: Connie Hagar of Rockport*. College Station: Texas A&M University Press, 2001.

McFall, Kerby. "The Texas Delta of an American Nile." *National Geographic Magazine* 74 (July–December 1938).

Melville, Elinor G. K., and Bradley Skopyk. "Disease, Ecology, and the Environment." In *The Oxford History of Mexico*, edited by William H. Beezley and Michael C. Meyer. New York: Oxford University Press, 2010.

Mertz, Richard J. "No One Can Arrest Me: The Story of Gregorio Cortez." *Journal of South Texas* 1 (1974).

Middleton, Beth A. "Effects of Hurricane Katrina on Tree Regeneration in *Taxodium distichum* of the Gulf Coast." *Wetlands* 29, no. 1 (March 2009).

Mild, Christina. "From Threatened to 'Threatening.'" *The Sabal* 27, no. 5 (May 2010).

Molleman, Freerk, Roy H. A. Grunsven, Maartje Liefting, Bas J. Zwaan, and Paul M. Brakefield. "Is Male Puddling Behavior of Tropical Butterflies Targeted at Sodium for Nuptial Gifts or Activity?" *Biological Journal of the Linnean Society* 86, no. 3 (November 2005).

Monday, Jane Clements, and Frances Brannen Vick. *Petra's Legacy: The South Texas Ranching Empire of Petra Vela and Mifflin Kenedy*. Kingsville: Texas A&M University, Perspectives on South Texas, 2007.

Montejano, David. *Anglos and Mexicans in the Making of Texas, 1836–1986*. Austin: University of Texas Press, 1987.

Muckleroy, Anna. "The Indian Policy of the Republic of Texas, 1." *Southwestern Historical Quarterly* 25, no. 4 (April 1922).

Nelson, Edward W. *Wild Animals of North America: Intimate Studies of Big and Little Creatures of the Mammal Kingdom*. Washington, DC: National Geographic Society, 1918.

Nicol, Scott. "Broken Promises and Border Walls Push Jaguarundi Closer to the Brink." http://notexasborderwall.blogspot.com/2013/01/broken-promises-and-border-walls-push_13.html

Norris, W. Clyde. *History of Hidalgo County Texas*. Kingsville: Texas A&M University, 1942.

O'Shea, Elena Zamora. *El Mesquite: A Story of the Early Spanish Settlements between the Nueces and the Rio Grande*. College Station: Texas A&M University Press, 2000.

Parker, Mary O. "Birds, Brush, and Fire." *Texas Parks and Wildlife*, May 2009.

Parsons, Elsie Clews. "Curanderos in Oaxaca, Mexico." *Scientific Monthly* 32, no. 1 (January 1931).

Peña, José M. *Inherit the Dust from the Four Winds of Revilla: A 250-Year Historical Perspective with Emphasis on Ancient Guerrero, Its People and Its Land Grants*. Bloomington, IN: Xlibris, 2006.

Perry, Ann. "Studying Streambanks Reveals Their Weaknesses and Strengths." *Agricultural Research*, February 2011.

Petsche, Jerome E. *The Steamboat Bertrand: History, Excavation, and Architecture*. Washington, DC: US Department of the Interior, National Park Service, 1974.

Pierce, Frank A. *A Brief History of the Lower Rio Grande Valley*. Menasha, WI: George Banta, 1917.

Pollen-Bankhead, N., A. Simon, K. Jaeger, and E. Wohl. "Destabilization of Streambanks by Removal of Invasive Species in Canyon de Chelly National Monument, Arizona." *Geomorphology* 10, no. 3 (2009).

Pope, Dorothy Lee. *Rainbow Era on the Rio Grande*. Brownsville, TX: Springman-King, 1971.

Pruitt, Kenneth D., David G. Hewitt, Nova J. Silvy, and Steve Benn. "Importance of Native Seeds in White-Winged Dove Diets Dominated by Agricultural Grains." *Journal of Wildlife Management* 72, no. 2 (February 2008).

Ramírez, Emilia Schunior. *Ranch Life in Hidalgo County after 1850*. Edinburg, TX: New Santander Press, 1971.

Rappole, John H., Gene W. Blacklock, and Jim Norwine. "Apparent Rapid Change in South Texas Birds: Response to Climate Change?" In *The Changing Climate of South Texas 1900–2100, Problems and Prospects, Impacts and Implications*, edited by Jim Norwine and Kuruvilla John. Kingsville: Texas A&M University Press, 2007.

Reid, Nick, Jorge Marroquín, and Peter Beyer-Munzel. "Utilization of Shrubs and Trees for Browse, Fuelwood and Timber in the Tamaulipan Thornscrub, Northeastern Mexico." *Forest Ecology and Management* 36 (1991).

Richardson, Alfred, and Ken King. *Plants of Deep South Texas: A Guide to the Woody and Flowering Species*. Kingsville: Texas A&M University Press, 2011.

Richter, Conrad. *The Sea of Grass*. Cleveland: World Publishing, 1946.

Rivera, José A. *Acequia Culture: Water, Land, and Community in the Southwest*. Albuquerque: University of New Mexico Press, 1998.

Robbins, Robert K., and Paul A. Opler. "Butterfly Diversity and a Preliminary Comparison with Bird and Mammal Diversity." In *Biodiversity II: Understanding and Protecting Our Biological Resources*, edited by Marjorie L. Reaka-Kudla, Don E. Wilson, and Edward O. Wilson. Washington, DC: Joseph Henry Press, 1997.

Robertson, Brian. *Wild Horse Desert: The Heritage of South Texas*. Edinburg, TX: New Santander Press, 1985.

Robinson, Willard B. "Colonial Ranch Architecture in the Spanish-Mexican Tradition." *Southwestern Historical Quarterly* 83, no. 2 (October 1979).

Romero, Yolanda. "Migrant Housing and Labor Camps in Northwest Texas, 1930s–1940s." In *Tejano Epic: Essays in Honor of Félix A. Almaraz, Jr.*, edited by Arnoldo De León. Austin: Texas State Historical Association, 2005.

Rowe, James. "History of the King Ranch." In *King Ranch: 100 Years of Ranching, 1853–1953*. Corpus Christi, TX: Caller-Times, 1953.

Russell, Carl P. *Guns on the Early Frontiers*. Lincoln: University of Nebraska Press, 1957.

Sáenz, Andrés. *Early Tejano Ranching: Daily Life at Ranchos San José and El Fresnillo*. College Station: Texas A&M University Press, 2001.

Salinas, Martín. *Indians of the Rio Grande Delta: Their Role in the History of Southern Texas and Northeastern Mexico*. Austin: University of Texas Press, 1990.

Sánchez, Mario, ed. *A Shared Experience: The History, Architecture, and Historic Designations of the Lower Rio Grande Heritage Corridor*. 2nd ed. Austin: Los Caminos del Río Heritage Project and the Texas Historical Commission, 1994.

Santos, John Phillip. *Places Left Unfinished at the Time of Creation*. New York: Penguin Books, 1999.

Schmidly, David J. *Texas Natural History: A Century of Change*. Lubbock: Texas Tech University Press, 2002.

Schmitz, Mark, and Price V. Fishback. "The Distribution of Income in the Great Depression: Preliminary State Estimates." *Journal of Economic History* 43, no. 1 (March 1983).

Scott, Florence Johnson. *Historical Heritage of the Lower Rio Grande*. 1937. Reprint, Rio Grande City, TX: La Retama Press, 1965.

Selections from the Collected Papers of the Lower Rio Grande Valley Historical Society, 1949–1979. Vol. 1. Harlingen, TX: Lon A. Hill Memorial Library, 1979.

Seton, Ernest Thompson. *Lives of Game Animals*. Vol. 1. Boston: Charles T. Branford, 1953.

Shaw, Charles. *Indian Life in Texas*. Austin, TX: State House Press, 1987.

Showers, Wayne A. "The Vegetable Industry in the Lower Rio Grande Valley, Past, Present, and Future." *Journal of the Rio Grande Valley Horticultural Society* 25 (1971).

Sjoberg, Andre F. "The Bidai Indians of Southeastern Texas." *Southwest Journal of Anthropology* 7, no. 4 (Winter 1951).

Small, Michael F., Timothy H. Bonner, and John T. Baccus. "Hydrologic Alteration of the Lower Rio Grande Terminus: A Quantitative Assessment." *River Research and Application* 25, no. 3 (2009).

Smith, Austin Paul. "Miscellaneous Bird Notes from the Lower Rio Grande." *Condor* 12, May 1910.

Smith, Margaret Harrison. "The Lower Rio Grande Region in Tamaulipas, Mexico." PhD diss., University of Texas, 1961.

"Spanish-Language Newspapers." Texas State Historical Association. www.tshaonline.org/handbook/online/articles/ees18

Stambaugh, J. Lee, and Lillian J. Stambaugh. *Historical Heritage of the Rio Grande Valley of Texas*. Austin: Jenkins Publishing, 1974.

———. *The Lower Rio Grande Valley of Texas: Its Colonization and Industrialization, 1518–1953*. Austin: San Felipe Press, 1974, reprint from 1954.

Stewart, Kenneth L., and Arnoldo De León. *Not Room Enough: Mexicans, Anglos, and Socioeconomic Change in Texas, 1850–1900*. Albuquerque: University of New Mexico Press, 1982.

Stewart, Omer C. *Forgotten Fires: Native Americans and the Transient Wilderness*. Norman: University of Oklahoma Press, 2002.

Straker, Mary Helen. *The Hills of Home: Five Generations of a Pioneer Ohio Family*. Nashport, OH: New Concord Press, 2008.

Strecker, John K. "The Extension of Range of the Nine-Banded Armadillo." *Journal of Mammalogy* 72, no. 3 (August 1926).

———. "The Trade in Deer Skins in Early Texas." *Journal of Mammalogy* 8, no. 2 (May 1927).

"Studying Streambanks Reveals Their Weaknesses and Strengths." *Agricultural Research*, February 2011. http://www.ars.usda.gov/is/AR/archive/feb11/streambanks0211.htm

Sutherland, Mary A. *The Story of Corpus Christi*. Edited by Frank A. Harrison. Corpus Christi, TX: Corpus Christi Chapter, Daughters of the Confederacy, 1916. http://www.cclibraries.com/localhistory/oldbayview/index.php/component/content/article/61/513-e-t-merriman

Sutton, George Miksch, and Olin Sewall Pettingell Jr. "Birds of the Gómez Farías Region, Southwestern Tamaulipas." *The Auk* 59, no. 1 (January 1942).

Swanton, John R. "Linguistic Position of the Tribes of Southern Texas and Northeastern Mexico." *American Anthropologist* 17, no. 1 (January–March 1915).

Taber, F. Wallace. "Expansion of the Range of the Armadillo." *Journal of Mammalogy* 20, no. 4 (November 1939).

Taylor, Richard B., Jimmy Rutledge, and Joe G. Herrera. *A Field Guide to Common South Texas Shrubs*. Austin: University of Texas at Austin, Texas Parks and Wildlife Press, 1997.

Terneny, Tiffany Tanya. "A Re-Evaluation of Late Prehistoric and Archaic Chronology in the Rio Grande Delta of South Texas." PhD diss., University of Texas at Austin, 2005.

Texas Forest Service. *Famous Trees of Texas*. 1st ed. College Station: Texas A&M University, 1970.

Thompson, Jerry. *Cortina: Defending the Mexican Name in Texas*. College Station: Texas A&M University Press, 2007.

Tijerina, Andrés. *Tejano Empire: Life on the South Texas Ranchos*. College Station: Texas A&M University Press, 1998.

Tijerina, Andrés, and Martha Doty Freeman. "A History of El Capote." In *Pharr Reynosa International Bridge: Continued Archeological and Historical Research at El Capote Ranch Community, Hidalgo County, Texas*. Austin: Prewitt and Associates, 1994.

Torres, Eliseo. *The Folk Healer: The Mexican-American Tradition of Curanderismo and Green Medicine*. Zurich, Switzerland: Nieves Press, 1984.

Tremblay, Thomas A., William A. White, and Jay A. Raney. "Native Woodland Loss during the Mid 1900s in Cameron County, Texas." *Southwestern Naturalist* 50, no. 4 (2005).

Turner, Matt Warnock. *Remarkable Plants of Texas: Uncommon Accounts of Our Common Natives*. Austin: University of Texas Press, 2009.

Vigness, David M. "Indian Raids on the Lower Rio Grande, 1836–1837." *Southwestern Historical Quarterly* 59, no. 1 (July 1955).

———. "Nuevo Santander in 1795: A Provincial Inspection by Félix Calleja." *Southwestern Historical Quarterly* 75, no. 4 (April 1972).

Villaseñor-Gómez, José Fernando. "Habitat Use of Wintering Bird Communities in Sonora, Mexico: The Importance of Riparian Habitats." In *Birds of the US-Mexico Borderlands: Distribution, Ecology, and Conservation*, edited by Janet M. Ruth, Tim Brush, and David Krueper. Special issue, *Studies in Avian Biology*, no. 37 (September 2008). Cooper Ornithological Society.

Volanto, Keith J. "Burying White Gold: The AAA Cotton Plow-Up Campaign in Texas." *Southwestern Historical Quarterly* 103, no. 3 (January 2000).

———. *Texas, Cotton, and the New Deal*. College Station: Texas A&M University Press, 2005.

Vora, Robin S. "Plant Communities of the Santa Ana National Wildlife Refuge, Texas." *Texas Journal of Science* 42 (1990).

Wakild, Emily. "Border Chasm: International Boundary Parks and Mexican Conservation, 1935–1945." *Environmental History* 14 (July 2009).

Walker, Laurence A. "Wood from Five Forests of Texas." *Texas Natural History*, Summer 1985.

Warren, L. E., D. N. Ueckert, M. Shelton, and A. D. Chamrad. "Spanish Goat Diets on Mixed-Brush Rangeland in the South Texas Plains." *Journal of Range Management* 37, no. 4 (July 1984).

Washington, Ann Reed. “Ranches in the Rio Grande Valley of Texas.” *La Porcione* 1, no. 2 (December 1986).

Webb, Walter Prescott. *The Texas Rangers: A Century of Frontier Defense.* Austin: University of Texas, 1965.

Weniger, Dale. *The Explorers' Texas: The Animals They Found.* Vol. 2. Austin, TX: Eakin Press, 1997.

Wheeler, Margaret L. *A Bird Watcher's Guide to Mexico*. Mexico: Minutiae Mexicana, 1967.

Wheelock, David C. “Regulation and Bank Failures: New Evidence for the Agricultural Depression of the 1920s.” *Journal of Economic History* 52, no. 4 (December 1992).

Whisenhunt, Donald W. *The Depression in Texas: The Hoover Years.* New York: Garland Publishing, 1983.

Wilbarger, J. W. *Indian Depredations in Texas.* Austin, TX: Hutchins Printing House, 1889.

Wolf, Blair O., and Carlos Martínez del Río. “Use of Saguaro Fruit by White-Winged Doves: Isotopic Evidence of a Tight Ecological Association.” *Oecologia* 124 (2000).

Wright, Robert. “Sacred Sites: Building Churches and Communities in 19th Century South Texas.” *Heritage* 17, no. 1 (Spring 1999).

Zorrilla, Juan Fidel. *Tamaulipas: Fértil planicie entre sierra y laguna. Monografía estatal.* 2nd ed. Secretaria de Educación Publica, Impreso en México, 1994.

Index

Note: Page numbers in *italics* denote photos, tables, or figures; numbers in **bold** denote maps.

absentee landlords, 15, 102, 107, 145, 149
acequias (ditches), 44–45, 63
A Crisis in Conservation (pamphlet), 14
adaptations by animals, 35, 38, 39, 49–50
adaptations by plants, 36, 38, 39, 113
aerial images, study of, 11, *56*, 58
African Americans, 105
Agostadero del Gato grant, 1, **5**, **46**, 65, 99, 101, *107*, 126. *See also* Domínguez family; Treviño family
Agricultural Adjustment Act, 16
agriculture: Anglo domination of, 126, 136–37, 141; citrus industry, 16, 46; commercial, impact of, 141–45, 152; corn crops, 25, 141; cotton industry, 15, 16, 22; crop destruction by waterfowl, 25; land development schemes 1900s, 140–41, 143–47; migrant workers, Depression era, 15–16; post-Depression expansion, 11, 22–23; post–World War I depression of, 145–46; regional history and lack of records, 7–8; subsistence farming, 63, 73–74; sugarcane, 136, 142. *See also* irrigation; ranching
Agua Negra, 119
Alamo, Texas, 4, **5**, 125, 139–40, 145
Alamo Land and Sugar Company, 143, 145, 146
Alamo Tract, 21, 140, 142, 143–45, 146
"A List of Indian Nations That Were in Nuevo León but Have Vanished" (De León), 31
Almonte, Juan, 90, 92
Alonzo, Armando, 7, 112, 128, 132
American Rio Grande Land and Irrigation Company, 136, 140, 143
Amistad Reservoir, 34
amphibians, 86
anacahuita (olive) trees, 61, 73
anacua trees, 61, 72, 86, 121
Anglo ascendancy in South Texas, 101–2, 107–8, 126, 136–37, 141
animales de uña (aminals with claws), 91
Apache Indians, 64, 78–81, 89
armadillos, 47, 110–12
Armstrong, F. B., 41
Army Corps of Engineers, 16–17, 18, 150
artificial flooding experiment, 86–87
ash trees, 18, 34, 77, 118, 131, 151
auctions (tax), land, 96–97, 99–100
Audubon, John James, 92
Audubon Christmas Bird Count, 22, 25, 86, 157
Audubon oriole, 82

bald cypress, 60–61, 150
Balli Cavazos, Victoria. *See* Leal, Victoria Balli
Balli family: family connections and background, 8, 64–66, 95, 104–5, 116, 139; Fransisco, 64, 65, 97, 106, 128; José Isidro, 97, 104, 123; Juan Antonio, 49, 94, 102; livestock of, 94, 103. *See also* Llano Grande grant
ball moss, 70, 118
balloon vine, 86
bancos (river channel curves), 33
barbed wire, 112
barrenground willow, 86
Basse, Elisha, 96, 97, 99, 100
beardless flycatchers, 21
Bell, P. H., 95
Bentsen-Rio Grande Valley State Park, 27
Berlandier, Jean Louis, 40, 91, 95
Big Ebony, 68, *69*, 70
birding and clubs, 14, 148. *See also* Rio Grande Valley Nature Club

Bird-Lore, 8, 22
bird populations: brushland, 111–12, 117–18; Christmas Bird Count, 22, 25, 86, 157; flooding cycles, impact on, 86–87; habitat types, 39–40; hunting pressure, 13–14, 18, 19; and insect predation, 42–43; irrigation and habitat creation, 13–14; migratory, 18, 149–50, 153–54; overgrazing, impact of, 114; predatory, 121, 131, 151, 153; songbirds, 154; waterfowl, 25, 86, 129, 154. *See also individual species*
blackbean tree, 68. *See also* ebony trees/wood
black-bellied tree ducks, 18, 25
black mimosa, 71
black vultures, 53
black willows, 58
Blalock, Peter Ebenezer, 127, 137, 139, 143
Blalock Town and Improvement Company, 139
blue heron, 84
Bobcat Trail, 86
bobwhite quail, 38, 154
boom-and-bust population dynamics, 37
Borderlands history, 6–7
border patrols, 17, 57, 148
border wall/fence, 185*n* 30
Borrego Indians, 63
borrow pits, 17–18, *19*, 21, 28
Boundary Commission. *See* International Boundary Commission
boundary issues, 83, 149–50. *See also* survey markers
Bourland and Miller Commission, 95–96, 100, 101
bóveda (tomb), 67, 148. *See also* cemetery, Guzmán; cemetery, Leal
Box, Lina Helen, 120
Bracero Program, 17, 162*n* 6
brands, livestock, 102, *107*, 109, 123, 124, *131*, 134
brasada (Nueces Strip), 62
breeding censuses. *See* nesting censuses
Brewster, William, Jr., 138
Brewster, William J. T. G., 124
bricks, handmade, 74–76
bristlegrasses, 154
broad-winged hawk, 153
Brownsville, Texas, *96*, *99*
Brownsville hurricane 1933, 11, 16
Brush, Timothy, 14, 117
brush country ecosystem, 35, 111–12, 117–18, 153–54. *See also* chaparral ecosystem
brush fires, 112, 117
buff-breasted sandpipers, 14
buffelgrass, 152
bull-nettles, 77
bulrushes, 60
burn offs of vegetation, 21, 59, 112, 141
burros, 49
butterflies, 37, 42–43

caballada (horse herd), 81
caballerias (irrigation grants), 44
cabrito (goat meat), 132–33
Calleja, Félix, 51
Camargo (Ciudad), Mexico, 16, 34, 45, 65
Cameron County: agricultural expansion in, 23; Brownsville profiles, *96*, *99*; chachalacas in, 20; Depression era profile, 15–19; historical records, 80, 81, 109; population boom, 115, **133**; racial tension in, 137; woodland loss in, 11
Camp Ebenezer, 139
canaba (needlework), 138
canals, irrigation, 44, 136, 137, 141
canopy height, importance of, 20, 34
Cantú, Carmen, 64
capul (granjeno berries), 57
caracaras, 84
carrion eaters, 52–54
carrizos (reeds), 60
Castillo, Charles David, 84, 151
cat brier, 86
Catholic churches, 108–9, 110, 116
Cattail Lake, *26*, 98, 129. *See also* West Lake
cattails, 25, 129, 131
"Cattle Queen of Texas," 116
cattle ranching: brands, registered, 102, *107*, 109, 123, 124, *131*, 134;

classification system for herds, 112, 116; decline in, 125, 136; drives, 115; expansion of, 9, 48–49, 113, 115–17; fever ticks, 17, 114; hides, trade in, 90, 115; impact on ecosystem, 22, 26, 56–57, 112; management best practices, 9, 48, 132, 134; predators, 52, 91; rustling, 89, 103, 180*n*18; seed dispersal by, 94; Spanish era profile, 44, 48–51, 52. *See also* grazing, domestic; ranching
Cavazos family: background and family connections, 64–66, 105, 119; and Indian raids, 79; loss/sales of lands, 102. *See also* La Blanca grant
cedar elm, 18, 20, 34, 55, 118, 131, 151
cedar trees, 152
cemetery, Guzmán, 125
cemetery, Leal, 67, 108, 109, 116, 123, 148
cenizo (purple sage), 50, 72
census data. *See* population/census data
chachalacas, 19–20, 37, 84, 156. *See also in* color plates
channelization, 21. *See also* flood control programs
chaparral ecosystem, 35, 49–50, 72, **130,** 131–32. *See also* brush country ecosystem
Chaparral Wildlife Management Area, 117
Chapin, D. B., 139
Chapman, Helen, 87
charcoal, 58
chickens, domestic, 120, 121
chili peppers, 72
Chloris sp. (grasses), 154
cholera, 112
Christmas Bird Count, 22, 25, 86, 157
churches, 102, 108–9, 110, 116, 143
citrus, native, 152
citrus industry, 16, 143, 146
Civil War: Leal family involvement, 106; mounted traffic, 88–89, 103; and ranching boom, 9, 113, 125; and Rio Grande steamboats, 84; and steamboat operations, 87
claiming ceremony, 156
clearing of land: and armadillo habitat, 111; clear-cutting, 9; and commercial agriculture, 141–42; flood control programs, 16–17, 21, 150, 151; Spanish era settlement, 51. *See also* fires; woodland loss
Cleary, Ed and Laura, 140–41
climate, challenges of, 38–39, 54, 76–77, 84, 125, 140–41
Closner, John, 136, 142, 143
clothing, cleaning and cloth making, 62, 77, 138
clovers, 86
clubhouse building on refuge, *56,* 147
Coahuila province, 31, 47
Coahuiltecan Indians, 31
coastal germanders, 86
colchas (quilts), 62
cold weather, 125
collectors, impact of, 14
Comanche (steamboat), 88
Comanche Indians, 78–81, 89, 92
coma tree, 70
community development: 1880s, 119–25; land development schemes 1900s, 140–41, 143–47; urbanization, 138
competition and adaptation, 36, 93, 114
conservation movements, 14, 23, 149–54
continuity of habitats, 25, 27, 36, 153. *See also* transition zones, ecological
controlled burns, 112–13, 118
cooking and food preparation, 61, 76–77, 132
coots, 129
coral snakes, 78
corazon huisache, 77
corn crops, 25, 141
corridas de caballada (roundups), 89–90
corridors, wildlife, 117, 153–54. *See also* transition zones, ecological
Cortez, Rosalía and Gregorio (son), 180*n*18
Cortina, Juan Nepomuceno, 103
Cortina War, 103–4, 106
Cortinistas, 103, 106
cotton industry, 15, 16, 22
cougars. *See* mountain lions

coyotes, 73
crafts, 62, 111, 121, 138. *See also* bricks, handmade; clothing, cleaning and cloth making
cranes, 14, 149
Craven, Earl, 4, 39, 114, 118, 148
crop destruction by waterfowl, 25
crossings/fords, 67, 91
crows, 150
cultural identity, 95, 126, 127
curandero (healer), 77–78
custodianship and land ethic, 134–35, 155–56
cypress trees/wood, 60–61, 150

dams, 18, 23, 34, 37, 149
Davis, Anna May, 22. *See also in* color plates
Davis, Irby: background and contributions, 8, 18, 22–24, 162*n* 6; on collectors, 14; on flood control programs, 21, 150; map of Santa Ana Tract, 2–3; nesting censuses, 2, 8, 18, 19, 21–22, 82; on Santa Ana Grove speculators, 146. *See also in* color plates; Rio Grande Valley Nature Club
deerskin trade, 48, 73
deforestation, 59, 60–61. *See also* woodland loss
defunción (death record), 80
De La Garza, Beatriz, 164*n* 2, 168*n* 13, 172*n* 25, 178*n* 31
de la Garza, Diego, 49
De León, Alonso, 31
De León, Arnoldo, 132, 137
Derramadero Rancho, 125
desecration of graveyards, 148
desert ecosystem, 32
desert willow trees, 61
Dicliptera vahliana, 36–37. *See also in* color plates
disease, 17, 32, 112, 119
dispersal of seeds, 86, 94, 117, 152
ditches, irrigation, 44–45, 63
documentation, lack of, 3–4, 6–7
domestic livestock: early increases in, 48–49; and forest habitat, 56–58; goats, 49–50, 52, 56, 132–34, 148–49; management best practices, 9, 48, 132, 134; sheep, 49, 51–52, 132; Spanish era profile, 44, 48–51, 52; stealing of, 79, 81, 89–90, 103, 180*n* 18. *See also* cattle ranching; grazing, domestic; horses
Domínguez family: background and family connections, 66, 97–98, 98–99; claiming ceremony, 156; loss/sales of land, 8, 98, 101. *See also* Los Toritos grant
doves, 13–14, 21, 40
doveweed, 38, 40
drought, severe, 27–28, 114, 118, 136
drought-flood cycle: artificial/managed flooding, 86–87, 131; damage to by flood control, 151; and environmental dynamics, 26–29, 33, 39, 87; refuge staff observations, 9, 11. *See also* drought; flooding
Dry Lake Ranch, 115
ducks, 18, 25, 86, 154
dwellings, 59–60, 61–62, 67, 74–76

ear marks, livestock, *107, 131*
East Lake, 27, 28, 129, *130*. *See also* Pintail Lakes
ebony trees/wood, *56,* 58, 67–70, 75, **130,** 141
edge habitats, 35, 42, 56, 147. *See also* transition zones, ecological
Edinburg, Texas, 99–100, 106, 108, 110, 139. *See also* Hidalgo, Texas
egg collecting, 14
egg predation, 19–20, 121
eggs, domestic flocks, 120
ejidos (common land), 51
El Agostadero del Gato grant. *See* Agostadero del Gato grant
El Capote Ranch, 8, 74–76, 119, 120–21
El Cintinela (Rio Grande Sentinel), 80
El Desierto, 45
elf owls, 27
El Gato grant. *See* Agostadero del Gato grant
elm trees, 18, 20, 34, 55, 118, 131, 151
El Sauz Ranch, 120
El Toro grant. *See* Los Toritos grant

endangered species, 3, 11, 13–15, 20, 40, 149, 157
environmental activism, 14, 23, 149, 150–54
environmental knowledge, 38, 62, 71, 72. *See also* medicinal plants
erosion, *10*, 88, 111, 127, 147
Escandón, José de, 32, 44, 45–46
escopeta (musket), 47–48
Esenbeckia runyonii, 151. *See also* jopoy tree
esteros (estuaries), 35, 97
evapotranspiration, 88
extinction, dangers of, 14
"eyes" *(ojos des agua)*, 48
eyra, 41

Falcon Dam/Lake, 23, 34, 37, 149
falcons, 121, 131
farming, commercial. *See* agriculture
farming, subsistence, 63, 73–74
Farm Service Agency, Hidalgo County, 11
Federalist Wars, 93
fences, 17, 57, 112, 135
ferruginous pygmy owl, 27
ferry services, 100, 107
fever ticks, 17, 114
fiddle anecdote, 122–23, 139
firearms, 47–48
fires, 112–13, 115, 117, 118–19
firewood, 70, 75–76, 83–85, 87–88, 143
"first lift," 67
fish and drought, 53
flamingos, 14
Fleetwood Raymond, 67, 71, 129, **130**, 152
flood control programs, 16–18, 21, 23, 61, 144, 149, 150–51
flood cycles. *See* drought-flood cycle
flooding: artificial/managed flooding, 86–87, 131; catastrophic, 110, 143, 145; and erosion, *10*, 127, 148; flood times, profile of, 85–86; river flooding, 35, 37, 145; and seed dispersal, 152. *See also* drought-flood cycle; hurricanes/storms; river flooding
flycatchers, 21
flyway, coastal, 18
folklore and nature, 37–38, 70, 77
forest ecosystem: characteristics of, 3, 33–35, 55; and flood control, impact of, 150–51; non-exploitation of Santa Ana, 143, 146–48
Forto, Emilio A., 136, 137, 139
Foster, Garfield, 140
foxtails, 154
fragmentation of habitats, 25, 27. *See also* continuity of habitats
fresno tree (Rio Grande ash), 77
frijoles (beans), 63, 141
Fuertes, Louis Agassiz, 111
Fulton, George W. and family, 120
Fulton's Store, 120
"Fulton's Strip," 120
funnel effect of coastal flyway, 18
fur trade. *See* hides/skins, trade in
Fusselman, John, 124

game bird hunting, 149–50
game laws, 23, 24
gardens, subsistence, 63, 73–74
garza (heron), 71–72
Garza family, 72, 74–76, 133
General Land Office (GLO), 95, 97
germanders, 86
Gilbert, Minnie, 23–24, 27
Glavecke, Adolphus, 97
goats, 49–50, 52, 56, 132–34, 149
Goldman, Luther, 4, 9–10, 25, 85
gordo lobo (fat wolf herb), 77
grackles, 53–54
granjeno (spiny hackberry) trees, 38, 57–58, 121
Grant, Ulysses, 92
grants. *See* land grants
grasses (species), 36, 59–60, 152, 154
grasshoppers, 42
grassland ecosystem: characteristics of, 35–36; and fire, 112–13; historic narratives, 33–34; refuge management of, 154; regenerative capability, 39–40. *See also* grazing
grass poaching, 114
graveyards. *See* cemetery, Guzmán; cemetery, Leal

grazing, domestic: competition among domestic animals, 93; competition with wildlife, 114; leases, 113, 114, 128, 149; management best practices, 9, 48, 132, 134; Spanish era, 48–51, 54. *See also* overgrazing
great blue herons, 71–72
"Great Cotton Plow-Up," 16
Great Depression years, 15–19, 136, 145–50
great tailed grackles, 53–54
grebes, 129
Guajardo-Vela site, El Capote, 75
guayacán tree, 38, 50, 71
Gulf coastal flyway, 18
gulf cordgrass, 59
guns, 47–48
Guzmán, Estéfana Garza, 75, 137
Guzmán, Julio, Sr., 9, 125–29, 132, 134
Guzmán family: background and family relationships, 75, 134–35, 137–38; brands/ear marks, registered, 131, 134; La Pechuga, development of, 125–29, 132–35; overviews, 9, 12; ranch life, 75, 132–35; sales of land, 137

habitat destruction: agricultural expansion, 11, 22–23; flood control programs, 16–17, 16–18, 21, 23
hackberry trees, 34, 38, 57, 87. *See also* *granjeno* (spiny hackberry) trees
Handy, Thomas James, 105
hardwoods, 11, 58, 71. *See also* ebony trees; mesquite trees/wood
Harlingen, Texas: profile of, 22–23
Harlingen Valley Morning Star, 23–24
Hatchee Eagle (steamboat), 84
hawks, 121, 131, 153
healers, 77–78
health issues. *See* medical and health issues
heat, extreme, 39, 54, 76–77, 84
heating of homes, 76
height of canopy, 34
herbs, 72, 76, 77
herons, 71–72, 84
Hidalgo, Texas, 75, 99–100. *See also* Edinburg, Texas
Hidalgo Advance, 142
Hidalgo County: brick making culture, 75; creation and profile of, 100–109; Depression era profiles, 15–19, 24–26; historical records, 6, 81, 123, 124–25, 127; land developers in, 140–45; location of Santa Ana grant/refuge, 4, 11, 66; population boom, 115, **133, 144**; racial tension in, 137; ranching boom, 117, 120–22; Spanish era, 32, 36, 39, 51, 78
Hidalgo County Marks and Brands, 134
Hidalgo County Water Improvement District #2, 143–44
Hidalgo Irrigation District, 27–28
hides/skins, trade in, 48, 51–52, 73, 92, 115
Hinojosa family: background and family connections, 64–65, 105; Rosa Maria de Balli, 116; Sonny, 33. *See also* Llano Grande grant
The History of the Prestigious Balli Family, 8
homes. *See* dwellings
hooded oriole, 81–82, 148. *See also in* color plates
"hoot-owl traffic," 17
Hord, Robert H., 96, 99, 100
horned lizards, 35
horno (outdoor oven), 67, 76
horses: breeding of, 49, 89, 93–94, 125, 129, 134; impact on ecosystem, 90, 94–95; as jaguar prey, 90–92; Mexican and early Texas era profile, 88–90, 92–95; Spanish era profile, 49, 52; stealing of, 79, 80, 81, 89–90, 92. *See also* grazing, domestic
Houston, Sam, 92
huisache trees/wood, 20, 58, 77, 118
human corpses, 53
hunting: collectors, impact of, 14; conservation and game laws, 14, 23, 24, 149, 150–54; and decline in bird populations, 13–14, 18, 19; game birds, 149–50; market hunting, impact of, 14, 19, 24, 149–50; native peoples, 31–32; of predators, 48, 111, 128; Spanish era practices, 47–48; subsistence, 47–48, 73, 121, 128, 148

hurricanes/storms, *10*, 11, 16, 18, 60, 85–86, 112, 147

illegal border crossing, impact on ecosystem, 17–18
Indians, North American: fire, use of, 112; irrigation and cultivation techniques, 44–45; mixing with Spanish and Mexican peoples, 63, 105; peoples, 31–32; raids by, 64, 70, 74, 78–81, 89; trade with, 48, 50
inheritance laws and heirship culture, 123, 136, 137–39
"Inland Lake," 67, 119
insect life, 22, 33, 42–43
"Inside Ranch." *See* Rancho Adentro
Interdependence: and domino effects, 19–20; plant-animal, 25, 39–40; predator-prey, 42–43; in settler communities, 78
intermarriage, 103, 105, 120, 122
"internal pasture" of refuge, 113, 114, 128
International Boundary and Water Commission, 151. *See also* International Boundary Commission
International Boundary Commission, 16, 21, 146, 150, 151
invasive species introduction, 152
ironwood trees, 71
irrigation: and catastrophic floods, 143; and commercial agriculture, 141, 149; and creation of bird habitats, 13–14; early settlement systems, 63, 73; and habitat creation, 13–14; Indian methods, 44–45; and land development schemes, 140, 141, 143; pump irrigation, 136, 142–43; Spanish methods, 44–45, 51, 63
I Would Rather Sleep in Texas (Amberson, McAllen and McAllen), 8, 66, 100

jacales (thatch huts), 59. *See also in* color plates
Jackson, Eli and Columbus, 105
Jackson, Nathaniel, 85
Jackson Ranch, 119, 120
Jackson Ranch Church, 102, 108, 143
jaguars and horses, 90–92. *See also in* color plates
jaguarundi, 40–42, 121
Jaramillo, Pedrito, 77
javelina, 90, 118
J. C. Engelman Land Company, 140
J. E. Roberts (steamboat), 84
Jones, Thomas Walter, 107
jopoy tree, 152. *See also in* color plates

Kenedy, Mifflin, 87
Kickapoo Indians, 89
Kidder family, 98, 101, 105, 120, 122, 161*n* 9
King, Richard, 87–88
King Ranch, 115
kitchens, outdoor, 61, 76–77

La Blanca grant, **46**, 65, 100, 101, 102, 103, 119. *See also* Cavazos family
ladrillera (brickyard), 75
La Esperanza Ranch, 7, 37
La Feria Border Scope, 27
La Feria grant, **46**, 54, 140
Laguna Seca, 115
La Habitación (Hidalgo), 99–100
La Joya, Texas, 51
Lake Pechuga, 34–35, 128. *See also in* color plates
lakes and ponds. *See resacas* (lakes)
land development schemes, 140–41, 143–47
land ethic and custodianship, 134–35
land grabs and tax issues, 95–102
land grants: grazing, 51; irrigation, 44, 51; maps, **5**, **46**; Mexican, 64–67, 95–102; Spanish, 45–47; town (common), 51. *See also individual grants*
landmarks as boundary markers, 1, 42, 60
land ownership, importance of, 126, 127, 156
land rush of early 1900s, 142. *See also* land development schemes
la partera (midwife), 78
"La Patrona," 116
La Pechuga, 125–29, 132–35
La Sal del Rey, 51

lead trees. *See tepeguaje* tree
Leal, Cristóbal (adopted son), 74, 81, 94, 104–5, 106, 123, 148
Leal, Cristóbal (Benigno's father), 64
Leal, Cristóbal (grandson), 105, 119, 122–23, 136, 139
Leal, Cristoval A., 63
Leal, José Benigno, 64, 74, 80–81, 106, *107,* 173*n* 32. *See also* Leal family and homestead
Leal, Joseph, 59
Leal, Juan Antonio, 59
Leal, Rafaela Treviño, 66, 105, 119, 148
Leal, Victoria Balli (Benigno's wife): background and family connections, 64–67, 134–35; death of, 110, 123, 136; profiles, 116–17, 119, 123; will, 106, 123. *See also* Leal family and homestead
Leal family and homestead: brands/ear marks, registered, *107,* 109, 123; contemporary descendants, 155; demolition of homestead and facilities, 118; homesite selection and arrangement, 67; interrelationships and connections, 64–67, 74, 97–99, 104–5; livestock of, 94, 113, 116, 120; loss of land due to fraud, 96–97, 99–100; overviews, 9, 30, 59; reclaiming auctioned land, 100–101; sales of lands, 102, 106, 136; structure and diversity of, 63. *See also* Santa Ana grant
leases, grazing, 113, 114, 128, 148
Lee, Robert E., 93
levees, 17–18, 21
lightning fires, 112–13
lime/lime paste, 60
limoncillo tree, 151–52. *See also in* color plates
Lipan Apache Indians, 64, 78–81, 89
literacy and schools, 121, 122
livestock. *See* domestic livestock
Llano Grande grant, **46,** 54, 64, 79, 105, 119, 125, 139. *See also* Balli family; Hinojosa family
Los Toritos grant, 1–3, **5,** 8, **46,** 65, 98, 101, 105. *See also* Domínguez family; Kidder family
Lower Rio Grande Valley National Wildlife Refuge System, 153
lynchings, 96, 141

mala mujer (Texas bull-nettle), 77
mallards, 154
market hunting, impact of, 14, 19, 24, 149–50. *See also* hides/skins, trade in; hunting
marsh wren, 129
McAllen family, 8, 115
McCulloch, Ben, 89
medical and health issues: disease, 17, 32, 112, 119; healers, 77–78; medicinal plants, 71, 72, 73, 77–78
Merriman, Eli T. and family, 100, 102, 107, 124
Merriman v. Blalock, 1, 127
"Merryman's Ranch," 102, 106, 107
mesquite trees/wood: characteristics and importance of, 57–58, 62; as food, 31, 94; as fuel, 75–76, 143; hardiness and adaptability, 113. *See also in* color plates
mesteñeros (mustangers), 90
metates (grinding device), 76
Methodist churches, 108
Mexican-American War, 83–85, 93
Mexican ash, 18, 118, 151
Mexican colonization act, 64
Mexican repatriation, 15
Mexican Revolution, 17, 141, 148
Mexican War of Independence, 65
midwifery, 78
Mier (Ciudad), Mexico, 34, 59, 60, 63
migrant workers, Depression era, 15–16
migration, bird, 18, 149–50, 153–54
Migratory Bird Conservation Act of 1929, 149–50
Migratory Bird Treaty, 149
Mild, Christina, 37
military conflict, impact on ecosystem, 83–85, 93, 103
Military Road, history of, 1, 88, 103
Military Telegraph Trail, 88
Miller, Mary A., 146
mimosa trees, 71

Mission Rise, *133*, 135
missions, Spanish, 31, 45, 63
Mission San Joaquín del Monte, 31, 45, 63
Mission Times, 23
mistletoe, 70, 77
molcajetes (grinding devices), 76
monte (hill/mountain), 35
Montezuma bald cypress, 60–61, 150
Montgomery Onion Patch, 142
mosses, *55*, *69*, 70, 82, 118
mottes (groves), 36
mountain lions, 42, 73, 77
mules, 51–52, 90
muskets, 47–48
"muskit tree," 62. *See also* mesquite trees/wood
mustangs, 89–90, 92–93

National Association of Audubon Societies, 14
National Audubon magazine, 8
National Geographic magazine, 153
National Wildlife Refuge System, 13
native peoples of Santa Ana, 31–32. *See also* Indians, North American
nest collecting, 14
nesting behavior and tree availability, 19–20, 21, 25
nesting censuses, 2, 8, 18, 19, 21–22, 82
New Guide to Spanish and Mexican Land Grants in South Texas, 96
New York Times, 88
nine-banded armadillo, 110–12
North Lake, 27, **130**
Nueces River, 51
Nueces Strip, 62
Nuestra Señora de Guadalupe Church, 138
Nuestra Señora de Santa Ana Church, 116
Nueva España, 4
Nuevo León province, 31, 45–47
Nuevo Santander, 32, 45–57. *See also* Tamaulipas, Mexico

Oblate priests, 62
"The Oblate Trail," 108
ocelot, 73
ojos de agua (springs), 48
olive trees, 73
Olmstead, Frederick, 112
onion crops, 142
oral history projects, 8
orchard oriole, 82
orioles, 81–82, 148. *See also in* color plates
ornithological clubs and birding, 14, 147–48, 150. *See also* Rio Grande Valley Nature Club
oropendula (orioles), 82
overgrazing, *26*, 128; avoiding through stewardship, 9, 48, 132, 134; and grazing leases, 128, 148–49; impact on ecosystems, overviews, 95, 114–19
Owen-White, Jennifer, 85
owls, 27, 149
Owl Trail Resaca, 86–87
oyster shells, 60

Palo Alto, Texas, 83
paloverde bush, 38
Partisan Rangers, Confederate, 106
passerine birds, 42
pastores (shepherds), 132
"Pasture of the Cat," 41. *See also* Agostadero del Gato grant
paths and trails. *See* trails and paths
patos maizal (black-bellied whistling duck), 25
Peña, Cristóbal, 104. *See also* Leal, Cristóbal (adopted son)
Peñitas, Texas, 51
pequin peppers, 72
persimmon trees, 151
Petra's Legacy, 8
Pharr-Reynosa Bridge, 8
pigeons, 34
Pintail Lakes, 3, *126*, 128, 129–32. *See also* East Lake
Pintail Lake Trail, *126*, 131
plantings, non-crop, 61, 72–73
plovers, 14
poaching of grass, 114
pobladores (settlers), 48
ponds. *See resacas* (lakes)

population/census data: 1750, 47, 49, 89; 1850, 74, 96, 99; 1855, 63; 1860, 103, 104; 1870, 65; 1880, 119, 141; 1900, 138, 141; 1930, **133**; boom, Reconstruction era, 115; native peoples, 32
poultry, domestic flocks, 120
prairies, 39. *See also* grassland ecosystem
predators: birds, 121, 131, 151, 153; of domestic animals, 52, 90–92, 121; financial, 96–97; habitat cover for prey, 35; hunting of, 48, 111, 128; reptiles, 19–20, 121. *See also* jaguar
prejudice against Mexicans, 17, 126, 127, 137–38
preservation of food, 76
prickly pear cactus, 49, 118
puddling of butterflies, 43
pumas. *See* mountain lions
pump irrigation, 136, 142–43
purple sage, 72
pygmy owls, 27
Pyle, Ernie, 147

quail, 38, 154

raccoons, 121
racial issues, 17, 126, 127, 137–38
railroads, 60, 117, 138, 139–40, 142–43, 145
rails (birds), 149, 154
rainfall, 38, 39
Ramírez, Emilia Schunior, 132
ranching: 1880s profiles, 119–25; decline in Tejano ranches, 136–39, 141; expansion, Reconstruction era, 113, 115–17; histories of, 7–9; Spanish era settlement, 51
Ranch Life in Hidalgo County after 1850 (Ramírez), 132
Rancho Adentro: 1860 census profile, 104; 1880s profile, 119–20, 122–24; homesite, 67. *See also* cemetery, Leal; Leal family and homestead
Rancho Relámpago, 103
raptors, 121, 131, 151, 153
rattlesnakes, 78
recertification of land titles, 95–102, 100–102
recovery management, 114, 118
red-billed pigeons, 21, 34, 156, 157
red-winged blackbirds, 129
reeds, 60
refuges and conservation movement, 23
Reinosa Viejo, 33. *See also* Reynosa, Mexico
Relámpago Rancho, 119, 122
religion. *See* churches
Resaca del Gato, 128
resacas (lakes): artificial flooding experiment, 86–87; damming and draining of, 145; definition, 33; and drought-flood cycle, 27–28; lack of on Los Toritos grant, 98; overviews/description, 3, 34–35
retama, 38, 70
retirement communities, 146
Reynosa, Mexico: brick making culture, 75; as haven from Indian attack/wars, 79–80, 103; history of, 33, 45, 50–51; Leal family in, 63; salt trade in, 51
Rinehart, Ann, 145–46
Ring, Lonnie, 23
Rio Bravo, 88
Río Bravo del Norte, 33. *See also* Rio Grande
Rio Grande: changes in and impact on ecosystem, 11, 33, 37; dry channel periods, 38–39; as national border, 83; at refuge boundary, *10, 28*; steamboats, 83–85. *See also* flood control programs
Rio Grande ash, 34, 77, 131
Rio Grande City, 100
Rio Grande Land and Irrigation Company, 136, 140, 143
Rio Grande Sentinel, 80
Rio Grande Valley Nature Club: overviews and background, 8–9, 162*n* 6; role in saving Santa Ana Groves, 13–14, 16–17, 23–24, 25–26. *See also* Davis, Irby
riparian forest, 34. *See also* forest ecosystem
riverbank alteration, manmade, 150–51
river flooding, 35, 37, 144. *See also* flooding

riverine forest, 33. *See also* forest ecosystem
River Riders, 17, 57
roads, development of, 88, 103
rock salt, 51–52
Roosevelt, Franklin, 23
rose-throated becards, 14
roundups, feral stock, 89–90
Rubalcaba, Santo(s) and family, 119
rustling of livestock, 79, 81, 89–90, 103, 180*n* 18

sacahuiste (saw grass), 59
sacas de agua (water bags), 44
sage plants, 72
Saint Anne, 30, 65
St. Louis, Brownsville and Mexico Railroad, 143
Salado River, 60
salt cedar, 152
salt trade, 51–52
Salyer, J. Clark, 18, 24, 26, 150
San Antonio and Rio Grande Railway, 143
San Antonio de los Esteros Ranch, 79
San Benito and Rio Grande Valley Railway, 145
sandstone, 61
San Joaquín del Monte (mission), 31, 45, 63
San Juan de Carricitos Ranch, 79. *See also* Cavazos family
San Juan River, 45
Santa Ana, Antonio López de, 93
Santa Ana grant, 1, **5**, 17, *19*, **46**, 99, 113. *See also* La Pechuga; *Leal family entries;* Merriman, Eli T. and family; "Merryman's Ranch"
Santa Ana Groves land venture, 145–47, 148
Santa Ana Lake. *See* Lake Pechuga
Santa Ana National Wildlife Refuge: aerial images, study of, 11, *56*, 58; federal creation of, 26, 29; historical overview of land, 3–6; maps, **2, 5, 130**
Santa Ana Ranch. *See* Rancho Adentro
Santa Anita Ranch, **46,** 66, 103, 115
San Tomás de la Blanca grant, 65. *See also* La Blanca grant
saw grass, 59
scaled quail, 38
scavengers, carrion, 52
schools, 121, 122
scissor-tailed flycatcher, 84
seasonal revitalization, 81, 113
"second lift," 13, *133*, 144
seed dispersal, 86, 94, 117, 152
seepage erosion, 88
Seminole Indians, 89
Sennett, George A., 82
Sennett oriole, 81–82. *See also in* color plates
Setaria sp. (grasses), 154
shade, value of, 56–57, 61–62, 73
shared experience concept, 6, 159–60*n* 4
Shary, John, 143
"Sharyland," 143
sheep, 49, 51–52, 132
Sierra Madre Oriental range, 33, 59
sitios (distance measure), 64
skins, trade in. *See* hides/skins, trade in
skunks, 47
smallpox, 32
snails, 53–54
snakes, 19–20, 78, 121
soaptree, 71
songbirds, 154
South Texas Wintering Birds Program, 117
spadefoot toad, 86
Spanish bayonet (yucca), 72
Spanish colonial era, 4, 32, 36, 39, 44, 45–57
Spanish-language newspapers, 80
Spanish moss, *55, 69,* 82, 118
sparrows, 154
species diversity, 11, 14, 22, 87, 152. *See also* endangered species; seed dispersal
"Spiderweb" railroad (San Benito and Rio Grande Valley Railway), 145
spiny hackberry, 57
spotted owl, 149
Sprague, W. F., 143
Starr County, 143, 155

Statistical Report on Texas (1835) (Almonte), 90
steamboats, 83–85, 87–88
stereotyping of Tejanos, 127, 137
Stillman, Charles, 87
stores, retail, 120
subsidies, agricultural, 16
subsistence farming, 63, 73–74, 121
subsistence hunting, 47–48, 73, 121, 128, 148
sugarcane, 136, 142
sugar hackberry trees, 34
survey markers, 1, 42, 60, 107, 139–40, 150
Swainson's hawk, 153

Tamaulipan Mezquital ecoregion, 33, 102
Tamaulipan thorn scrub, 33
Tamaulipas, Mexico, 32–33
Tamaulipas crow, 149
tax issues and land grabs, 95–102
Taylor, Zachary, 83–84
teals, 154
The Tejano Community, 132
Tejano cultural identity and land ownership, 126, 127, 156
tepeguaje tree, 18, 34, 71, 86, 131
Texas Almanac and State Industrial Guide, 15
Texas bull-nettle, 77
Texas ebony, 18, 20, 58
Texas horned lizard, 35
Texas indigo snake, 19–20
Texas-Mexican War, 93
Texas persimmon, 151
Texas Rangers, 89, 137, 148
Texas Revolution, 78, 93
Thomas, William A., 106
Thomas's Rangers, 106
Thompson, Jerry, 97, 106
thorn forest/scrub, 3, 33, 56, 70
tigre (jaguar), 91
toads, 86
totora (cattail), 131
trade practices, Spanish era, 50, 51–52
trail entrance habitat, 56–57
trails and paths: 1900s, 147; Bobcat Trail, 86; cattle drive, 115; Dicliptera Trail, 37; domestic animal, 17, 22, 50; Indian, 31–32; Leal homestead, 68, 70; and military conflicts, 84; Military Road, 1, 88, 103; neighborhood, 127–28; "The Oblate Trail," 108; Pintail Lake Trail, *126*, 131; trail entrance habitat, 56–57, 115
transition zones, ecological, 35, 42, 43. *See also* edge habitats
trapping, fur trade, 73
Treaty of Guadalupe Hidalgo, 83
tree ducks, 18, 25
tree snails, 53–54
Treviño family, 4, 65–66, 98–99. *See also* Agostadero del Gato grant
trumpeter swans, 14
tuberculosis, 119
tule (grass), 60
tunas (prickly pear), 49
turkeys, 142, 154
Turner, Josiah W., 124

undercutting of banks, 88, 150–51
understory trees, 57–58
upland plovers, 14
urbanization, 138

vado (ford), 67, 91
Vallin family, 49. *See also* Balli family
Vela, Macedonio, 115
Vela grant, 8
Villa de la Santa Ana de Camargo, 65. *See also* Camargo (Ciudad), Mexico
violin anecdote, 122–23, 139
Volanto, Keith, 15
vultures, 52–54

Wahl, Kimberly, 152. *See also in* color plates
warblers, 154
water bags, 44
water clover, 86
waterfowl, 25, 86, 129, 154. *See also individual species*
Weaver, Sarah Sanborne, 141
weaving, 62
Webber, John Ferdinand, 101, 120

Webber Ranch, 119, 120
West Lake, *26*, 27, *130*. *See also* Cattail Lake
whistling ducks. *See* black-bellied tree ducks
white-winged doves, 13–14, 18, 21, 40, 156
whooping cranes, 14
wildflowers, *36–37*
Wild Horse Desert, 90
wild horses, 89–90, 92–93
willow trees, 58, 61, 86
windmill grasses, 36, 154. *See also in* color plates
windmills, 142
women, roles in family/community, 62, 63, 72, 76–78, 138
wood, knowledge and use of, 57–58, 60–61, 71. *See also* firewood
wood ducks, 86
woodland loss: agricultural expansion, 11; deforestation, 59, 60–61; die offs of trees, 150–51; firewood, 75–76, 83–85, 87–88; flood control programs, 17–18. *See also* clearing of land
woodlands. *See* forest ecosystem
wool industry, 51–52
World War I and agricultural depression, 144–45
wrens, 129

yellow fever, 112, 124
Young, John, 100, 101
yucca plants, 72, 86

Zacatal Ranch, 104–5

Other titles in the Kathie and Ed Cox Jr. Books on Conservation Leadership, sponsored by The Meadows Center for Water and the Environment, Texas State University

Money for the Cause: A Complete Guide to Event Fundraising
Rudolph A. Rosen

On Politics and Parks
George L. Bristol

Hillingdon Ranch: Four Seasons, Six Generations
David K. Langford and Lorie Woodward Cantu

Green in Gridlock: Common Goals, Common Ground, and Compromise
Paul W. Hansen

Heads above Water: The Inside Story of the Edwards Aquifer Recovery Implementation Program
Robert L. Gulley

Fog at Hillingdon
David K. Langford